LUTHER'S WORKS

LUTHER'S WORKS

VOLUME 29

LECTURES ON TITUS, PHILEMON, AND HEBREWS

JAROSLAV PELIKAN
Editor

WALTER A. HANSEN
Associate Editor

CONCORDIA PUBLISHING HOUSE · SAINT LOUIS

Contents

General Introduction

T HE first editions of Luther's collected works appeared in the sixteenth century, and so did the first efforts to make him "speak English." In America serious attempts in these directions were made for the first time in the nineteenth century. The Saint Louis edition of Luther was the first endeavor on American soil to publish a collected edition of his works, and the Henkel Press in Newmarket, Virginia, was the first to publish some of Luther's writings in an English translation. During the first decade of the twentieth century, J. N. Lenker produced translations of Luther's sermons and commentaries in thirteen volumes. A few years later the first of the six volumes in the Philadelphia (or Holman) edition of the *Works of Martin Luther* appeared. Miscellaneous other works were published at one time or another. But a growing recognition of the need for more of Luther's works in English has resulted in this American edition of Luther's works.

The edition is intended primarily for the reader whose knowledge of late medieval Latin and sixteenth-century German is too small to permit him to work with Luther in the original languages. Those who can, will continue to read Luther in his original words as these have been assembled in the monumental Weimar edition (*D. Martin Luthers Werke.* Kritische Gesamtausgabe; Weimar, 1883 ff.). Its texts and helps have formed a basis for this edition, though in certain places we have felt constrained to depart from its readings and findings. We have tried throughout to translate Luther as he thought translating should be done. That is, we have striven for faithfulness on the basis of the best lexicographical materials available. But where literal accuracy and clarity have conflicted, it is clarity that we have preferred, so that sometimes paraphrase seemed more faithful than literal fidelity. We have proceeded in a similar way in the matter of Bible versions, translating Luther's translations. Where this could be done by the use of an existing English version—King James, Douay, or Revised Standard—we have done so. Where it could not, we have supplied our own. To indicate this in each specific instance would have been pedantic; to adopt a uniform procedure would have been artificial — especially in view of Luther's own inconsistency in this regard. In each volume the translator will be responsible primarily for matters of text and language, while the responsibility of the editor will extend principally to the historical and theological matters reflected in the introductions and notes.

Although the edition as planned will include fifty-five volumes, Luther's writings are not being translated in their entirety. Nor should they be. As he was the first to insist, much of what he wrote and said was not that important. Thus the edition is a selection of works that have proved their importance for the faith, life, and history of the Christian Church. The first thirty volumes contain Luther's expositions of various Biblical books, while the remaining volumes include what are usually called his "Reformation writings" and other occasional pieces. The final volume of the set will be an index volume; in addition to an index of quotations, proper names, and topics, and a list of corrections and changes, it will contain a glossary of many of the technical terms that recur in Luther's works and that cannot be defined each time they appear. Obviously Luther cannot be forced into any neat set of rubrics. He can provide his reader with bits of autobiography or with political observations as he expounds a psalm, and he can speak tenderly about the meaning of the faith in the midst of polemics against his opponents. It is the hope of publishers, editors, and translators that through this edition the message of Luther's faith will speak more clearly to the modern church.

J. P.
H. L.

Introduction to Volume 29

THE commentaries contained in this volume are all the direct product of Luther's work in the lecture hall at the University of Wittenberg as a professor of Bible. Unlike most of the other commentaries in our edition, however, they were not polished up and reworked for publication, either by Luther himself or by his students or by later editors. In fact, it has only been in the twentieth century that these lectures have been prepared for publication at all. Although they are separated by about a decade and are quite different both in method and in content, both show Luther the expositor engaged in the interpretation of his favorite apostle (whom, at the time, he believed to be the author also of the Epistle to the Hebrews).

The lectures presented here as the *Commentary on the Epistle of Paul to Titus* (Weimar, XXV, 6–69) and as the *Commentary on the Epistle of Paul to Philemon* (Weimar, XXV, 69–78) followed by less than a week his *Lectures on the First Epistle of St. John* (*Luther's Works*, 30, 219–327). The last of the lectures on 1 John had been delivered on November 7, 1527 (ibid., Introduction, p. xi). On November 11, "after the completion of the Epistle of John," Luther immediately set himself to the task of expounding the Epistle to Titus, following this immediately with his comments on the Epistle to Philemon. He completed this assignment in a series of 16 or 17 lectures during November and December. The sequence of these lectures seems to have been as follows:

Titus 1:1-2	November 11
Titus 1:2-6	November 12
Titus 1:6-7	November 13
Titus 1:7-9	November 18
Titus 1:9-13	November 19
Titus 1:13-15	November 20
Titus 1:15–2:4	December 2
Titus 2:5-8	December 3

Titus 2:9-13	December 4
Titus 2:14 – 3:2	December 9
Titus 3:2-4	December 10
Titus 3:4-8	December 11
[Titus 3:9	December 12]
Titus 3:10 – Philemon 1	December 13
Philemon 1-6	December 16 [not 15]
Philemon 7-16	December 17
Philemon 17-24	December 18

Thus Luther seems to have followed his custom during those years of lecturing on Mondays, Tuesdays, and Wednesdays. (The date given in the manuscript for the lecture on Philemon 1-6 is December 15, which was a Sunday; this is almost certainly a mistake for Monday, December 16.) In addition, apparently to make up for the lectures he had missed during the last week of November and to complete the course before Christmas, he delivered one or two extra lectures, on Thursday, December 11, and perhaps on Friday, December 12; the latter of these seems unfortunately to have been lost. The transcript of Luther's lectures was yet another labor of George Rörer, whose industry and devotion made him in many ways the Reformer's most faithful amanuensis. But because neither Rörer nor any later editor ever revised these lectures for publication as a finished commentary, there are elisions, abbreviations, and other problems in the text. Many of these also testify to Rörer's fidelity as a scribe, reflecting as they probably do Luther's own manner of delivery; others are undoubtedly the result simply of stenographic error and of haste. In our translation we have endeavored, whenever we could, to stick to the original, so long as it was possible to make sense of it as it stood. Where this proved impossible, we have supplied what seemed to be a reasonable conjecture, indicating such editorial liberties by the use of square brackets.

The *Lectures on Hebrews* (Weimar, LVII-3, 97 – 238) are in many ways even more difficult to handle satisfactorily in a modern English translation. At the time, Luther was still following the medieval pattern of providing "glosses" as well as of delivering his lectures in the form of "scholia." (The glosses are reprinted in Weimar, LVII-3, 5 – 91). Glosses were marginal and other com-

ments on individual words or passages, some of them grammatical
or philological, others doctrinal or moral; scholia were the connected and sustained exposition of the text. There is virtually no
way to translate the glosses in their entirety. Most of them make
sense only in relation to the Latin (or even the Greek) text of the
epistle, while others are cryptic and fragmentary. On the other
hand, experience has demonstrated that selecting from the glosses
those which seem theologically interesting is unavoidably arbi-
trary and quite tendentious. Moreover, the ideas contained in
the glosses are usually repeated and developed in the scholia.
Throughout our edition we have made it a practice to prefer the
printed version of Luther's exegetical works to the manuscript
version in those cases where we happen to have both. At the risk,
therefore, of losing from our edition certain phrases in the glosses
that may be of special interest to some readers (most of whom are
probably conversant with the Latin), we have translated only the
scholia, or, as the manuscript of student notes on the lectures
calls them, the *Commentariolus.*

That manuscript was found in the Vatican Library (to which
it had been brought from the Palatinate during the Thirty Years'
War) at the turn of the present century. It was edited, with introduction and notes, by Johannes Ficker, who was certainly the outstanding palaeographer among the Luther scholars of this century.
Like Ficker's work on Luther's other early commentaries, this
edition of *Hebrews* is a model of editorial care and scholarly
thoroughness. In the translation of the text we have followed
Ficker's deciphering of the manuscript throughout, indicating in
a few places where we might be inclined to diverge from it. Our
notes, too, owe much to his painstaking research into the sources
of Luther's comments. We have endeavored, with the help of
Ficker's notes, to identify all citations and all verbatim quotations.
But we have not identified all the allusions, parallels, and echoes
to which Ficker calls attention; nor have we indicated the source
of the various translations from Greek into Latin to which Luther's
commentary refers, except where there was special reason to do
so. In a very few cases we have also succeeded in identifying
Biblical and patristic passages that managed to escape Ficker's
careful sifting of sources, or in correcting his identifications; but
we have not called attention to these in particular. In conformity
with our general practice, however, we have called attention to

Biblical and other references which are cited erroneously in the original itself.

Luther lectured on the Epistle to the Hebrews from April 1517 to March 1518. Ordinarily he lectured twice a week, on Mondays and Fridays, and apparently in the noon period. His glosses were intended to be copied directly into a specially printed edition of the Latin text of the Epistle. His scholia do not seem to have been written out in full, but to have been delivered from quite extensive notes, containing, for example, the quotations from John Chrysostom which are so frequent in the lectures. Unfortunately, neither Luther's own copy of the Latin text with glosses nor his lecture notes for the scholia have been found, so that we remain less reliably informed about his *Lectures on Hebrews* than about his *Lectures on Romans*. But it remains abundantly clear that both in its form and in its content this material comes from the man who, during the very months that he was lecturing on Hebrews, was also achieving notoriety as the author of the Ninety-five Theses.

The arduous task of translating the Latin of Luther's *Lectures on Hebrews* into English was the last work of the longtime associate editor of the exegetical works in the American Edition, Professor Walter A. Hansen, who died on November 28, 1967. It manifests that combination of classical learning and stylistic sensitivity for which so many other volumes of our edition—and their editor—are indebted to Walter A. Hansen.

J. P.

LECTURES ON TITUS

Translated by
JAROSLAV PELIKAN

FOREWORD

A FTER the completion of the Epistle of John,[1] I have been think-ing about our next series of lectures, so that we are not idle and do not eat our bread in vain, especially because Paul admonishes us (cf. 1 Tim. 4:7): If we have a talent from the Lord, let us train ourselves in godliness. The highest work of godliness is to meditate on the Word of God in order that we may teach and exhort one another.

The Epistle to Titus is short, but it is a kind of epitome and summary of other, wordier epistles. We should be imbued with the attitudes that are taught in it. Paul is the sort of teacher who is engaged most of all in these two topics, either teaching or exhorting. Moreover, he never exhorts in such a way that he fails to mingle didactic, that is, doctrinal, instruction with it. And so while this epistle is obviously a hortatory one, yet he writes in such a way that he superbly mingles doctrine with exhortation, and in double measure. He is a true teacher, one who both teaches and exhorts. By his teaching he sets down what is to be believed by faith, and by his exhortation he sets down what is to be done. Thus by doctrine he builds up faith, by exhortation he builds up life. He begins with exhortation, yet he mingles instruction with it. Therefore this is a hortatory epistle, yet not exclusively so.

---

[1] Just four days earlier, on November 7, 1527, Luther had completed his lectures on 1 John; cf. *Luther's Works,* 30, pp. x—xi.

1. *Paul.* For such a short epistle this is a rather long salutation, almost equal to that in the Epistle to the Romans. In other epistles it is not his custom to present so long a salutation as he does in Romans and Galatians. The apostle foresaw that his epistle would be preserved in the church of God. Even in the very salutation he teaches faith. All his words are framed in such a way that they can be weapons for the right hand and for the left (cf. 2 Cor. 6:7). Everything glows with great stress and emphasis. His first assurance is that he calls himself a minister. Every minister ought to glory in this, that he is an instrument of God through which God teaches, and he ought not doubt that he is teaching the Word of God. Peter says (1 Peter 4:11): "As one who utters oracles of God." If he does not know that what he is saying is the Word of God, let him keep silence; for "God has spoken in His sanctuary" (Ps. 60:6). Therefore heretics should keep silence, because they are utterly uncertain. Whoever is certain that he has an oracle of God knows that he is pleasing to God, because he speaks what God has given to him through His Holy Spirit from heaven. Paul boasts of that assurance here.

A *servant of God* is more general than "apostle." He is not a servant of the Law; nor is he a servant of men so far as the assurance and the certainty of his doctrine are concerned; nor is he a servant intent on imposing the slavery of the Law. Thus whoever is faithful in his own function is a servant of God. Moses was a servant of God. Therefore we read in Rom. 1:9: "Whom I serve." "Servant of God" is a magnificent and outstanding title. The words "servant of God" should be pondered carefully, for such a person has an office assigned by God. He is saying this to make us certain that his word is the Word of God, as Moses and the other prophets said: "Thus says the Lord." This boasting was truly necessary, because Paul brought a new doctrine about the will of God and needed to stop the mouths of those who said:

"Paul was a man, etc." Augustine said: "If anyone wants to teach, let him be sure of his calling and of his doctrine."[2] 1 Peter 4:11 says: "Whoever speaks, [let him speak] as one who utters oracles of God."

An apostle. Not only do I serve God, but I have an office with which I have been commissioned. This is another kind of certainty. Not only does he know that he serves God and that he speaks the Word of God, but also that he has been sent and commissioned by God and that an obligation to teach has been laid upon him. To know the Word of God and to teach it are two different things. He who has the Word of God does not immediately teach it unless he is called. He should not teach as an interloper. Here you see what it means to serve Christ and what sort of kingdom Christ has, namely, a spiritual and an invisible one. His kingdom is not seen; therefore His ministers are those who rule by the Word and who bring the Word. Hence the kingdom of Christ is ruled, and Christ is recognized, solely by the Word. Now he announces what sort of ministry he has, namely, a spiritual and invisible one. For what purpose are you an apostle? What is it that you bring?

It is not without reason that he adds the words "an apostle of Jesus Christ," for the prophets and Moses were also able to boast that they were servants of God, as Heb. 3:5 says. So it is said of David too (cf. 1 Sam. 16:12-13). Moses had an office, and he taught, as Ex. 19 and 20, 2 Cor. 3:7, and Heb. 12:21 declare. "I am frightened, and I tremble." Not only were the people terrified by his teaching, but he himself was. He did not have faith at the Waters of Contention (Num. 20:12-13), and he died before the entrance into the Promised Land (Deut. 34:5). But Paul is not the sort of servant that Moses and the prophets were. He brings better things, as he says in 2 Cor. 3:7-11. Therefore he adds "an apostle of Jesus Christ," as he also says in 2 Cor. 5:20; and here he adds: "To proclaim the faith." We ought to be excited by this word, as by the title in the Gospel (Matt. 1:1), "the book of the genealogy of Jesus Christ," which means that we listen to One who is present and whom kings and prophets expected so eagerly. By design He first serves the Jews. The name "Jesus"

---

[2] Cf. Augustine, *De doctrina Christiana*, Book IV, ch. 4, par. 6, *Corpus Christianorum, Series Latina*, XXXII, 119—120.

was hateful to the Jews, who called Him "Thola." [3] Acts 17:5 says this; and in Acts 25:24 the Gentiles, specifically Festus, attest to this. Somehow the servant of the great Lord was an exception to this, as can be seen throughout the epistles. "No matter how hateful I am to you, I am still the apostle of Him who was promised to the fathers." "And he who does not hear My messenger [does not hear Me]" (cf. Luke 10:16).

According to faith. These are extraordinarily outstanding words, and they are full of doctrine. Here one could discuss the sum total of the Christian life. These words contradict false dogmas. Usually he joins faith and truth, as in 1 Tim. 4:12. In Eph. 4:13-15 he says that we become truthful by attaining to the unity of the faith and of the knowledge of the Son of God, and again (Titus 1:15) that "all things are pure to those who know." Faith is that by which we believe in the Lord Jesus through the word of the apostles. It is that by which we have the forgiveness of sins and righteousness through Christ, as the canticle of Zechariah says (Luke 1:77): "To give knowledge." The first part of our doctrine is to know that through Christ we have the forgiveness of sins, as 1 Cor. 1:30 says: "God made Him our wisdom." From this faith there obviously follows the knowledge of the truth. For if I have knowledge, I live in the kingdom of mercy. If I slip and fall, I rise again. It follows that outward things contribute nothing to righteousness, such as where we are or what we wear, etc. In Gal. 2:21 he himself concludes: "If it were by works [then Christ died to no purpose]." Therefore "neither circumcision counts for anything nor uncircumcision" (1 Cor. 7:19); nor do monastic vows, the use of Masses, and the things that can be called "the elemental spirits of the universe." To know this now is to know the truth. Thus from faith there flows this knowledge, which is true, and is certain that whatever outward thing there is besides faith does not justify. Forms of worship were instituted in such variety among the Jews and among us that they are beyond number. "Go and learn what this means" (Matt. 9:13), that what is most important to you nevertheless does not count for anything. Therefore those who want to please God through sacrifices are in error. And to the disciples who were plucking grain on the Sabbath, Christ said (Mark 2:27): "The

---

[3] On the meaning of this term, cf. *Luther's Works,* 14, p. 269, n. 25.

Sabbath was made for men." Here the righteousness that consists in the observance of days, even of the Sabbath, is rejected.
"I do not care," He says, "for a greater one is here" (Matt. 12:6);
that is, the Sabbath does not justify, but faith in Christ does. To
believe that the Sabbath justifies is to believe something contrary
to the truth. But what of the new moon? This does not count for
anything either, Paul says (Col. 2:16). This is the truth. Why do
we fast frequently? We are "sons [of the bridechamber]," He
says (Matt. 9:15). This was a good and a true fasting, not like the
fasting mentioned in Matt. 6:16. Nevertheless, he rejects it. Fasting
does not justify, but faith in Christ does. If you have this, then
you are pleasing to God, whether you fast or not. Eat whatever
God has given. "Nothing is to be rejected," Paul says in 1 Tim. 4:4.
And why did David eat the bread of the Presence? (Matt. 12:3-4)
Nothing is pure or holy apart from faith. To us all things are holy,
even sins committed against human traditions. Thus touching
the chalice or taking off the cowl are great sins, but they become
the very opposite, the ultimate in righteousness. But there is
neither condemnation nor salvation in outward things, but only
in believing. Therefore we say in accordance with the mind of
Christ that nothing justifies except believing in Christ. Therefore whatever else has been instituted for the purpose of justification is an error. Therefore the decretals of the pope and the
rules of the fathers are in error, because they established outward
ceremonies concerning food. They are in error because they conflict with the doctrine that "Christ was put to death [for our tres-
passes and raised for our justification]," Rom. 4:25. Thus with
one word all pomp and all traditions are overthrown. Therefore
faith and truth extend far and wide. I do not preach on the basis
of fasting or the Sabbath; I am not an apostle on the basis of altars,
Masses, and vigils. Therefore nothing is conducive to righteousness except faith and knowledge. Whoever entrusts himself to
Christ has this knowledge, as has been said above. This is the
great light, as Christ shows by His example in the Gospel, when
He rejects everything that they bring from the Law of God and
from the traditions of men: "In vain do they worship Me" (Matt.
15:9); as was said above, Paul expresses the same thing even more
forcefully with his thunderbolts. To know the truth is to know
that those things are free. It is a great thing that a wretch such
as I am under obligation to say against the pope and against all

[W, XXV, 9, 10]

the clergy that they are in error. And yet it is true, for either they
are liars or Christ is. You see how blind they are; therefore they
do not understand "an apostle in accordance with faith and the
knowledge of the truth." We have this knowledge, that everything
which is outside of Christ is free, be it the Law of Moses or the
law of the pope. If you get married, you have not sinned; nor
have you sinned if you eat fish on Friday. 1 Cor. 3:21, 23: "All
things are yours," with this exception, "you are Christ's." What
you apostles teach — if I like it, I will keep it; if I do not like it,
I will not keep it. In any case, it is a danger to our souls if we do
not believe in Christ; it is not a danger if you fail in your obedience. That is why he says "in accordance with faith."

Of the elect of God. Why this? It seems that this epistle was
written near the end of the apostle's life and that he was sorely
troubled. His word was being despised just as that of Jeremiah
the prophet had been. He was called a seducer and a heretic;
he was accused of destroying Moses and the temple. They stirred
up hatred against him among the Gentiles so that people were
disgusted at the apostle, as 1 Cor. 4:13 says, and the false apostles
were undermining whole churches. What was one to do? "I preach
and pray amid great danger. I give them the greatest of blessings,
and this is how they requite me. So the Gospel suffers slander,
and from our school there arise heretics. Nevertheless, I do not
for the sake of all this stop preaching the Gospel, even though
Jews blaspheme, heathen persecute, and heretics arise. Nevertheless, I shall go on teaching because I know that the elect will
accept it." With this word he looks into the tragedy which the
Word of God suffers. They will fall by the wayside. "I am doing
everything for the sake of the elect." We ought to be acting the
same way. The papists slander us. They are stubborn and attack
the manifest truth, and still they slander us. Moreover, those who
have worked with us and planted with us are stirring up sects.
The Anabaptists, the Sacramentarians, original sin,[4] and many
such fanatics have come. Thank God that He did not disclose to
me that such heresies were to follow, for I would never have begun. We have this comfort: "We did not begin this for the sake
of you who are stubborn nor for the sake of the Sacramentarians,

---

[4] Presumably Luther is referring to those who denied original sin, viz., certain
of the Anabaptists, who opposed infant Baptism on the grounds that it was not
necessary.

and we shall not quit for your sakes. We began for the sake of those who are yet to come." Thus the Word of Christ is full of sects and stumbling blocks; that is, it stands in the midst of these things, and sects arise; but it prevails. The enemies of the Gospel throw up this objection to me: "What good is arising from your gospel? The people are degenerating into beasts. It is accomplishing nothing that is good. Wars and all sorts of evil are being provoked. Heresies and discord arise." Let it happen as it is happening. I preach the faith to the elect. Therefore let no one be offended if he sees that persecution follows the Word or that sects arise. "Not all have faith" (2 Thess. 3:2) is our consolation, as Paul certainly consoled himself with this word. If the others do not accept this faith, it is still present among the elect of God. He has said a great deal in a few words. Faith prevails against all works, efforts, the stumblings of the elect, persecutions, the cross, etc.

The faith. Paul is stinging the false apostles. Not the Law, circumcision, works such as those of Moses, the traditions of the fathers, ceremonies such as those of the Pharisees, rosaries, vows, Masses, vigils, monastic works such as those of the papists, the abandonment of property such as that of the Anabaptists — but faith! Here the Old Testament and all forms of worship and of righteousness throughout the world are abolished. And we see what preaching deserves the name "apostolic," as in 1 Cor. 1:17: "Christ did not send me [to baptize, but to preach one Gospel]"; that is, they preach a Word which does not require works but faith, the Word spoken of in Rom. 10:10. Look at the sermon in Rom. 3:23: "All have sinned." And in Acts (1:8): "Go into the world."

The truth which accords with godliness. Here again he distinguishes between "bodily training" (1 Tim. 4:8) and a godliness which avoids extremes and is on the proper way. Godliness means to serve God and to worship Him. The worship of God among Christians is not the sort of trumpery which wears out the body by chanting at night, fasting, and torturing the body. God knows nothing of such worship; but where His Word is diligently used, there He is being worshiped purely. Souls are aroused to faith, love for God and one's neighbor is taught. To believe in Christ, to be moved to compassion for the poor and the weak, and to persist in these things — this is our religion, that is, the Christian

religion. And if a cross follows, this is perfect Christianity. Godliness is to believe in Jesus Christ and to love one's brother. It
belongs to this that faith should be trained through the Word.
Here God is being served because habitations of the Spirit are
prepared for Him. For this godliness great exercise of the body,
such as fasting, is not required; what is required is that I meditate diligently. This is the work of the soul, and speaking is the
highest exercise of the body. Godliness [5] is the feeling which
fathers have for their children and vice versa. This knowledge
of the truth is a kind that is not idle; for it "accords with godliness," that is, it teaches and has godliness, and godliness is located
in it. He calls Timothy "a good minister of Christ" (1 Tim. 4:6).
When I teach that only faith in Christ is righteousness, and that
to be a servant, a celibate, or a husband is good, and that other
things are free, then this is truly godliness, because I am instruct-
ing souls so that they may know how they ought to believe. Therefore there is no godliness except in faith and in truth, because we
know that nothing binds the conscience. For while this thought
is useful for the present life, its purpose is to redeem not only from
sins but also from death. Sin has deserved death, and "the wages
of sin is death," as Rom. 6:23 says. Our doctrine is the godliness
which we teach, and it prepares us for eternal life. This is the
boast of our doctrine. Those who have been taught are free of all
human traditions and exercise themselves with these supreme
benefits of Christian doctrine.

In hope. We do not yet see the life which we attain through
godliness. First we must fall asleep. Our life is prepared, but in
hope. That which is hoped for, however, is not seen (cf. Rom. 8:24).
Our cross must be understood in hope at the same time; for where
there is the exercise of godliness, there the cross is not lacking.
Because everything is condemned, there is not peace but a cross
(cf. Matt. 10:34). Therefore if we employ the Word, we bear the
reproach of evil both from the whole world and from our brethren,
and the devil accuses us. But under the cross which we experience,
eternal life lies hidden. If it did not lie hidden, it would be the
present life. Therefore we have it in hope. When I am aware of
my sin, I am aware of life even in the midst of my sense of sin,
and even in death I think to myself: "I am alive, and I shall live."

---

[5] Here Luther is harking back to the meaning that *pietas* had in Roman usage,
where it meant (to use the closest English equivalent) "filial piety."

If a martyr is to withstand, he must not judge according to how he feels. Otherwise he despairs. Instead, he should say: "Even though I am aware of my sin, Jesus Christ intercedes, and He does not accuse us." His intercession must be grasped by faith, which senses in fact that Christ is accusing, but which expects in hope that Christ is interceding for it. In that death there will be life for me, for Christ is the Lord of death. "Even though I walk through the valley of the shadow," Ps. 23:4 says. Of course, he realizes that he is being overcome. Nevertheless, he says: "I fear no evil." Here hope is aroused, contrary to external appearances, and he does not believe that God is wrathful. We, too, experience the cross, and death appears to us, as Rom. 8:38 states, if not in fact, yet in our conscience through Satan. Death and sin appear, but I announce life and faith, but in hope. Therefore if you want to be saved, you must battle against your feelings. Hope means to expect life in the midst of death, and righteousness in the midst of sins; for no one can conceive of a life in which there is no sin. It is useless for you to run to a Carthusian. Instead, you should say: "I am a sinner and can never set myself free. I have been ungrateful for the blessings of God. But in the midst of sin I have the hope of eternal life." That is a great proclamation. "Hope which is seen is not hope" (Rom. 8:24).[6]

You have heard the salutation of this epistle, in which Paul exalts his ministry and boasts of it, but with a kind of holy pride, which is a sure confidence in God and a boasting over against the traditions of men which teach the contrary; these are "a reed shaken by the wind" (Matt. 11:7). It is my task to teach the faith of the elect, the knowledge of the truth, in which there is genuine godliness, which is profitable not only for the present life, for the feeding of the belly, but for life eternal, which is in hope. These are grand and priceless words, and they are understood by faith alone.

Which God, who never lies, promised ages ago. This is also a word of confidence, because he is speaking against those who are timid and weak in faith when he says "who does not lie." For to believe that in hope one has a life that is eternal, this passes all understanding (Phil. 4:7), even that of the godly. The ungodly

[6] This is the end of the first lecture, delivered on November 11, 1527, and the beginning of the second, delivered on November 12.

ridicule this proclamation when they hear it. So did the heathen; it was folly to them (1 Cor. 1:18). The Sadducees did not believe that there is an afterlife. All of them ridiculed the idea of a life after death. This is especially what Pliny and his associates believed. So did Suetonius.[7] But the godly strive to believe this, because it is the greatest of doctrines to believe in eternal life. To buoy up those who are weak in faith he says "who does not lie," which sounds more effective than if he had said "who is truthful." A negative way of speaking is a more forceful way to express feelings. "He will not lie to me." Thus the weak should be buoyed up with these words: "Do you not think that He will live up to what He has said?" Thus Christ gives the consolation in Luke 12:32: "Fear not, O little flock." This consolation has always been necessary for all believers; for if a man looks about him, he stumbles at the idea of eternal life. Our primary impression is that we are sinners, but it is a sublime thing to believe that God has prepared eternal life. He raises the poor up from the dirt and leads him from sin and death; He crowns the unworthy. Thus He says in John (John 14:1-2): "Let not your heart be troubled. In My Father's house, do not doubt. Eternal life is promised to you. It is a grand thing, but do not fear. You are a little flock, but you should have the courage to believe; for it has pleased the Father. Besides, if dwelling places were not prepared, I would prepare them for you now."

Which He promised. Here again He does away with merit. We have not merited it; we are not worthy. God wants us to be humbled and cast down in our glory and our powers, but He manifests His love and mercy. The light was given, not after we prayed for it, but "ages ago." Thus Christ says in Matt. 25:34: "Prepared for you." This is a word in the New Testament which always contradicts the idea of merit, as in Galatians (3:18): "God gave it to Abraham by a promise and before the Law." Therefore the promise is sheer mercy, because no one asked Him to make the promise. It is the greatest of consolations for weak consciences that He does not base eternal life on our virtues or merits. If He had done that, no one would be saved; for we are so fragile, unstable, and unsure that after one hour we become ungodly and unbelieving. Therefore in order that our hope might be solid and sure, life eternal is based upon the promise of God, which cannot

7 Perhaps Luther is referring to Pliny's letter to Suetonius, *Epistolae,* I, 18.

lie. There it is certain and firm. The foolish man builds upon the sand (Matt. 7:26). The term "ago" also contradicts the idea of merit in order to show that God does not vary. Neither the promise nor God is temporal. He promised freely, when there was no one to ask or to merit. He promised within Himself, and the promise was complete in God before the world, but it had not been manifested. What good would it have done if He had promised eternally and had not manifested it to us? Therefore God manifested this faith and godliness at the proper time, that is, at the time of the coming of Christ, who was sent to manifest this Word. Indeed, He did so long before this through Jacob and Daniel. Against our fanatics he says: *His Word through preaching.* He is speaking of the oral Word. Next, *with which I have been entrusted* means that he did not do it on his own. Paul was not entrusted with the inner Word, which the Holy Spirit alone preaches by inspiration. "Through" means that He let it be preached.

Through preaching. Here he clearly explains what kind of servant of God and apostle of Christ he is, not one who worships God, as he once did, through the observance of the Law, according to Phil. 3:9, as the Jews had imagined and the papists still do; but "through preaching," as we read in Acts (10:42). What sort of kingdom does Christ have? A spiritual and invisible one. He Himself is visibly absent, and yet through His Word He rules and administers His kingdom. Therefore it is not a political kingdom, as the fanatics suppose, and He has servants who are not armed but who teach in weakness, as Gal. 4:13 and 1 Cor. 2:3 state. It does not consist in ceremonies, in external pomp, in special places and persons, as the papists suppose, who, even if they preach, yet do not preach faith but only their own imaginings.

He comes full circle in that he calls himself an apostle again. He is not talking about ceremonial elements, but the Word concerning faith and truth teaches godliness. *By command,* by delegation, something with which he has been commissioned. He wants to say that every herald ought to bring a mandate, a command, an order that is issued; there must be a mandate, an authority, or a right to instruct and teach, as the lawyers say. "I have a mandate to preach. God the Savior has given me this mandate." This is a very beautiful salutation in which the sum total of the Christian doctrine has been made known in very few words, even though the epistle is a hortatory one. Paul is an apostle, not from men but entirely from God. Therefore he brings a Word which is the Word of God.

To Titus, my true child, the salutation continues. "True," that is, sincere, or in German *rechtschaffen.* This commendation applies not only to Titus himself—he was such a one—but Paul is also considering the false apostles; he had met with many of these, as he complains in all his epistles. Where he had instructed many sons, some of them became illegitimate, degenerate, and false sons—sons only in name, not in fact. But of Titus he says that he strove to take the same steps with Paul (2 Cor. 12:18), that he taught the same thing, that in everything he expressed the image of Paul both in word and in deed. If they teach, think, say, do, live, and express everything the same concerning Jesus, they never stir up heresies. In addition, they have the same crosses and sufferings, and each has compassion with the other, so that there is no dissembling either in spirit or in public behavior; they have the same attitude, judgment, life, cross, suffering, and compassion. With this word he also taunts the false apostles, sons who imitate Paul in part, that is, in their baptizing but not in their teaching. They taught that there was no resurrection of the dead (1 Cor. 15:12). Therefore Titus was true and not like the others, who were degenerate. To avoid the impression that he means a natural son, he adds *spiritual:* "I have taught you, and through my doctrine you have been regenerated in faith. Thus I am your spiritual father, and you are my son." Just as a son gets the substance and nature of his father from his father's body, so the spiritual son gets his faith from Paul, his teacher. Thus he has the same likeness that his parent has, that is, faith, which you and I also have. Christ forbids us to call anyone "father" or "master" (Matt. 23:9-10). What are we to say to this? "Do not be called." And James says (3:1): "Let not many of you become teachers." Why does he say here that he is the father of Titus, and to Timothy (1 Tim. 2:7) that he is "a teacher of the Gentiles"? There is a similar expression in 1 Cor. 4:15. And 2 Peter 3:4 says: "The fathers fell asleep." Here he calls the apostles "fathers." Anyone who is a father in Christ does not divide the fathers into many fathers. Paul the teacher was the vicegerent of Christ. Arius is a different kind of father from Paul; they disagree both in their teachings and in their life, and the form of unity in Christ is severed. If there is to be only one father, then Christ is our father in Paul, in John, or in Peter. Thus all of us are sons in Christ, because John teaches nothing different from Peter. Therefore they can be called fathers in Christ, but not in themselves, because I listen to Christ speaking to me, not as the apostle himself speaks but as my Lord speaks through his mouth. And so I call Paul "father," not for his own sake but for Christ's. Thus he says to the Corinthians (1 Cor. 11:1): "Be imitators of me as I am of Christ," not merely "of me" but "of me as, etc." Here he unites himself with Christ, so that there is one example and pattern which both Christ and Paul set forth. In this sense we are fathers, provided that our fatherhood redounds to Christ, our Head. For through the apostles He speaks to us and rules us. Neither the pope nor the heretics do this. They do not say: "Be imitators of us as we are of Christ." Christ did not speak of observing days, etc. If the pope were to say: "It is not my desire that you imitate me to the extent that I imitate Christ," then the text would apply (John 10:5): "Sheep do not know the voice of strangers." This pertains to any father or preacher in whom I do not hear the voice of Christ.

Grace and peace. In his other epistles he makes a practice of combining these two; and writing to Timothy (1 Tim. 1:2), he puts "mercy" between them. I believe he did this to express a more vigorous feeling against the false apostles. Others say that he was a bishop in battle. Because Paul is being utterly assailed by the trial that he has preached in vain, and that the Word remains in only a very few, therefore he expands upon his greeting. "May God grant you His mercy," he says. He is speaking with the same feeling here. "I am losing those whom I have served every day, and every day I am acquiring enemies from among my sons. You are the only one who remains." Thus he expands upon his greeting because of his emotion and because of the intensified trial. I for my part would do the same thing and would express my increased emotion because of the dangers.

Grace is the favor of God by which He has forgiven us all our sins. Mercy is that by which He pities and overlooks if in any way you fall and are imperfect, and increases His gifts. The third benefit is the assurance of conscience. Here he attributes the same honor to Christ and to the Father. And he proves that Christ is true God by nature, because it is the distinctive office of God to grant these three benefits. Therefore when grace proceeds from Christ, this is a work by which it is proved that He is God;

for God does not turn over to anyone else the granting of these
three gifts and works. So far the salutation and superscription.

This is why. Here you see that the epistle is a paraenetic and
hortatory one, for it teaches and instructs about morals. In other
epistles he would have begun by speaking about the mercy of
God which has been shown to the human race through Christ.
Under the obligation of the necessity to visit other churches, he
had left Titus in Crete. He could not stay as long in Crete as he
had intended; he had not yet ordained elders who would teach
the Word after his departure. He had appointed some, but not
in all the cities. In the midst of this task he is compelled to break
off and to go elsewhere. "Therefore," he says, "I left you there.
Otherwise I would have taken you with me. You were to amend
what was defective." Paul indicates that he had arranged many
things, but that he had left some things to be arranged by Titus,
things which he himself was unable to do. Therefore he tells him:
"If you see cities in which there are no parishes, establish and
ordain elders. Appoint whatever there is to be ordained; for though
all are priests, not all are ministers."

Christians are all priests, as 1 Peter 2:5, 9 says. Jer. 31:34 says:
"They shall all know Me," and Is. 54:13 says: "All your sons shall
be taught by the Lord." It is the office of the priests to teach, to
pray, and to sacrifice. The first of these is well known; the second
is taught in the statement "Whatever you ask, etc." (John 14:13);
the third is taught in Heb. 13:5 and in Rom. 12:1. But not all are
elders, that is, ministers, as he has commanded Titus. First he
gives Titus the general commission to appoint elders. Then he
prescribes what kind of men they ought to be.

Christians all have a priesthood, but they do not all have the
priestly function. Although all can teach and exhort, nevertheless
one ought to do so, and the other ought to listen, so that they do
not speak at the same time. Therefore it should be noted that it
was Paul's ordinance that he should select "elders" (in the plural)
in each city, and they are called bishops and elders. Therefore
at the time of the apostles every city had numerous bishops. Then
Christianity was in outstanding condition. This meaning of the
word "bishop" disappeared, and it was subjected to very long
and very distorted abuse. Now it is called the human ordinance
by which a man is in charge of five cities. Thus human traditions
are never harmless, no matter how good they may be. Bishop

Alexander began to be the chief over all the rest,[8] and from this
there developed the title and authority, with the result that no
feature of the episcopacy has remained. The apostolate has now
become the office of acquiring property and of putting on pomp.
There is no doctrine, not to speak of words and deeds. Every city
ought to have many bishops, that is, inspectors or visitors. Such
an inspector should be the parish clergyman along with the chap-
lain, so that they may share the duties and see how people live
and what is taught. He would see who is a usurer, and then he
would speak the Word of healing and correction. This apostolic
type of episcopacy has long since been done away with. In Acts
20:28 Paul speaks of the bishops of a single church: "Take heed . . .
in which the Holy Spirit has made you bishops." All bishops
nowadays are of the devil. There is no hope of salvation in any
of them. They sit in the seats of bishops, and no one of them is
a teacher. If they do not function in the office of a bishop, one
cannot tell who is feeding the sheep.

In every town, that is, many in each town. Elders are those
who have authority in the Word. We are called bishops by apostolic rite, and that is what we are. We teach Christ, and we see
who believe and who live in a Christian way; on the other hand,
we rebuke those who do not do so, and if they refuse to change,
we exclude them from the fellowship of Christians and from the
sacraments. "Imitate my pattern. You have seen me ordain several
elders in each city. Do the same thing. Moreover, I do not want
you to ordain just anyone indiscriminately." Ordination was not
performed as our bishops do it, but the elders gathered and performed it by the laying on of hands.

6. *If any man is blameless.* "See to it that you do not appoint
thieves and robbers, scoundrels." Jerome thinks that only someone who has lived a pure and holy life since his baptism should
become a bishop.[9] Whoever is such a man, we shall commend
him. He should be someone who cannot be accused. According
to the list Paul makes, he should not have public guilt which

---

[8] It is not clear whom Luther means here by "Bishop Alexander," unless perhaps Alexander I, bishop of Rome 105—115 or 109—119; more commonly he
attributes this development to Pope Gregory I (590—604).

[9] Jerome, *Adversus Jovinianum*, Book I, ch. 35, *Patrologia, Series Latina*,
XXIII, 270—271.

causes people to stumble. Paul is referring to public vices which can be made the subject of an accusation. But this does not mean, does it, that they should be without any guilt at all, without any flesh and blood? "He himself is beset with weakness," as Hebrews says (Heb. 5:2). But Paul is speaking about public vices, where the state is obliged to say and to give testimony about him that he is doing me an injustice and that a detractor will find something to cavil at; that is, he should be the kind of person who cannot be accused openly and publicly. He must pray: "Forgive" (Luke 11:4).

The husband of one wife. Despite everything that has been said about celibacy, an apostolic bishop elected by God can have a wife. If this divine ordinance and apostolic regulation does not have more validity than the ordinance and regulation of the pope, who can contradict it? They take it to mean that a diocesan, a parish priest, can have many vicars but cannot have two parishes, and that a bishop cannot have two dioceses at the same time.[10] Are these not shocking and obvious monstrosities? Who ever heard of anything like this? These human traditions were a darkness thick enough to be felt (cf. Ex. 10:21). We know what celibacy achieved. The Archbishop of Mainz has two wives who are incompatible,[11] and the pope has as many concubines as Solomon had. No one is allowed to be both a husband and a bridegroom except Christ alone, as John 3:29 says. Thus Christ alone is one flesh with His church, and He alone has washed it with His blood. Fie on their dirges and their darkness! If anyone had ever said: "What do you mean, a wife?" the answer would be that by divine ordinance he should be the husband of one wife.[12]

A man who is to be selected as bishop should be blameless and the husband of one wife. I have said that this text is a kind of divine oracle against the great pretense and argument which our conscience sets forth, namely, the custom of so many centuries

[10] Comments attributed to Augustine, explaining "husband of one wife" this way, had been collected in the *Glossa ordinaria* on this passage, whence they had passed into Gratian's compilation of the canon law.

[11] Either Luther is referring here to the gossip he knew, and cited elsewhere, about the personal life of Albert of Mainz, or he is speaking of the conflict of interest between Albert's position as archbishop of Mainz and his position as elector of Brandenburg.

[12] This is the end of the second lecture, delivered on November 12, 1527, and the beginning of the third, delivered on November 13.

and the examples of so many saintly fathers. The fathers observed celibacy freely, without coercion by any law; later on it was enacted into law. Nothing could have happened that was more monstrous than celibacy. In the kingdom of the pope a bishop is blameless when he is without a wife. If he is punishable for other vices, that does not count. Let him associate with harlots; one can do penance for this. And so it follows. I am saying this in order to strengthen consciences, for the saintly fathers lived as celibates. This has been discussed, and if someone arises and gets married, he also knows that on the Last Day God will approve this through the apostle Paul. Look at Paphnutius at the celebrated council of 318 bishops at Nicea.[13] Among the other articles there was also celibacy. The majority wanted celibacy to be legislated. Paphnutius alone resisted, and he was a martyr. He opposed a universal council. He did not want to give occasion to lust but wanted "the marriage bed [undefiled]," as Heb. 13:4 says. Afterwards they did not dare to establish celibacy, even though the first bishops voluntarily lived as celibates: "If you wish, live that way." Nevertheless, at this time anyone who wants to get married should do so, in order to confirm the oracle of God. At that time, too, there was no obligation of a vow; but the monks could return home from the desert. Thus this text speaks of "his children." They maintain: "We grant that husbands were selected as bishops, but they did not get married afterwards. So it was with Peter and the bishops whom Paul ordained, whom he found in the state of matrimony." I reply: "What was permissible once is permissible always. If it is permissible that he be a husband, why is it not permissible that he become one?" Paul says and argues that the marriage of a priest is approved. It is the same regardless of whether he is a husband or becomes one. 1 Cor. 7:7 is a perfectly clear text: "I wish that all were [as I myself am]," where he says that he is a celibate; and in chapter 9:5 he says in argument: "Do we not have the right [to be accompanied by a wife]?" Here he reserves the right and makes the claim that it is possible for an elder to become a husband. Therefore their argument is the mere quibbling of sophists. The issue here is a station in life which is approved by God, for the Gospel did not come into the world to destroy the works of God but to restore

[13] The source of Luther's information about Paphnutius is probably Cassiodorus, *Historia tripartita*, Book II, ch. 14, *Patrologia, Series Latina,* LXIX, 933.

them, not to amputate the limbs or to destroy the body. The Epistle to Timothy (1 Tim. 4:3) speaks of those "who forbid marriage." The Gospel confirms and establishes God's creation. And the text clearly states that marriage is a creation of God; therefore the Gospel confirms it. It is said that someone may be a husband before he becomes a bishop but may not become one afterwards. Yet the episcopacy is an ordinance of the Gospel; it does not abolish God's creation. It is not permissible to establish human traditions contrary to that which has been ordained by God. Thus it is not permissible to set up a so-called vow as a commandment contrary to the commandment to honor parents. The same thing applies here to the divinely ordained liberty of marrying or remaining unmarried. Therefore it is not permissible to make a vow contrary to this ordinance of liberty or to establish rules contrary to it. Hence Paul calls it a "doctrine of demons" and a "pretension," a lie, a departure from the faith, a false appearance, because it is directly contrary to the divine ordinance (1 Tim. 4:1-2). For Christ wants a minister of the Word to have a wife, but the pope does not. You can see which of them has the spirit of demons. So we should console those who are timid and afflicted with scrupulosity, those who do not see the Word, but, imitating the example and behavior of others, get married. We must gather and be filled with the evident authorities, namely, Scripture. We should say: "Go and argue with Paul. And if that is not enough, go to Christ. Fight it out with Him, 1 Tim. 4:1, 1 Cor. 9:5." "But the pope prohibits it, and you are opposed by the example of so many fathers and by the practice of the whole world." Yet they are not greater than Christ. If they are, you have won; but if they are not, then I have won. The practice of the saintly fathers was voluntary, as the Council of Nicea proves. Later on they changed this freedom to necessity. In this way weak consciences are to be encouraged, so that they can respond to the Word. Do this in every temptation. If the Word is not available, you are immediately done for. But if you are armed with the Word, Satan has been conquered. Therefore he does everything he can to remove the Word from your heart, so that he may have an idle soul to work on. On the other hand, "Resist the devil and he will flee from you" (James 4:7). *His children are believers.* Therefore a bishop ought to be the kind of man who keeps watch over his flock. What do our monks and nuns do? All those canonical clergy, vicars,

altarists, monks, and whoever they all may be — who among them
does any teaching or any reading?! Yet they all lay claim to the
title "elder." They are ignorant, they despise the Word, all they
do is persecute. If they dropped their titles and called themselves
men of the world and were honest about it, there could be hope
for them, but not as long as they claim to be elders and to want
to live as such. But you may say: "I have said Masses." Christ
and Paul did not establish this. It is horrible to say what happens when these texts are examined. Before God all temples,
monasteries, and academies are drowned. On the basis of this
passage some argue that it is not permissible for a bishop to live
as a celibate.[14] Paul does not force either marriage or celibacy
upon anyone. At that time those who were ordained as elders
were almost all from among the Jews, among whom it was not
permitted to live a celibate life. Paul only wants to establish that
it is permitted either to be married or to be celibate. The matter
is within our power. For the sake of setting an example, a minister
of the Word could get married to spite the pope. That is how I proceeded, for I was not in a mood to get married.[15] Because a bishop
is to be set up as a light of the world and an example to the state,
therefore nothing in his home ought to be contrary to the faith
or unchristian. Otherwise both Gentiles and Christians are offended. If he had no children, would he still be a bishop? The
matter is free. If God gives children, he has them. But how can
it be a matter of his decision to have them? If they are not believers, let him put them away and not acknowledge them. He
recognizes immediately from their fruits whether they are believers, if they read the Word gladly.

Not open to the charge of being profligate: They should
be free of the accusation not only of lust but also of profligacy.
'Ασωτία means that one lives a wild life and carouses, as the youth
usually do. The Greek people were especially addicted to ἀσωτία.
They would drink until midnight and then they give themselves
over to sexual immorality and to revelry. Consider how young
people live and how drunk they are, that is, which of them can
be accused of ἀσωτία. But on the contrary they ought to be subject

---

[14] This may have been Jovinian's exegesis of this passage; cf. Jerome, *Adversus Jovinianum,* Book I, ch. 34, *Patrologia, Series Latina,* XXIII, 270.

[15] As these comments suggest, it had been with some reluctance that Luther
had married Katherine von Bora on June 13, 1525.

to their parents, obedient, retiring, well-disciplined, so that they obey their father. If they are not this way, let him put them away and thus show that he is a father to them. We have the example of the sons of Eli, who were notorious for their ἀσωτία. They devoured any sacrifices they wanted and consorted with women. They really led a wild, profligate, and shameless life. But he did not correct them: "No, my sons" (1 Sam. 2:24). But a father says: "You accursed scoundrel!" Therefore God says that he has honored his sons more than God, and therefore he died. If a son does not improve, put him away. To Timothy it is written (1 Tim. 3:4): "He must manage his own household well," not as the pope and the bishops do now, who gather treasures, adorn their churches, and increase their revenues. All of this is physical. But it means to rule his children, his wife, and his household in the fear of God, so that they may be children of modesty, not of ἀσωτία, "profligacy." Our noblemen are children of ἀσωτία; they are gluttons and drunkards and carousers. They do not know how to behave or how to dress. They are intractable and incorrigible, and they do not let anyone tell them anything or restrain them. They are not restored to orderliness. Not only are they insubordinate, but they refuse to be subject. They fight against the orderliness to which they ought to return, and instead of allowing themselves to be corrected, they insist on charging headlong all the way.

7. *For a bishop as God's steward must be blameless.* This means the end of the adornments of Aaron and of his sons. The adornments of the priests of the New Testament are described here. "If it were empty." [16] We have vestments of another kind because we are priests of another kind. Here is the alb: that he should be pure before the world, that he should be beyond reproach. And now there come various precious stones. Here he calls the man a bishop, earlier he spoke of elders. Therefore in Paul bishop is the same as elder. The established usage is contrary to this. A bishop, that is a minister of the Word, should wear the alb, as the minister of a family. Christ is the Head of the family, and the bishop is the minister. He is the steward to whom the Lord has entrusted everything. If a bishop thinks about his calling, he sees that he is a bishop by the rite, the oracle, and the command of God, and, secondly, that he has in his hand the possession

[16] The phrase "Si vacaret" in the text seems to contain an allusion known to Luther's hearers, but not to us.

and the property of Christ. What is that? It is the Gospel and the sacraments. He has been appointed a minister of the Word for this, that he should distribute these things to his family, to his brethren, that is, that he should diligently preach the Gospel and administer the sacraments, instruct the ignorant, exhort the instructed, rebuke those who misbehave, moderating and tempering them by the Word and ministering to them with prayer and the sacraments. And he ought to make gain, so that the property of Christ grows and increases. Then the Gospel will be in many thousands, while previously it was hardly in one. This is what it means to use the Lord's talent. We know that we have the riches of Christ, and we faithfully dispense them and do battle against our enemies. We are in a true ministry. Therefore we expect that "when the chief Shepherd is manifested [we will obtain the unfading crown of glory]" (1 Peter 5:4). But woe to us if I have seduced the family of Christ and we have filled ourselves with gluttony, as the fanatics and the pope do. They have the title of pastor, and they sit in the household of God, but they do not administer food and drink at the proper time.

To be violent means to trouble consciences and to enact laws so that no conscience is safe, while they meanwhile live in drunkenness. Here is a picture of the church of the pope. It has Scripture, and it has the sacraments, because it is in the temple of Christ; it has the office of administering the Gospel, because, Paul says, "he takes his seat in the temple of God" (2 Thess. 2:4). Therefore he is not to be rejected entirely, as the fanatics maintain. And we see that our side has grown and will continue to grow, that is, that we are the servant to whom the entire possession of the Father has been entrusted, so that we might serve others and make it grow. This happens when by our teaching we lead men to Christ.

Not arrogant. These are the precious stones that are on the chasuble. This clings by nature to all honors. Αὐθάδης refers to the thought by which I myself am pleasing to myself. This refers to that stern and haughty attitude which looks at itself in the mirror and despises others. The behavior of pride is described in this saying, that it admires itself and is puffed up by the gifts of God which it has, by contrast with someone who does not have them, and that it wants to be feared and looked up to. Christ stands in opposition to this vice. "He emptied Himself," as Phil. 2:7 says.

He could have said: "I am holy, and you are a sinner. I am the
Son of God, and you are the son of the devil." But ["He emptied
Himself"]. "But I am sorry for you. I shall make it possible for
you to become the opposite." This is how a bishop ought to act.
Seeing an ignorant brother, he should not think: "I am more
learned. This other man amounts to nothing. In comparison with
me he is a peasant king." This is the pride not of an aristocrat
but of a peasant. When a peasant has a hundred florins in his cof-
fers, he tries to let everyone know about it. If you have a skill,
you should know that you do not have it in order to ridicule or
insult your neighbor but in order to build him up. This is how
our fanatics behave. They want to give the impression that they
know everything, but that we know nothing. But if I do know
something and am a faithful dispenser of it, I should know it for
the benefit of my brother and share it with him, not simply seeking
grace, comfort, or praise for myself but desiring the salvation of
my brother. It means, purely and simply, sharing with him what
he himself does not have; it does not mean pleasing oneself, which
is, according to Paul, "grasping" (Phil. 2:7) the gifts of God. The
gift was given to me in order that it might serve my neighbor.
But if I want others to pay attention to me, then I am changing
what was given to me into something to be grasped. I ought to
distribute it to others and to share it with them, but instead I am
grasping it for myself. Thus I take pleasure in being praised and
in being called pious and learned; but if, on the other hand, I am
accused of something, I become angry. This is a great and an
unspeakable vice. It brings with it vainglory, envy, the spirit of
self-love, and a grasping after the gifts of God. It is "a coated
onion." [17] When a preacher has a greater gift than someone else,
he should refuse to teach [18] unless he is set free from vainglory,
that pestilence. I myself have done this in order to remove from
myself the vainglory that is in my heart. Surely everyone ought
to do it. Other sins can be acknowledged, but not this one. When
the Lord makes a man learned and appoints him, this is not intended to let him please himself or be vainglorious or steal the
glory of God. You commit an abomination and a sacrilege, as
Rom. 2:22 says; for it is sheer sacrilege to use your gifts for nothing
but your own pleasure. Such people do not care whom they serve.

[17] Cf. Persius, *Carmina*, IV, 3.
[18] Although the text has *doceri*, we have read *docere*, as the sense demands.

But Christ demands of us that these gifts and virtues be for the sake of service, even though they be very small. And a bishop is the kind of man who does not please himself but pleases the other person, yet in the sense that he serves to build the other up.[19]

Whoever is *arrogant* is also *quick-tempered.* The virtues are said to be linked together, and so are the vices. Whoever pleases himself and takes delight in himself and in the gifts he has received will be easily offended at the deficiency of a brother. Therefore when a bishop is appointed as someone to be looked up to in the midst of his brethren, of whom some are firm and learned, while others are quite different, and when he has wolves in his circuit and is set in the midst of devils, it is impossible for him to avoid being constantly tempted by all sorts of trials and being presented with many reasons to lose his temper. He should take great care not to be quick-tempered toward his brethren; that is, he should be gentle and meek in order that he may be able to bear the weaknesses and all the diseases of their souls. But someone who pleases himself is soon offended when things do not go as he wants them to. If he sees someone who is the least bit reluctant, he wants to excommunicate him, as our bishops do. Yet no one is allowed to mumble or complain against them on account of their tyranny. But a bishop should have a fatherly and motherly attitude. Peter explained it this way: "Not as domineering over those in your charge" (1 Peter 5:3), as though they were your own inheritance, simply wanting to have dominion over the church, so that everything goes according to your crazy ideas, so that you can glory in your every word. As I have already said, this is how the pope and our bishops behave. "Not to have dominion over you," Paul says, "but as your servants for Christ's sake" (2 Cor. 4:5). I have not been appointed to rule over any Christian as his lord but to be his servant. Only One is the Lord. Although they are servants, nevertheless we ought to obey them and humble ourselves before them for the Lord's sake. On the other hand, they ought to serve us and bear our infirmity, also for the Lord's sake. Therefore anyone who pleases himself cannot avoid being offended and exercising tyranny. If someone is appointed as bishop, it is necessary that he be in honor and good reputation. Otherwise the Word would be despised. For who

[19] This is the end of the third lecture, delivered on November 13, 1527, and the beginning of the fourth, delivered on November 18.

[W, XXV, 23, 24]

would listen to someone with a bad reputation, especially among those over whom he is in charge? And then one is immediately in danger, because flesh and blood are tickled by praise and bend it to their own purpose. On the other hand, if my brother does not praise me, then he himself sins. "If you are praised, you are in danger; if you are not praised, your brother is in danger," as Augustine says in his commentary on the Sermon on the Mount.[20] Therefore we must have the presence of the Holy Spirit to moderate us toward one another, so that the bishop gives the glory to Christ and the hearer honors him for Christ's sake, as Heb. 13:7 says. Therefore let a pastor or a bishop think as follows: "Although you occupy a superior place and have been endowed with better gifts, nevertheless the judgments of God are unsearchable (Rom. 11:33). It can happen that He looks down upon someone in a lowly place while you are in a high place, and yet the one in a lowly place pleases God more. One denarius from him can be more pleasing than 10,000 talents." There is an instance of this in Luke (7:36-48). One man had performed inestimable works and had treated Him publicly with great praise, while the sinful woman does none of these things. Yet Christ repudiates the splendid and magnificent works of the Pharisee. He praises and boasts of the things which the sinful woman has done and places upon the miserable Pharisee the burden of many sins. Yes, yes, that is the sort of one you are. Therefore let everyone be afraid, for He despises the proud and regards the humble, but is not a respecter of persons. Therefore our humility is not the monastic kind, which is a pride and a humility in itself, not in Christ; it is the pretense of humility. Those who are most humble are in fact the most proud. But your humility should be the kind which does indeed have very great gifts but nevertheless fears God, because He judges in a wondrous manner. I could perish with all my gifts, fame, and honor. Those who acknowledge Christ have the proper relation to you. One should have honor and value his brethren very highly, but he should pass through life as though he did not see these things, but he should think: "I am a servant, and I shall strive to serve my brother, even the least of them." Thus one should humble oneself through Christ. Anyone who feels this way cannot be proud, because this spirit does not tolerate pride. He says:

---

[20] Augustine, *De sermone Domini in monte,* Book II, ch. 1, *Corpus Christianorum, Series Latina,* XXXV, 91—92.

"I do indeed know more than others, but what does it profit if by one word of mine someone else [falls]? Thus the proud peacock casts off his feathers. I shall glory in Thee, because I understand and know Thee (Jer. 9:24), not in my gifts." By such means pride is forbidden.

Drunkard. This is written to the Greek bishops, because the Greeks have a reputation as carousers; hence the expression "to play the Greek." [21] That nation was given over to carousing; Daniel called them goats (Dan. 8:5). *Not a drunkard.* This vice follows when a tyranny is established and the sovereign has begun to be quick-tempered and assumes control over his inheritance; he soon thinks that he is permitted to do anything. Once he has acquired tyranny, he soon thinks that he is permitted to do anything and that he need not be concerned "about the grief of Joseph"; but, as Amos says, "like David, they invent for themselves instruments of music" (Amos 6:6, 5). The flesh does not do otherwise. Our bishops were paupers at first, but later on riches were contributed to them; now kings do not have greater wealth than they have. Since they do not have a spiritual attitude, so as to be afraid of Jesus, they would do the same thing to us. This means that a bishop should be sober. He may drink wine, but he should not be given over to wine. *Violent.* This word they interpret in various ways. [22] He is not speaking about violence with the hands but about violence of words and behavior. "You do violence to their conscience, since it is this way, and you crush it," as Corinthians says (1 Cor. 8:12). It does not always refer to physical harm. [23] In the church violence is done to brethren with the word, that is, when they are "bitten," which means that they are rebuked without mercy. And it is a great vice of preachers that when they are in the pulpit, they rail against the faults and the person of their hearers. They strive for the favor of the mob, and they want to appear bold. The mob enjoys listening to them, especially when they attack the magistrates, and men of this kind are held in honor, as though the common people were sound and without fault. On the other hand, those who attack the common

[21] Cf., for example, Plautus, *Mostellaria*, I, 1, 22 and 64—65.

[22] Jerome, *Commentaria in epistolam ad Titum, Patrologia, Series Latina,* XXVI, 601—602.

[23] Here, as elsewhere in these lectures, Luther breaks into German: "es stehet y nicht ubel."

people and flatter the magistrates are commonly seditious, especially if they were to have the chance. Both are to be rebuked, the common people as well as the magistrates. But if one party is tickled, the other is attacked; soon afterwards there is a reversal. But it is not proper for the other party to ridicule, and a rebuke should not be divided in such a way that they portray one person, so that all eyes are turned on him. He should be admonished privately, as Matt. 18:15 says. This means that one should be sharp even in the case of those who do not need it. For he supposes that one should take this from him particularly if one is innocent. If one is guilty, this should be done in the proper order prescribed by Matt. 18:15-17. The public attack should always wait. John 16:8 says that the Holy Spirit "convicts," but He does this in private. It is another matter to do violence to someone by an evil example or a scandal, of which Paul speaks to the Corinthians (1 Cor. 5:1). The common people see bishops keeping company with harlots and not doing anything that bishops ought to do, and they are told: "You must honor us even if we are wicked, for it is not up to you to pronounce judgment." Relying on such license, they imagine they can do anything they please. So consciences are offended to do evil. This is doing violence by a work. But a bishop ought to comfort the weak, bring healing to those who are contrite in heart, and admonish "in a spirit of gentleness," as Gal. 6:1 commands.

Not greedy for gain, that is, one who does not seek after filthy lucre. Where shall our pontiffs take refuge? What sort of gain do they have from their vigils and Masses, and from the cult of the saints? This does not even deserve to be counted as filthy lucre, for it was the most violent, accursed, and abominable usurpation, because people are seduced into trusting in their works and Masses and into bringing all their possessions as tribute. The pope is not glorious enough to be accused of such filthy lucre. What he has is usury, which comes from mixing into the affairs of usurers. This is a scandalous business which brings shame to the Word. A bishop's livelihood should be honest, the kind that no one can impugn. I do not know a single canonical clergyman who does not live by filthy lucre. This property is exceedingly corrupt. Those who have land or who get salary from the magistrates have an honorable means of support and property. But the other property is usury. The various kinds of filthy lucre cannot even be numbered. Therefore let the bishop see to it that his property is [acquired in an honorable way]. Thus the apostle has set forth mostly negative prescriptions.

8. *Hospitable,* because a bishop is appointed as an observer who welcomes others when they come to him. In the time of the apostles, to be sure, bishops were wealthy, but I believe this was because wealthier men were elected as bishops. Therefore the bishop should be available to everyone for service in matters of the soul, but especially also in matters of the body. It will happen that false brothers will come who will take away what the true brethren ought to have. The word "hospitable" requires that he accept both the saintly and the evil ones. *Lover of goodness* means that he should love good people. According to Jerome, he is commanded to be zealous for good things, but especially to be zealous for good people.[24] Many good people will come to his attention, and he will often be deceived; nevertheless, let him be concerned to help the good and to turn away from the evil. Let him be prepared to advance such causes as piety, sacred letters, peace, harmony, and friendship among neighbors. Let him support good causes and turn away from evil ones. Let him be zealous to help good persons and good issues. Even with officials and princes he can see to it that they support orphans and widows, casting aside the evil ones and helping the good.

Σώφρων. Rom. 12:3 speaks of sober judgment. The Greek means "a modest man," a reasonable man, a man not passionate and drunk with his own opinions. For there are some who go ahead recklessly, while others act moderately, with a sober mind, not giving attention to considerations of comfort or glory. This means that one should act modestly and moderately in his activities. This modesty should be present not only in food and drink but in business and in human relations, so that a man does not break into things with an excited mind and an impetuous heart, but is one who can listen and reflect, and only then act. This virtue is especially important for an emperor. In the writings of Paul this term is employed very often. Thus when Frederick spoke with people, he was extremely σώφρων.[25] Some are drunken in

---

[24] Jerome, *Commentaria in epistolam ad Titum, Patrologia, Series Latina,* XXVI, 602—603.

[25] Frederick (cf. *Luther's Works,* 13, pp. 157—159) had died in 1525; he was named "the Wise," and Luther seems to be alluding to that sobriquet here.

their mind, while others are sober and thoughtful. In German we say that they are *vernunfftig*. This refers to someone who acts sensibly in the matter. Paul praises this term very greatly, and later on he lays great stress on this virtue for every social station, namely, that one be modest.

Upright, because he has been appointed to rule over men's souls. Cases come to him for adjudication. He must see to it that he is not deceived by feelings of partiality, but that he is objective, free of all feelings. He should not be afraid of the loss of his own money, but should go straight ahead without respect of persons, as Moses did (cf. Deut. 1:17), not distinguishing between the rich and the poor. If he is upright, he will not be influenced by poverty and will not decide the case against a poor man. Thus he will establish peace and serve concord.

Holy is not used in the sense of ἄγιος, the holiness that applies to holy things. Every Christian is holy, that is, set aside from profane things, so that he belongs to Christ and not to the devil. ῞Οσιος means someone who is zealous in holy things, so that he teaches, lives, and prays in a holy way, and does other works which pertain to holiness, in his teaching and meditating. He abstains from profane thoughts and speech, and from worldly actions and customs, as Rom. 12:2 states. If a priest swears, he is profane. A "holy" man is one who performs, speaks, sees, hears, and carries out holy things. This, therefore, is the practice of holiness.

Self-control refers to his entire moderation, that he be moderate in food, drink, and sex, and not be wanton for another woman. He will do this in word and in deed, as 1 Cor. 9:27 says. These virtues ought to be the fruits of faith in bishops.

9. *He must hold firm.* This is the most important of all. The virtues are beautiful. A bishop is appointed in the midst of the nation (cf. Phil. 2:15), but especially in the midst of heretics. If someone becomes a pastor, especially in a prominent place, and presents the Word, he will have them. Therefore he admonishes that a bishop be ready for both, that he have a trowel in one hand [and a weapon in the other], as in Nehemiah (Neh. 4:17). There are not many such; many teach, but few fight. A certain tenacity is signified here, that is, that he not put the Bible aside, but that he give attention to reading, as the Epistle to Timothy says, adding: "Practice these duties" (1 Tim. 4:13, 15). The reason he

ought to be provided for by the church is that he ought to tend to reading and stay with it not only for others, but that he ought to meditate constantly for himself, that is, ought to immerse himself completely in Scripture. Such study will enable him to fight back. It is impossible for someone who reads Scripture studiously to meddle in worldly matters, but he should have the strength to be the kind of man Paul has described here. If he does not diligently study Holy Scripture, which he knows, the result will be a kind of rust, and a neglect of and contempt for the Word will arise. Even though you know Holy Scripture, nevertheless it must be read over and over again, because this Word has the power to stimulate you at all times. I have been preaching the Gospel for five years, but I always feel a new flame. For 12 years I have prayed the Our Father.[26]

That he may be diligent in it, that he may be sure of that Word which avails for instruction. Let him avoid sophistic disputes about useless and unsure myths, but [let him concentrate] on those things about which there is no question. There are questions which are diseased and doubtful, mere opinions; for example, the fanatics fall into questions without understanding what they are saying, as 1 Tim. 1:7 says. What does it matter to me what Augustine or the pope says? These are uncertain sayings, but Holy Scripture is well-founded and is "according to doctrine," that is, it avails for instruction. Whoever knows something well can teach it well. Words will not follow upon the wrong content. Eloquence is joined to wisdom. God, who gives wisdom, also gives the word, so that we can speak. Those who do not understand something cannot speak about it. Thus also our fanatics do not teach anything, because they wander around in their own hearts and thoughts. The fanatics know much to babble about but nothing to say and teach. Christ says (Luke 21:15): "I will give you a mouth and wisdom." Where there is wisdom, there even the fanatics may speak. They jabber all right, but they do not speak. What I have known, therefore, on that I will stake my life. And so he who has the right to teach must be "an apt teacher," that is, he must not only be diligent in teaching but also able. But he cannot teach unless he is certain. I have not read any book of my oppo-

---

[26] It is not clear in what sense Luther says he has been preaching since 1522 or praying since 1515; if "12" is a slip of the pen for "21," he could be referring to his ordination in 1507.

nents through to the end except the *Diatribe* of Erasmus,[27] because at the very outset I see them wandering about foolishly
and lacking a sure word.[28]

So that he may be able. These two things are particularly
necessary for a bishop, especially in the office of teaching, because this is by far the chief office of a bishop. Other virtues adorn
his person, but this one adorns his work, his ministry. First, let
him have a sure word and be sure that he has the Word of God,
as 1 Peter 4:11 says. Earlier (v. 7) he spoke of "God's steward."
Let no one presume to teach anything in the church of God unless
he is certain. Once he has this Word, then he will not only teach
but is able to teach and to denounce or to convince, because if
someone is certain of anything, he knows: "I am saying this."
But someone who is uncertain is capable neither of teaching nor
of polemics. So it is with the sectarians; they talk a great deal,
but when one reads a book of theirs, it has no content. I have read
Jerome; but when the reading was finished, the time had been
wasted, for he says nothing to comfort the conscience. I have
read through the books which Augustine wrote before his conflict
with Pelagius [and the same is true of them]. The fanatics present sophistic arguments which are altogether irrelevant to the
subject matter. [This passage means that the bishop should be]
strong and robust, versatile in his exhortation. Paul laid the foundation and gave instruction; those who build upon it are exhorters,
lest the doctrine once handed down be consumed by rust. Jude
says: "Contend for the doctrine once handed down" (Jude 3).
We should labor over this faith and contend for it to the end. The
flesh becomes sluggish; it sees to it that we forget the Word and
grow tired of it. The bishop should not worry that he is often teaching the same thing. The word "sound" is a word peculiar to Paul,
who speaks of "sound doctrine" or "sound faith," by contrast
with wasting time on questions. He opposes diseases of doctrine;
that is, doctrine should be right, stable, and constant. If someone
is idle, his body neither lives nor dies. Thus those who do not
have a doctrine that is sure and constant do not teach. He is al-

[27] Luther is referring to the treatise *On the Freedom of the Will*, which Erasmus had directed against him in the autumn of 1524 and to which Luther had
replied in his treatise *On the Bondage of the Will* in 1525.

[28] This is the end of the fourth lecture, delivered on November 18, 1527, and
the beginning of the fifth, delivered on November 19.

luding not only to the Greek adage about "sound advice" [29] but also to the Hebrew saying (Ps. 119:1): "Blessed are those whose way is blameless." When the Latins say: "Blessed is he who is sound," this is a Hebrew and a Greek way of saying that someone is blameless. This is said in opposition to the uncertain opinions of reason, first, in order that he may serve his pupils with sound doctrine, and, secondly, in order that he may convince his adversaries. It is necessary that the Word of God should have gainsayers. No one contradicted the rules of the fathers and the articles in monastic disciplines and in collegiate churches, for they were demonic and human. But the Word of God receives such treatment as soon as it is taken up, as happened when John Hus came along and disputed over papal abuses; for Satan is on the watch. The bishop should know that his word will soon meet with opposition, if not from those on the outside, then from his own brethren, as Acts 20:29-30 says. Before Christ could be crucified by Pilate, it was necessary that there be a Judas. He does not say it in this way to restrain them. No, a heretic has never been completely overcome. The Jews still cry out that it is impossible to prove on the basis of the Scriptures that Jesus is the Messiah. Our sophists say that they are not convinced by sound Scripture that the pope is the Antichrist, that both kinds in the Sacrament are permitted, and that monasticism is wicked. Therefore we are not commanded to stop their mouths so that they yield permanently. Christ stopped the mouths of the Sadducees, and yet they did not yield, but took counsel how to kill Him. Therefore if a bishop is unable to convert and to restrain the gainsayers, he should merely declare that they are in error. Thus he can preserve his flock from seducers, so that they are not devoured by the wolves. Therefore the faithful shepherd is one who not only feeds his flock but also protects it. This happens when he points out heresies and errors. Thus it is only by his reproof, not by his victory, that he rescues the church, just as today we protect the church against Sacramentarians; but they remain utterly invincible. Carlstadt was refuted on the word τοῦτο, and still he told his associates that the argument was not valid. In the same way others cannot prove their interpretations of the words "represents"

[29] Luther may be referring to the familiar classical adage, known in both Greek and Latin versions, *mens sana in corpore sano,* or to such literary formulations as Aristotle, *Nicomachean Ethics,* Book VI, ch. 9.

and "body." [30] We are not the victors there, for we did not convince them; but we are the victors in ourselves, because we serve the brethren in the simplicity of the Word. There are two glorious qualities which a bishop has in his office: when he holds to a sure word, and when he is powerful. This is the description of a holy and divine priest. If he is lacking in personal virtue, let not his virtue as a bishop be lacking. If he must choose, let him rather choose a fault in the former regard, so long as there remains the purity of a sure word, the power to denounce, and the office of exhortation. The Lord has branded us with this office. We exhort and denounce our enemies. If I am holy, righteous, etc., this is my personal quality, by which others are not greatly edified. But if I teach in a holy way, this is the most important. God has given this to us. Let us give thanks to God and distribute this gift in such a way that our brethren become the better for it. And we save many through Jesus, who is with us. There is always an infinite number of fools, but very few people today are publishing pious books. On the other hand, the insubordinate men, the vain talkers, and the φρεναπάται are writing the books. They know for certain that, according to Rom. 6:23 and 1 Cor. 12:3, they are corrupting faith and consciences.

10. *For there are.* Here he gives the reason why he said that it was impossible for a bishop to avoid opposition and enemies. For he will have a domestic Satan who suggests many false thoughts and speculations to him, as well as external enemies, through whom he stirs up sects. Under the papacy parish priests and mendicant friars competed for confessions and for funerals, which brought money to parish priests, while the monks looked down upon the priests as far inferior to them. Thus among the Jews a Sadducee despised a Pharisee, later on a monk despised a monk, as Herod despised Pilate. The devil is always a liar and a murderer (John 8:44). He started this in Paradise. "His goods are in peace" (Luke 11:21).

Insubordinate men, whom nothing can persuade. They refuse to allow their sins to be restrained; they are beyond conviction or persuasion; they are a Headlong Hans.[31] Moses said (Deut. 9:6): "You are a stubborn people." "Your forehead and neck are an

---

[30] Cf. *Luther's Works,* 37, p. 30 and passim.

[31] A familiar phrase, "Hans mit dem kopff hin durch"; cf. *Luther's Works,* 21, p. 23, n. 9.

iron sinew" (Is. 48:5). The prophets use these metaphors to indicate the invincible stubbornness of people. Look at the Sacramentarians! The papists, too, are stubborn, and yet they recognize
that we are in the right.[32] But they refuse to believe this because
"their forehead is brass." One kind in the Sacrament is defended
by them "with an iron neck." They refuse to listen to anything.
The circumcision. This refers to the stubborn Jews. No matter
what is preached to them, it does not help a bit. They should be
warned that they are dealing with intractable men, but they should
have inflexible men over them. Therefore they will not try to convince their opponents, but they will try to denounce and convict
them, so that your brethren may acknowledge that they are con-
victed. He gives this title to a heretical and false Christian. Arius
is not simply to be adjudged a heretic, but he was a stubborn man.
They are called inflexible and unconvincible.

Empty talkers is a very fine title. They cannot be described
more accurately. They want to be theologians when they cannot
even sing. Anyone who does not know how to sing always wants
to sing. Arty masters always see that something is missing in
a work. This is their genius. They butt in because they are impatient with their knowledge. Some men who have been ordained
here to preach at a particular place were unable to stay here.
This is second nature to them. An ungodly teacher is first of all
a stubborn one; then, thinking that "what you know is nothing
unless someone else knows it also," they will begin to meddle.
They do not wait for the opportune time, and in their speaking
they put on the appearance of sanctity. "You must be circumcised,"
they said to Paul, who was the newest of the apostles. Christ did
not abolish the Law (cf. Matt. 5:17), and yet [He had to endure]
empty talk. They speak about a thing which they do not understand. Thus our fanatics are most truly stubborn men and vain
talkers. They speak about a thing which they themselves have
not experienced: "The external Word is nothing. One must first
receive the Spirit." They say a lot of things like this about the
Spirit, and it is sheer vanity. We have the sure Word, which
tells us what to do. "The man believed the word," John 4:50;
see also Rom. 10:17. The truth is a sure Word, while their word
is a seduction.

[32] See, for example, the reference cited in *Luther's Works*, 13, p. 352, nn.
2—3.

Seducers. He is not speaking about physical seduction, but about those who cause hearts to go astray. They do nothing but seduce consciences. They are murderers and deceivers of conscience. They do not try to seduce the eyes, but they penetrate to what is within, to what is most precious in Christians, namely, a pure heart, conscience, and mind. They are stiff-necked, empty talkers, thieves and robbers of consciences. They refuse to admit that this is what they are, but they brag that they are the kindest of physicians, spiritual guides, teachers of erring consciences. They have those three virtues: they are incorrigible; they are impatient with silence, as Job 5 and Job 32 show; and they are dangerous. If they had only the first two virtues, it would not be so bad; for then only they themselves would be going to jail and to the devil. But the third thing is the most dangerous of all: they are scattered throughout the world, and they take very many people along with them.

The circumcision party were not only Jews but also Christians. There were some Gentile preachers who had been deceived by the Jews. It is easy to recognize from Acts 15:5 what a great deception arose from the council: "It is necessary to circumcise." One should not disregard this text. They came from Jerusalem as emissaries of the apostles, saying: "You cannot [disobey this]." Paul and Barnabas, coming up to Jerusalem, declared: "You must [disobey it]." There only Peter stood with Paul and Barnabas; the majority remained opposed to the apostles. The demand was placed upon Paul that Gentiles should be circumcised. This is the way our fanatics proceed. Where we preach the Gospel, they pollute it. Why do they not come to the papists? This [circumcision] party was strengthened by noble people among the Christians.

The circumcision party. He calls them this as a derogatory reference to their authority, as though he were saying: "Tell the bishops not to be impressed by their authority when they say: 'We are your teachers and the disciples of the apostles, whom we have seen observing the Law of Moses. Are you better than they? Our teaching is sound.'" It is as though he were saying: "They will say that they belong to the circumcision party, and the Gentiles will think: 'They have read Moses from the beginning, while we have read nothing at all. Paul does not amount to anything.'"

11. *They must be silenced.* How can this happen when it is impossible to stop their mouths? For if even the council of the apostles was unable to stop their mouths, much less [can we]. That is, they are not [arising] among our adversaries, but among our own people, so that it is clear that within the church their arguments are undermining the authorities. We cannot make them shut up, but we can persuade our people not to listen to them. And this happens, as was said earlier, when one does not pay attention to their person or their kind. *Whole families,* because the church remains. When they are admitted into a home, they infect it all—father, mother, household. Therefore the church was gathered into a home. The Twelve gathered at home to hear the Gospel and to have communion. The dangerous doctrine was so successful because it always sought out those who were not powerful in Holy Scripture and who could be easily deceived. If, even after all our sermons, a fanatic were to come here, he could subvert everything in three weeks. The common people are not influenced [by us], and very few accept the Word, as though they wanted some day to stand in the battle. But those who have gone through this experience will become good preachers and bishops. Such people refute the arguments and stand firm, but there are very few of them.

Teaching. He does not indicate what they teach. It is as though he were saying: "Who could enumerate what different sorts of things they teach? But in summary, they teach things that they have no right to teach, that is, things that are forbidden." They are empty talkers, and they do not teach what is necessary for salvation. In addition, they teach *for base gain.* Is Paul carping at the preachers here? Who told him about this? Do they say: "We seek the salvation of souls and the glory of God"? That is what our men say today. Therefore it is difficult to accuse them of being out for base gain. Perhaps he had sometimes seen this with his own eyes, as he says in 1 Cor. 9:12: "If others have the right to a share in holy things, we have lived by our own hands." Therefore Paul calls that gain "base" which is sought to feed one's stomach. They came to satisfy their own stomachs; Rom. 16:18 has "their own belly," and Phil. 3:19 says that "their god is their belly." And this I can say: Let the fanatics swear all they please! They are vainglorious and have the appetite of beasts. By the authority of Scripture I conclude this, for it describes false teachers as those who devour. "They devour widows' houses" (Mark 7:11). They devour as though it were a handful of barley (Ezek. 13:19); Isaiah says (Is. 56:11): "The dogs never have enough"; and Amos calls them "cows" (Amos 4:1). Therefore Paul, by the authority and usage of the Scriptures and by his own usage and Spirit, concludes that every false apostle is a belly-server. And the Spirit says this. Any teacher in whom the Holy Spirit dwells seeks the things that are of the Spirit, the glory of God and the salvation of man, even at the cost of danger to his own stomach. Therefore the converse also follows: Where the Holy Spirit does not dwell, is where the flesh dwells. And where there is the flesh, there there is the zeal for one's own glory; they understand the things of earth, and they seek for the earth. Therefore Paul is not a slanderer; he is a completely sure judge. Every wicked teacher seeks his own glory, satisfaction of his own appetite, and base gain. This is what Paul calls it when they accepted money from you for their support. It is gain which is sought out of sheer baseness, because they are engaged in wicked doctrine and in the deception of souls. He wanted to make them hateful in the eyes of the bishops and to disparage their authority altogether. This explains the term "bellies": they seek base gain in order to have something to eat. 12. *Cretans.* This is an unusual passage because Paul quotes a heathen text. Here he builds silver on the foundation (cf. 1 Cor. 3:12). Truth comes from the Holy Spirit, regardless of who says it, especially the true sayings of the poets, when they show us our sins. The cause and the origin of this statement is always in Him; it is an emphatic statement. The Cretans worshiped Jupiter, whom they called the supreme god. They also said that they had the grave of Jupiter and that Jupiter was fed in their caves.[33] These two things do not agree. It is as though the poet were saying: "I certainly have some fine countrymen! They glory in a god who is simultaneously alive and dead." Today, too, that nation is remarkably lighthearted. And although Greece is a liar, nevertheless in history one hears testimonies to their trustworthiness, as the oration for Flaccus shows.[34] But among the Greeks the Cretans are the worst. The vice of that nation was that they were liars. On the other hand, when they had really been converted, they were far more truthful.

[33] Cf. Hesiod, *Theogonia*, lines 477 ff.
[34] Cicero, *Oratio pro Flacco*, IV, 9—10.

Thus if an Italian is found to be upright, he is truly upright. This is a natural sin and vice of the Greeks, to be frivolous and liars. All the Latins attribute this to them. "From one accusation you can learn them all," as the sixth book of the *Aeneid* says.[35] It is as though he were saying: "No wonder." "He has been instructed in the Pelasgian art." [36] Paul says this especially about the Cretans. He attributes three virtues to them: they are a frivolous nation; they cultivate lies; and they are influenced by lies. Therefore it was easy for them to let the false apostles in. "So you should give this your special attention." Our vice is our fierceness and our drunkenness, or our gluttony, so that we are like swine born in warfare and destined for slaughter.

Liars. Therefore it is not easy for them to keep their word; if they keep it, it is easy for them [to break it]. They are poisonous beasts, like the beasts in the forest, bears, lions, and serpents. Paul confirmed and experienced the truth of this. Apart from grace it cannot be otherwise. They are wrathful and ferocious; they are persecutors. Therefore a bishop will have vicious detractors and accusers. I could give you the example of our fanatics, who want to give the impression of being modest and of not condemning the Gospel. And yet look at the murdering and stabbings they commit. The best and most learned qualities of this sort are those of the Greeks and the Cretans, those vicious beasts. Christ calls them vipers (Matt. 12:34). Before men they shine with a beautiful appearance, but under it they stir up the worst kind of trouble. "If you say this," Paul declares, "you will arouse against yourselves lions, bears, and tigers, if you refuse to leave them alone in their lies."

Bellies. This is a beautiful synecdoche, an antonomasia,[37] that he calls them bellies and slow, lazy, greedy jackasses, who are good for nothing except the stable.[38] True doctrine teaches the mortification and denial of our own feeling. 13. [*This*] *testimony* [*is true*]. This is a confirmation. That verse is true, even though it was written by a heathen poet. These are spoils which we can

[35] Vergil, *Aeneid,* II, 65, not Book VI, as the text states.

[36] Ibid., II, 152.

[37] On the figure of antonomasia, cf. Quintilian, *Institutiones Oratoriae,* VIII, vi, 29 and 43.

[38] The German phrase *auff kobel* is obscure. We have followed the Weimar editors in referring it to a stable.

take away from them.[39] But it requires an art to apply these things to spiritual matters. Plato and Aristotle wrote well about political matters, Pliny described the works [of nature], etc. But do not undertake to have a heathen instruct consciences. Only Christ our Teacher is competent for this.[40]

Therefore [*rebuke them*]. He moves from the particular to the general. For now he begins a general exhortation, directed not only against the false apostles but also against his hearers. Therefore since Cretans are by nature frivolous and liars, it is all the more necessary to rebuke them; for vain speaking is added to their natural evil. Here two evils come together: a natural frivolity and an evil physician, a bad egg.[41] Where there is an evil teacher, there there will be very evil pupils. *Sharply* means in Greek concisely and thoroughly. He wants to say: "Denounce them in such a way that you do not leave anything unrebuked in them, just as when you prune a tree in such a way that no branch remains. Whatever you see in them that goes beyond sound doctrine, no matter how tiny it is, cut it off sharply, so that nothing is left of the content of human doctrine." The reason for this is that everywhere the apostle has the proverb about "a little leaven" (Gal. 5:9). One dare not fool around with the doctrine of men, for it always begins to expand. The first church council set down a certain human rule concerning what is strangled (Acts 15:20). Not even the first council was free of pollution, even though they set down their decrees with the aid of the Holy Spirit and observed them out of deference to the Jews. Nevertheless, this provided the precedent for many decrees. Later on Paul abrogated this rule, contrary to the decree of the apostolic council, saying (1 Cor. 8:4): "An idol has no real existence." In the Council of Nicaea there was a decree on celibacy,[42] which has now permeated

[39] On the basis of Ex. 3:22, Augustine had justified the use of pagan ideas as "despoiling the Egyptians," *De doctrina Christiana*, Book II, ch. 40, pars. 60—61, *Corpus Christianorum, Series Latina*, XXXII, 73—75.

[40] This is the end of the fifth lecture, delivered on November 19, 1527, and the beginning of the sixth, delivered on November 20.

[41] This is probably a reference to a proverbial saying about a bad egg producing a bad hatch; in view of the Latin phrase, "ab ovo usque ad mala," referring to a meal from eggs to soup (roughly the equivalent of the American "from soup to nuts"), it may be a play on words.

[42] Cf. p. 19, n. 13.

the whole world, because it was a "leaven." Therefore it is up to a pastor to take care that nothing remains unpruned, because a disease will begin to grow out of this. This is how Satan proceeds, for he is determined not to allow a single syllable to stand against him. If he makes a Christian deny anything, he will not let him alone until he denies everything. Thus Christ wishes that not one syllable of the doctrine of Satan remain unpruned. As we say in German: "Give a rascal your hand [and he will take your arm]." Likewise: "One should not ask the devil to stand as sponsor for one's children." They are to be rebuked sharply, that is, thoroughly, radically, absolutely, roundly, perfectly.

That they may be [sound in faith]. Let this be the purpose of your rebuke, that faith is not weakened—a phrase of Paul's—that it does not grow weary, that it is not mingled with some sort of trust in works; for then poison is released in the heart, and the result is the same as when a disease damages the body. Our faith depends solely on Christ. He alone is righteous, and I am not; for His righteousness stands for me before the judgment of God and against the wrath of God. If to this I add the declaration "I have vowed three vows," then immediately the plague has begun; for a foreign righteousness has been introduced as a covering. Cut it off completely! If you want good works, do them for the benefit of your neighbor. Those who want to poison are teachers of the plague.

Instead of giving heed [to Jewish myths]. He has combined two things into one. In large and golden letters this title should be written over the doctrines of men: "It is," he says, "their nature to reject the truth. Just as fire burns and consumes by nature, so the doctrine of men rejects the truth." The argument that is set in opposition to the doctrines of men should be noted. How? If I accept the command of men, then it is impossible for my conscience to avoid being offended. If it is a command, it requires to be observed. If it requires this, it is a sin not to observe it; if it is not required, one is free. A command of men says: "You cannot be saved unless you do this." If I say: "I prescribe for you that you freely eat meat on Friday," this is not a command that the works of Christians be performed. Therefore it is obvious that faith and the commands of men are in opposition to each other. Unless I do something out of deference to you, there is no command except the command of love, which is the freedom of

the Spirit and does not reject the truth; on this basis, you gather
that the command of men and sound doctrine are diametrically
opposed. If the abbot permitted me to wear my cowl voluntarily,
this would not conflict with sound faith. But he says: "Unless
you wear it, you will be damned." Then everything must be torn
up, because it conflicts with sound faith. Christian righteousness
says: "I know nothing except Christ" (cf. 1 Cor. 2:2). I serve my
brother through love, but I do not want to be saved through it.
I do so out of free deference to him, but I shall not be either saved
or damned and lost on that account. When those teachers who
bind consciences come, their commands should be trampled underfoot. Therefore the pope is the Antichrist, for he declares:
"We command by a strict requirement: If anyone, etc." [43] He
sets forth the wrath of God and of the saints, threatening the disobedient with damnation and promising salvation to the obedient.
You must denounce such things sharply and thoroughly, for they
are intolerable. *Sound* means that they know they are justified
in Christ alone, and that the works of love are completely free.
Therefore the commands of men ought to be even more free. If
loving your neighbor as yourself does not justify but you must
first be justified through Christ, it will justify much less if you
live according to the commands of men. I prefer to understand
not giving heed to Jewish myths as referring not only to Jewish
genealogies but even to the Law itself, including the precedents
of their elders and of the apostles. He says: "They teach circumcision, sacrifices, and other legal ceremonies. They allege the
precedents of the fathers and the apostles." Thus by tapinosis
he calls the Law *myths*, but he calls the traditions of the elders
commands of men, which were prescribed over and above the
Law, as we read in the Gospel (cf. Matt. 15:4-5). The summary
of all this, about which we must be certain, is that whether it be
the command of men or the Law, no righteousness avails except
that of Christ. Therefore through the righteousness of faith the
Law is abrogated in such a way that I do not sin if I fail to observe
the ceremonies of the Law, and vice versa. But no false apostle
teaches without imposing a necessity and saying: "We require
by a strict command." Thus a Mass is not a command; it is a voluntary ceremony which is open to our discretion as long as we

[43] This is a stock formula for introducing decrees in papal legislation and
canon law.

wish. But in the papacy there are nothing but commands, such as that "a layman dare not touch the chalice."

Or, to express it without tapinosis, the Jews almost surpass the Greeks in their myths. But I take this to mean that by "myths" he is referring contemptuously to the tradition of the Law as it is accepted by them. They ought to teach that "through the Law comes knowledge of sin" (Rom. 3:20). And by this [their traditions are refuted]. *Who [reject the truth]* refers to men. In the primitive church there were many such. Thus Spyridon, who is spoken of in church history, lived a life of freedom.[44] But the best examples and sayings have perished, while the worst are the ones that are recalled. In the Decretals we do not read expositions of Holy Scripture, but which bishop may ordain, who has jurisdiction, how a particular church is to be governed, how much income a particular one is to have, how the pallium is to be used. These writings, the worst of all, have been preserved, while the best have perished. Spyridon, Bishop of Cyprus, had a certain guest. When he wanted to feed him, he commanded his daughter to bring meat. She said that she would bring pork, and she placed it before the guest. This was during Lent. The guest said: "I am a Christian"; for he thought that a Christian was not permitted to eat meat during Lent. The bishop responded fittingly: "You are a Christian. This is all the more reason why you ought to eat it, for to the pure all things are pure." I believe that there were only a few such men. This one example was written down and deserves to be celebrated, of someone who dares with a very good conscience to eat meat contrary to the ceremony of others. The bishop's answer is also praiseworthy. There were others like him, but their story [has not been told]. If now you say to a monk: "Take off your cowl, marry a wife," he will reply: "But I am a Christian." Therefore consciences were held captive then, and how rare pure doctrine was!

All things are pure. Here you see why I felt that Paul was calling the Law of Moses "myths" in a contemptuous way, for this passage indicates what these myths concerning food, clothing, and drink were. Therefore they are the commands of men and Jewish myths. In the Law of Moses, however, there are prescriptions about clean and unclean animals, and these he calls

---

[44] On Spyridon, cf. Cassiodorus, *Historia tripartita,* Book I, ch. 10, *Patrologia, Series Latina,* LXIX, 895—896.

Jewish myths. That is what they are. They are not to be imposed upon men. Neither are the regulations concerning the washing of clothing, concerning things not to be touched, concerning all the different utensils. The commands of men reject the truth, but sound doctrine makes everything pure. This text ought to be written in golden letters. This single text is a thunderclap and a storm against all the straws of human traditions, against the law of the pope and the decrees of the councils, which declared that marriage was impure for priests. Because they themselves are impure, Paul says, they reject the truth. To the pure marriage is pure. The pope says that during Lent one must abstain from foods prepared with milk, from cheese, milk, and butter. To the papists and their followers these things are impure because they have made them impure; they are not impure to us, as Spyridon said. I read one decree of the pope which declared: "We command abstinence from milk and meat not because a creature of God is bad, but because it serves to bridle the flesh, for the sake of piety and temperance." [45] He did not see deeply. Commands are handed down for a twofold reason: that those who observe them may obtain righteousness, and the opposite. There are no such commands whatever. If you are speaking about righteousness in the sight of God, nothing obtains righteousness except Christ, who is the Mediator. His righteousness is our righteousness, as 1 Cor. 1:30 declares. Here no law avails, either of Moses or of the pope or of men. I do not stand for it that the pope with his commands should present me as righteous in the sight of God because I observe his commands. But none of you will be able to stand that way, for that is not what He requires. In the sight of God my three vows have no right to present themselves, for that would mean that I am treading the blood of Christ underfoot. But if there is a command, it is one of love. I do things spontaneously in deference to you, and I will obey you, but not in order that I may be saved or damned. One way of preaching is contrary to faith, while the other is in accordance with the principle of love; the first is to be rejected, the second is accepted. None of the false apostles recognize this, but they all proceed with laws. So it is with the iconoclasts: "I make the destruction of an image a basis for justification, and the failure to destroy it a basis for

[45] It is not clear whether Luther is referring to a papal decree of his own time or to one preserved in the standard collections of canon law and their glosses.

ungodliness." This shows that they do not admit [the truth] unless they are spiritual, as are we, who in the freedom of love neither want to be justified by this nor suppose that we are better than others. But without the Spirit they determine everything in such a way as to justify or to accuse. We do not allow this [prerogative] even to love itself. It does not justify me in the sight of God, even if I perform all the works of love; but it justifies me only in the sight of the world. Let the text stand just as it is. Those are pure who have a sound faith, who believe in Christ, who know that they cannot be defiled by anything. Faith in Christ soon produces love, which causes one to defer to his brother; but one is not justified by this. Paul himself explains what he means when he speaks of the *unbelieving;* therefore, by contrast, those who are pure are those who are believing. I do not need to enter into a dispute. Whoever does not believe is not pure. This conclusion is simply true. The Book of Acts says (Acts 15:9): "He made no distinction, but cleansed." He cleanses through faith. "Blessed are the pure in heart, [for they shall see God]" (Matt. 5:8); those who believe also see. Therefore to those who know that they are justified by Christ alone everything is pure, be it fish or meat. This is a storm against all traditions and councils. What were our monks and bishops doing when they read this and did not understand it: "To the pure all things are pure," and they made food and clothing impure? All the rest of them are faithless. Therefore the commands of men reject the truth. Paul proves this as follows: To the impure and faithless, that is, if anyone has done anything impure, he should know that he is faithless, one who necessarily rejects the truth and is therefore completely without faith. Therefore we conclude that the reigns of the pope and of the monks are reigns of faithlessness; they are heathen, because they live completely without faith and without righteousness, making things impure that are pure in the sight of God.

To the corrupt. This is an inversion. Here nothing is pure, because if someone has lost his faith, then everything is impure: God is impure, as are righteousness and his own heart. How does it happen? Whatever a conscience deals with without faith is polluted. If a monk goes to confession, goes to Mass, acts in accordance with his rule, is tonsured, obeys his rule, and has gone to Mass with the utmost devotion, his conscience must nevertheless conclude: "I do not know whether I am pleasing to God."

Here everything is impure, because in the sight of God he is not righteous. He senses this, and thus is already impure, because he does not believe that he is pleasing to God. Therefore his Mass, garb, tears, and prayers are impure. Thus when he observes chastity, poverty, and obedience, he is a dying man, because he must say: "I do not know whether [this is pleasing] to God." Here all vows are impure because they are all devoid of faith. He is not persuaded that they are pleasing to God. Thus if I speculate about Christ as He sits at the right hand of God and as He will judge you, rather than as Rom. 8:34 portrays Him, then Christ and God are impure to such a person.[46] In this way the use of every creature is impure. He does not think that it is pleasing to God that he uses the sun. Thus whatever he uses arouses doubt, and therefore the sun, light, food, drink, and life itself are impure. A conscience is impure when it does not believe that it pleases God in the work of using a creature. What priest can believe that his Mass is pleasing to God? For he does not have the Word but can only say: "It seems to me." I conclude in opposition to him: Where the Word is not present in the conscience, it is impossible to trust. As Rom. 10:14 asks: "How?" If you have the Mass without the Word, you have it without faith. Thus I say to a monk: "Do you have the Word for taking your vow?" Therefore no monk is able to say: "This life of religion is pleasing to God," because he cannot produce a Word of God which would say: "Whoever leads this life is pleasing to God." In a pure man, therefore, the conscience has faith, and vice versa. Therefore faith is the purity of conscience, which believes that it is pleasing to God in Christ; on the other hand, a conscience which seeks to please God otherwise and does so without the Word is always uncertain and polluted. On the Last Day its works, vows, and the creatures will all accuse it.[47]

We have heard in this passage how Paul condemns all the doctrines of men with very serious words which ought to be feared unless we are obdurate and blind, namely, that to the pure all things are pure. I have said to the impure and to those who lack faith that their best works are not pure but impure because they

[46] Luther's Latin is obscure here. We have followed the interpretation suggested by the Weimar editors.

[47] This is the end of the sixth lecture, delivered on November 20, 1527, and the beginning of the seventh, delivered on December 2.

cannot declare in their conscience that this is pleasing to God. Thus today our Sacramentarians have an impure faith and a perverse [48] doctrine. When they dispute concerning the resurrection and death of Christ, everything is impure, because they do not have it in their conscience that they are teaching these things correctly. Therefore because of the uncertainty and doubt of their conscience nothing is right.

But to the corrupt [*and unbelieving nothing is pure; their very*] *minds* [*and consciences are corrupted*]. Both things are impure. They do not recognize this, because they have been blinded by their impurity. The eye of their heart is full of impurity, just as the eye of the body does not see properly when it has been filled with blood and injured by impure water. Thus their mind, he says, is impure, and therefore their conscience is also. The mind is the judgment about things, as 1 Cor. 14:19 says, "with my mind rather than in a tongue." It refers to the mind or the spirit, the cognitive power in a man, which accepts [49] instruction. Their thinking, mind, and opinion are corrupt; therefore an impure conscience also follows, because as the mind judges, so the conscience dictates. The mind says: "If you eat meat on Friday, you sin." The conscience follows: "Therefore meat should not be eaten." The conscience always draws the conclusion, but the mind sets forth the minor premise. All sin is to be avoided; this is the major premise. But to eat meat on Friday is a sin; this is dictated by the mind. The conscience concludes that therefore [eating meat is a sin]. The major premise is always true, because it does not contradict the common sense of all men. Thus the fanatics say: "We ought to teach faith in Christ, love, and the avoidance of human traditions." This major premise is held in common by the entire human race. But they stumble on the minor premise. Thus [the false apostles of Paul's day] proclaimed: "Evil is to be avoided, and it is an evil that you are not circumcised." It is not an evil to obey God; but if you abstain from meat, [you are doing good]. If the minor premise is upheld, the conclusion follows. Everything good ought to be done; it is good to cast off the monastic life. Here is the conflict: The pope says no, and we say yes. Those who have a sound mind

[48] The text reads *universam,* but the context suggests that *perversam* was probably the intent of the sentence.

[49] The Weimar text has *reeipit,* but we have read *recipit* instead.

have a true [conscience]. The idea they have about holy things is impure; therefore their conscience is also impure. First of all, therefore, the conflict should not be about the conscience, but first we urge what pertains to the mind. If I persuade the pope that it is good to cast off the monastic life, then the conclusion easily follows. When the conscience and the mind are impure, then nothing can be pure. Therefore when they dispute concerning grace, this is not pure. Those who deny Christ in one thing deny Him in everything.

16. *They profess* [*to know God but they deny to know Him by their deeds*]. These are very impressive words. Someone who errs in mind and conscience cannot do a good work. This should be noted by all those who cling stubbornly to human tradition. Those who do not have a pure mind and a sound faith cannot possibly do good works. Nevertheless, he says that they have a greater appearance of the purity of religion than we do. They give testimony, they make a show of knowing God, they give with their mouths. Paul concedes to them an eloquence and a great boasting about Christian doctrine; they speak about the knowledge of God and say that they know Him. This is mere appearance and boasting. Look at our fanatics; they stuff their books with such words as the glory of God, the love of the brethren, the righteousness of faith. All these things are spoken in impurity, because they speak them with the intention of making their sacrament polluted. To speak these utterly pure doctrines concerning faith, etc., with an impure mind is to speak nothing, because they do so in order to pollute the Eucharist, Baptism, and the external Word, and to confirm their own dreams. They are men of an insincere heart, because they want to misuse these words in opposition to the glory of God, the Word of God, and the sacraments; [they speak of] glory, therefore, and yet they snatch God's glory away from Him. Therefore they snatch these words, these outstanding dogmas, these most sublime sentences, in order thereby to battle against the grace of God. Their speaking and jabbering is incessant, far more than ours; *but* [*they deny Him by their*] *deeds:* "You must be circumcised." *They profess* [*to know God*]; they teach righteousness, and yet by doing so they battle against righteousness and good works; for to establish good works in place of righteousness is to battle against righteousness. We agree on the major premise: "Good works ought to be performed."

This we affirm with our mouth, but the denial comes in the performance. It is the glory of Christ that one believe all His words. But in the words of the Lord's Supper He instructs us to eat His flesh. They say: "It is the glory of God and of Christ that He sits [at the right hand of God], and so for the sake of the glory of Christ we pollute the glory of Christ." Thus the Jews seek the righteousness of the Law, and by this they attack God. This is to deny God and the things that are God's under the pretext of [glorifying Him].

They are detestable. He says three things, and there are three very fine titles. First he indicates that they are true idolaters, who are represented by all the ancient doctrines. *Abomination* refers to idolaters. In their heart they have an alien mind and an impure conscience turned away from God. They do not correctly maintain any of the words and works of God. Therefore they stray from the words and works of God; they stray, and nevertheless they retain a true outward appearance. When anyone depicts God differently from the way He is, he is fashioning an idol, as when someone says: "On account of my chastity God regards me, and He will give me a greater reward than He will to other Christians. One is a bride of Christ on account of the chastity of the body; therefore even pagan virgins ought not [be condemned]." [50] Such thinking is a sheer idol of the heart. It does not describe the true God, but under the name of the true God it invents and describes an utter lie. And yet this idolatry and abomination comes to be expressed and is published in the church. *Detestable;* that is, they follow abominations and are abominable in the sight of God. They are idolaters, as were the Jews at that time, who said: "Circumcision saves you." It is the righteousness of Christ that saves you; that is where true righteousness is, and the contrary is idolatry and an abomination. He is not speaking only about ceremonies, as Erasmus maintains,[51] but about all laws which lead men to trust in their works on account of the spiritual abomination and idolatry in their hearts.

Unbelieving, or incapable of believing and of being persuaded. This is an outstanding quality, according to Paul. First they have been alienated from the mind of the Holy Spirit and from true understanding. Secondly, they are confirmed in that stubborn-

---

[50] Cf. Augustine, *De civitate Dei*, Book IV, ch. 10, *Corpus Christianorum, Series Latina*, XLVII, 106—108.

[51] Erasmus, *Paraphrasis in epistolam ad Titum, ad* 1:16.

[W, XXV, 41, 42]

ness, they persist with a stubborn heart, they are beyond persuasion. They refuse to be told anything. If a faithful teacher
attacks them, saying "You are in error, this is how the true God
is. Righteousness is the grace of God in Christ," they refuse to
hear or see it. This is what it means to be alienated from righteousness and then to refuse to come to one's senses. It is as though he
were saying: "I have often tried. I have wanted to call them back.
It was no use." When the fanatics are unable to give any reply
to the arguments that are set forth against them, they still are not
silent. Thirdly, that they are not only detestable and stubborn,
but their whole life is useless. *Unfit for any good deed.* And yet
they have an outstanding outward appearance. They perform
deeds of mercy and suffer a great deal. Why? Paul says that they
are unfit for any good deed. Just as by the appearance of their
words they claim to know things, so by the appearance of their
good works they give the impression of holiness. No one seems
less unfit for good deeds than they. We say that inasmuch as their
mind and conscience are in error, it follows that what they do is
not done for the sake of God but for the sake of their own glory.
The tree is bad; therefore [the fruits are bad]. The tree is bad
because their mind is impure, and to the impure nothing is pure.
Their heart is impure, and therefore their works are impure also;
therefore it is inevitable that they are unfit. Whatever they do,
they do on the basis of error. If they are cast into prison or die,
all these things are impure. A work is not pure unless it proceeds
from a pure heart and conscience. Not only are their efforts vain,
but they are unsound and evil, even though in appearance they
are very good and seem to be the works of Christians. They suffer, they perform works of mercy, they die, they imitate all the
works of Christians. But we tell them that they have an impure
mind. This text is a consolation to us, and it fortifies us against
their very fine outward appearance. For if the doctrine is impure,
then the conscience and its impressive works are too. To the Galatians he says (Gal. 3:4): "Did you experience so many things
in vain—if it really is in vain?" Therefore let us be cautious,
not too quick to accept doctrines. For when the Word of truth
is lost, this is an irretrievable loss. This is why I demand of them
that they prove that "is" means "represents." Satan is leading
them and taking them where he wishes. These three virtues are
the special and final ones: that they have an impure mind, that

they have an impure conscience, and that they speak [as they do] about God.

For any good deed. Nevertheless, they do a great deal, yes, more than the faithful, as Ps. 16 says, "but they," referring to the Baalites and to Achor.[52] And Ps. 14:1 says that "they are abominable in their deeds," not in their sins, "but in their striving." Therefore what follows is certain (Ps. 14:2): It is the manner of life that is judged by God.

---

52 Apparently an allusion to Joshua 7:26.

CHAPTER TWO

THE first chapter has set forth the antithesis between pious and impious ministers of the Word. This second chapter contains the duties of all the estates of society. It says: "Conduct yourself according to the model, and pay no attention to questionings and to Jewish myths. Remain in the right and sound doctrine, and thus instruct others." *Sound doctrine* is pure doctrine, to which all things are pure, which teaches how to have a pure mind and conscience, which makes men good, faithful, and charitable. *Bid the older men,* as well as other orders of society.

Temperate means wakeful, not lazy or snoring. They should bestir themselves and not be overly devoted to sleep. Those who are drunk sleep a great deal, but those who are wakeful are able to arise in the morning and are sober.

Serious means dignified, honorable, as distinguished from those who are frivolous. It means conducting oneself respectably and earnestly, not making light of things, after the manner of those who, when they are presenting a case, provoke laughter and tickle the carnal senses; it means that one should be serious-minded in word and behavior. Σεμνότης, dignity. This means that an old man should have such manners, actions, and dress that seriousness, not frivolity, is evident. He should not behave as though he wanted to be an adolescent, to dance, and to conduct himself in a way not appropriate to his age. The same thing applies to food. Σώφρων: modest, reasonable, a fine, upright man, one who is not intoxicated with his own passions and opinions. I have cited the example of our Prince Frederick, who was not blustering and stubborn.[1] This applies to external behavior and to the active life. Then he continues: *sound in faith, in love, and in steadfastness,* that is, those who are upright, not false, counterfeit, or lazy in faith. A good gold piece is an honest coin; the same quality pertains to an honest wine, one which has not been

[1] Cf. p. 29, n. 25.

adulterated. That is, they have a pure and sure faith, because they are under obligation to teach morality.

In love, that is, they ought to have a love without pretense — sincere, honest, and authentic, so that they love friends and enemies equally. A love which discriminates between persons is an inactive love not an active one, an inauthentic love not an authentic one. Rom. 12:9 says: "Let love be genuine." Nevertheless, there is nothing which is simulated to a greater extent in the world, because no one would be deceived unless pretense were added. *In patience.* There are three parts of a Christian life. The first is to be temperate and serious. This is still a heathen quality, because it really pertains to the outward person [2] and depends on one's behavior; the heart is not involved. But he who believes has righteousness. A justified person loves his neighbor and does the works of love. There follow the cross, imprisonment, and reproach. There you can see who are the true Christians, those who truly believe, those who love patiently. People say: "If Judas were to hurt me, I could easily bear it. But this is someone near to me, someone for whom I have done many favors!" This is a love that is not upright and sound. But love ought to be authentic.

3. [*Bid*] *the older women.* He instructs the men how they ought to live, and by the word "sound" he indicates that he wants them to be set apart from profane things. He wants their wives, the older women, to be adorned *with holy* and decent *deportment,* that is, deportment that is fitting for saints or for holy things. What is seriousness [*of conduct*] in men ought to be a seriousness of apparel in women. *Holy women.* He says this in opposition to old women who adorn themselves as though they were girls of fifteen, which is a sign of frivolity and lust. Adornment, but not profane and youthful lust, is proper for a youth and for a girl. In summary, they also ought to be serious and show themselves by this common adornment to be dignified in deportment. This means that they should not be frivolous in their words. This is especially the vice of women. A woman is naturally prone to derogatory speech. Especially old women pass judgment on one woman after another; according to them, no one is beautiful or chaste. When a woman is past forty, she is counted among the old

[2] The Latin word is *personale;* but since *persona* refers to one's public position and to his official role rather than to his private life, it means just the opposite of the English "personal."

women. She ought to provide an example to others in word and in deed. This refers to women who are guilty of detraction, disparagement, and slander, the vice of which women are especially guilty. A matron who is free of this vice is worthy of the highest praise. It should be preached that they abstain from this vice. *Slaves to drink.* In this country there was a great deal of wine. This vice is especially common among those of older age, and such women have a craving for wine. They ought to fight against this vice.

[*They are to be*] *good teachers.* "Good teachers" are those who are instructed, apt, and skillful at teaching, filled with good doctrines and exhortations, because he will appoint older women as the instructors of younger women. To what end? 4. *And so train the young women.* They should train by example and by word and should make them modest; that is, they should train them in modesty, so that they are sensible, not noisy and raucous but quiet and gentle. Any of them who is not modest should be taught and instructed by [an older] woman, so that the young women love their husbands and are devoted to their children. They should see to it that they take care of their husbands and children. (We have consulted the decretals, and we have found others.)[3] This is how they ought to behave. It is their duty. A woman was created for a man and for bearing children. This text is against all monks and nuns. She will not do this work of loving of her own accord, because Satan is present, and the flesh grows weary in less than one year and looks at another man. Therefore it is the greatest gift of God when she takes pleasure in her own husband and not in another, when she does not pay more attention to another man than to her own. *To love* [*their husbands and children*]. Is this not superfluous, since young women are the ones who love the most? This is directed against those who say that it is pagan to love in a physical way. People who say such things are rebuking, not teaching. These words mean that they should enjoy their husbands' bodies and provide for them.[4]

Thus he instructs matrons to be good teachers and to train younger women to love their husbands and children. I have said

[3] This is apparently intended ironically, as a jibe at the canon law.

[4] This is the end of the seventh lecture, delivered on December 2, 1527, and the beginning of the eighth, delivered on December 3.

what it means to love one's husband, namely, not merely to co-habit with him but to respect one's husband, to regard him as lord, to submit to him in all things, not to be domineering. This is a rare quality in a woman, for the female sex inclines naturally toward what is forbidden to it; it wants to reign, to rule, and to judge. From this there come marital discord, blows, and beatings. To love children means not only to educate them for the world but to see to it that they are provided for in body and in soul. For such love the rod and discipline are required, as Prov. 3:11 and 23:13 say; and Ecclesiasticus says (Ecclus. 30:1): "He will whip him often," because there is foolishness in the heart. Such love is also rare. People love their children for the sake of the pomp of the world. They adorn and save their possessions for them. They do not enrich their souls with the arts, with study, with sound literature. It is the duty of good parents to instruct their children from childhood in the fear of God on the basis of sound literature of Christian women. Here we see that a pig will train a pig, but that human parents do not know anything. Such a man is not even pagan; he is beastly. Matrons, Paul wants to say, have no need to wear themselves out with foolish and self-chosen works. They have tasks at home to keep them busy, but they turn away from these to pilgrimages and the like. It has been truly said that a father will find eternal life in his off-spring; that is, a father has plenty of opportunity in his house-hold to practice his piety, and if anything is left over, to distribute it to his neighbor. But let him see to it that he does not neglect his own household.

Sensible, that is, modest. They should be sensible women, not stupid clods and impudent in the house. They should manage everything soberly in relation to friends, enemies, their husbands, and their children. *Chaste.* Thus in the fifth chapter of Timothy (1 Tim. 5:2) he mentions "older women and younger women in all ἀγνεία, that is, chastity." This is properly marital chastity, that you abstain from lascivious words, gestures, and actions toward other men in the presence of people and especially of your own family. Marital chastity is very highly spoken of in Scripture, as, for example, in Heb. 13:4. Marriage has a great blessing also in the matter of chastity, for he who has the gift of marriage does not go insane with lust. Those who are devoted to their own wives do not lust for others. In those who are worthy of the blessing with which God blesses marriage, the madness of lust is extinguished. That is, they are content with their marriage and have the blessing of marriage, so that they do not grow tired of their own spouses and lose their desire for them. I have seen many who became disgusted with marital relations. Where this is not the case, there will be moderation in intercourse, to resist Satan. *Domestic.* According to Erasmus, the ancients pictured Venus seated on a tortoise.[5] By this the pagans wanted to indicate that it is the chief praise of a woman if she takes care of the house, because a tortoise [has a house] and therefore Venus [is seated on it]. This is a singular and worthy praise for a woman; it is also celebrated by the apostle. There are some who are "gadding about," as the fifth chapter of Timothy (1 Tim. 5:13) says. And as soon as the husband brings home one denarius, [she spends it], so that their property cannot grow. Such a man has a porter who goes out by the back door. Anyone who has a woman so frivolous that she does not care for the family possessions is in a desperate strait. Besides, decency and discipline in the household are in danger, because the household takes her as example, and thus the children, too, are ruined. These three things all add up to the same thing: that she enjoys staying home, that she willingly allows herself to recognize the sign,[6] that she enjoys being in the kitchen, that she does not enjoy going out, that she does not enjoy speaking with others. Such a woman can help her husband in preserving discipline, in adding to the family's property, and in preserving decency. Although these are everyday matters, they should be emphasized in opposition to the nuns. The Holy Spirit extols such matters, and therefore their praises should be sung in the church. When a woman is in the kitchen or when she is making a straw bed, this is an everyday thing. This does not bother the Holy Spirit. Women who do such work are ten times better in their lives than if they lived in a convent and meanwhile were filled with evil thoughts and lusts because they were idle. A wife is appointed for things that are very ordinary in the judgment of the flesh but nevertheless extremely precious in the eyes of God. Therefore such things are to be preferred to all the

---

[5] Luther's source is Erasmus, who had, in turn, derived his information from Plutarch; on this basis our suggestion in *Luther's Works*, 3, p. 201, n. 30, is to be corrected.

[6] In part, Luther seems to be paraphrasing Prov. 31:10-31.

works that are carried on in a convent, because such things have the testimony of the Holy Spirit.

Kind. We would say *gütig*, ready to help everyone, to bear, and to forgive. In this word he indicates and includes all those virtues with which she ought to shine toward her neighbors, while previously he has discussed those virtues that belong within the family. They all belong in the household, but if there is anything left over, she should be kind, friendly, and generous to others. *Submissive to their husbands.* This is now the law with which he concludes here. Women are a fragile sex and under authority; therefore they can suffer miserably. This is how she ought to live. The rule is perfect, but life is not; for it is now heedless and transgresses it.[7] Then there is the other rule about the "weaker vessel" (1 Peter 3:7): Weak though she may be physically, she is even weaker emotionally. Manly women are rare; women are usually weak, easily frightened, easily offended, easily angered, easily made suspicious. Then a man should be patient. One can always find more good than bad in women. We would want everything to be perfect in women. Why are these things commanded here? *That [the Word of God] might be preserved.* All these things should be taught in outward conduct, so that God may be glorified. As Matt. 5:16 says, "that they may see." This passage identifies the final cause of all good works. Through faith we are justified; through good works God is glorified. Let this, he says, be seen among you, for you are set in the midst of the wicked (cf. Phil. 2:15). And God wants to use your life to convert other nations, that the kingdom of Christ may be expanded. *That the Word of God may not be discredited:* Our good life is necessary to remove offense and to edify others, "that your light may shine" (Matt. 5:16). God Himself gives everything freely. But He demands that we not give offense to others who are to be converted and that we not alienate them from our doctrine. For if we have lived a wicked life, we alienate many; because the heathen cannot see our faith, they ought to see our works, then hear our doctrine, and then be converted. So he speaks elsewhere of "adorning the doctrine" (v. 10), so that the enemies do not have [a reason for complaint]. That is: "Live good lives, so that men are not frightened away from your doctrine." We should be a good ex-

---

[7] The Latin is somewhat obscure: "Sic debet vivere, Regula est perfecta, vita non, quia iam negligens est, supergreditur."

ample to others, "so that no fault may be found with our ministry," as 2 Cor. 6:3 says. Therefore if a Christian is greedy, lustful, or usurious, he offends others. "Is that what Christians are like? What good comes from their doctrine?" The offense that comes from the abrogation of the Mass is a Pharisaic offense, an offense that ought not to be avoided but sought. Christ said (Matt. 9:13): "I desire mercy, and not sacrifice." He condemned a righteousness that consisted in washing one's hands, in giving alms, and in fasting. He said (Matt. 15:13): "Every plant [which My Heavenly Father has not planted will be rooted up]." These are offenses one must let go. "They are [blind] guides," He says (Matt. 15:14). The offenses that are to be avoided are those that can accuse us in our conscience, as Galatians 5:19 says. But God is praised by our proper and beautiful lives. I see that among Christians adultery is punished and that the women behave in a reserved way. When the Christians were accused before Trajan, Pliny said that there was no guilt to be found among them; they gathered before dawn and were strongly opposed to adultery and violence.[8] It impressed a heathen that Christians lived a chaste and sober life, and he warned Trajan not to [punish them]. Thus Lucian says that Christians are good-natured, that they trust everybody, that they are not anxious, that they recognize their own mistakes; and therefore anyone who wants to be rich should go to the Christians.[9] This is how the wicked are compelled by their own consciences to think about Christians. But what testimony they could have against us! Thus both Münzer and our fanatics could justify their separation from us in the name of God, saying: "[The Lord will not hold him guiltless] who takes His name in vain." (Ex. 20:7)

Likewise urge the young men to control themselves, the young men or adolescents. He distinguishes between the aged men and the young men. Thus he commends the young men and the mature men with the same virtue. Σώφρων: those who are now in the years of flaming youth should be sensible. He has said the same thing about the old women and about the young women. There is no stage in life which ought not to be sensible. If they are sensible, they are virtuous enough. 7. *Show yourself in all respects a model of good deeds,* a type, an example, a pattern. Titus ought

---

[8] Pliny, *Epistolae,* Book X, ep. 96.

[9] Lucian, *Peregrinus,* 13.

to be a τύπος.[10] You who are placed in their midst should be a pure pattern. A bishop ought to be held up to public view. If anything is desirable in others, it ought to be found in him. In what respect? *In your teaching.* The text is confused here. Neither the Greeks nor the Latins agree on the distinction.[11] The chief thing in a bishop is that he set forth the Word correctly, because teaching is his principal work, and he is to be devoted above all to the conservation of doctrine. *Show,* that is, in your doctrine you will show integrity, gravity, sound speech, and irreproachability. All four of these should be shown in his teaching: integrity, gravity, sound speech, and irreproachability, all four in doctrine. This is the way I distinguish them. The Greek text distinguishes as follows: In teaching you will preserve and demonstrate integrity and incorruptibility, so that you do not adulterate the Word in teaching but teach a doctrine that is not mixed or diluted. This should be evident not only in your word, but in *yourself,* that you may be a sound teacher, one who is not at fault, one who does not vitiate the doctrine with his own opinions but presents the Word in its integrity as it has been entrusted to him. *Gravity:* Be fine and upright. Do not be frivolous in your teaching, as are those who with their eloquence and rhetoric only tickle their hearers to laughter, to serve their itching ears (2 Tim. 4:3), as on Easter.[12] You should teach the Word seriously, as Rom. 16:18 warns, and you should teach the things that are serious. He who preaches truly concerning Christ has a Word of salvation that is sweet not according to the tastes of the flesh but according to those of the Spirit, so that he does not make his appeal on the basis of myths. Just as you ought to preserve doctrine in its integrity without mingling anything with it, so you ought to proceed with gravity, that is, be upright and steady, to prevent the introduction of questions which arouse quarrels. This is what happens now. Those questions will overthrow and drive out the Gospel, so that one deals with the questions [instead of the Gospel].

[10] This play on words in both Greek and Latin cannot be reproduced satisfactorily in English.

[11] Most Latin manuscripts read "in teaching, in integrity, in gravity," but some agree with the Greek text.

[12] Luther is referring to the homiletical *risus paschalis* in the late Middle Ages, the custom of including *Ostermärlein* ("Easter fairy tales") in an Easter sermon to amuse the worshipers.

8. *Sound speech that cannot be censured.* It still causes offense, but because of the truth. I have not said or taught anything, but the Holy Spirit has. It is our aim that your word may be irreproachable. Why is that? That we may be justified by it? No, but so that the heathen are not alienated, but when they see you teaching as I have prescribed, are moved by your doctrine and are converted. If, on the other hand, the doctrine is not sound and they inculcate it, you will have many opponents—heathen with their philosophy, Jews with circumcision and the Law, and wiseacres who will create trouble. Therefore since you are set "in the midst of a crooked nation" (Phil. 2:15), who are not only offended but look for offenses, conduct yourselves in such a way that they do not find them. It happens to us that when our books are published, they would like to see [our doctrine] perish. Therefore we must be careful that our doctrine be irreproachable. And so live up to the four requirements.[13]

9. *Bid slaves to be submissive to their masters.* This kind of slave receives authorization here. It is confirmed that he is in a very good kind of life, regardless of how mean it may appear in the eyes of those who are holy and wise. The clergy despise them, but in the sight of God they are most acceptable. We passed over such mean, pious, and salutary things when we did our teaching according to the pope, where there was no piety in life except to become a monk, despising these very statements of Scripture in which the greatest commendation is given to being an old man, a matron, a wife, or even to being a slave. He is speaking about the slaves of ancient times, who were the property of their masters, as sheep are in our regions, who had been captured in war or who had been purchased. Nevertheless, he calls this a very good kind of life, in which they ought to live with a good conscience. How much better is the kind of life when a man is a servant to another man, promising fidelity and the duties of a servant! Here there is a voluntary fidelity by which such servants promise to perform their service. As he says to the Corinthians (1 Cor. 7:21), how much the more [such a man should serve]! It is a powerful testimony when you know that you are in a way of life which is pleasing to God. No cleric is able to say that. *They should be submissive and serve faithfully, giving satisfaction in every re-*

[13] This is the end of the eighth lecture, delivered on December 3, 1527, and the beginning of the ninth, delivered on December 4.

spect. He says the same thing in Ephesians (Eph. 6:5-8) and Colossians (Col. 3:22-24). They should give due satisfaction, have regard for what is good, and bear their servitude patiently, considering that this is the will of God and that their servile slavery is pleasing to the Divine Majesty. It should be pleasing also to us, who are only dregs ourselves; that is, we should be willing to be pleased with it too. The second [instruction] is that they carry out their duty in such a way that they avoid offending their masters and that they do what is pleasing to their masters. They should strive to please and to please perfectly, serving in such a way that they do not choose certain works in which they are willing to please and others in which they follow their own ideas. This kind of virtue is certainly rare, especially in those who are captive in life-long servitude. Then the flesh is indignant at being captive. If you read the comedies, you will see what the poets think about slaves — good-for-nothing fellows doing things in such a way that they neglect their duty to their masters.[14] With those who serve voluntarily, as our servants do, the situation is far worse. They reserve for themselves the freedom that if they do not like things, they can leave. Those who are truly captive could be thrown into jail by law and compelled to work. This is not possible now, because ours is a free kind of service. Therefore there is complaining throughout the land because they do not hear anything preached about service. I have never heard it said that a household staff should serve its masters and that this is the best possible thing to do. If servants knew that it pleases God when they pay attention to the things that belong to their service, they would act differently. But [they do not], because they do not know that they are in a very good station of life. Colossians says (Col. 3:23): "as serving the Lord and not men," because they are in a kind of life which He Himself had established. Let the servant strive to give satisfaction in all his duties without exception, doing exactly what his master wishes; if he does that, he is saved. It is not necessary that you go to Jerusalem. You should not think: "I am a poor servant. How am I ever going to do such good works as a monk does?" Let somebody else establish churches. Remain a servant, and pay attention to doing what gives satisfaction to your master. Then you will live in security, and

---

[14] Luther's favorite among these was the *Phormio* of Terence; cf., for instance, *Luther's Works,* 13, pp. 155—156.

you will expect the revelation of Christ, as he says below (v. 13). And so why do you look at how others live, when you are extremely rich in your own works? Remain at home, and be subject to your master. Yet these simple, common, and everyday matters are despised. Someone says: "I shall not be a servant any longer, but I shall become a monk." Thus we despise the piety that is set forth everywhere. The greatest virtue is to serve in such a way that one strives to give satisfaction to one's master. This is what Christians are able to accomplish.

They are not to be refractory. It is easy for them to grumble. This is the vice of servants. Ask the farmers how much trouble they have with their hired hands in taking care of cattle and fields. Servants live today as though they were masters. There is nothing but force and violence. The servants are tyrants. The Lord cannot stand for this, and therefore He sends the plague. They refuse to be instructed; or if they are instructed, they do not listen. If a servant is a Christian, he is a noble member of the kingdom of Christ. "If you have a good servant, let him be as your own soul," as Ecclesiasticus says (Ecclus. 33:31). Sarah was holy, and Hagar was holy; yet the latter, who was a domestic, wanted to be the lady of the house. She could hear the Word of God, and yet she rose up against her mistress. 10. *Not to pilfer.* They are not to embezzle. This kind of thievery goes on in many ways, and they do not regard losses to the household as a sin which can be prevented. They keep quiet, and in addition they steal. They should be looking out for their master's property. If they neglect it by not rising in defense of it, they are not taking care of it and are culpable. If they turn it to their own advantage and steal, they are robbers and thieves. Nowadays one hears the complaint: "Servants are disloyal. They take things for themselves. And when they do damage to their master, this does not bother their conscience, because it is not their own property." This is the reason why no one is being blessed. You see very few peasants who are prospering, because they have deserved the way they are being treated. Now God is recompensing them, and they are getting their reward. So it is on all sides that beggars, botchers, and bunglers continue. They are not being told that faith, that is fidelity, loyalty, or good faith, is counted by Gal. 5:23 among the fruits of the Spirit. As he says later, "They make it of no effect." *Faith* here does not mean trust in Christ, but fidelity, that they be faithful and demonstrate good faith *in everything,* that is, thoroughly; they are to take care of their masters' property faithfully. The matters themselves are ordinary, things like taking care of the cow and washing the dishes, worthless things like that. If a cleric looks at them, he magnifies his own works. But the Holy Spirit replies: "You are a holy priest, yet I ignore your magnificent works. But a servant girl who washes pots is serving Me, no matter how dirty they may appear in your eyes. And the angels themselves look at this service to Me, and rejoice." *In everything* occurs again in relation to particular forms of service. Thus some go more willingly into the garden and take care of the plants; if they are permitted to do what they wish, they are good. He does not say: "Do this or that," but "in everything act faithfully." These are simple words, and I do not have to read St. Thomas to explain them. If we had ten hands, we would have enough to do. But we keep looking for other things. We have the command to love our brethren, but we run to St. James's.[15] Why? I do not attribute righteousness to you on this account, but tell you to be good and faithful and to abound in good works because you have already been made righteous. Do this, so that there may be glory to God. You have your salvation and your food. Now act that God may be glorified through you. This is how Paul speaks. He is an orator who expresses the same thought in various ways. Earlier he called the Word of God "our ministry," here he says *that they may adorn the doctrine.* The meaning is the same, because if I am as he describes here, I adorn the Word. A heathen cannot say anything if he has a Christian servant who strives to give satisfaction in every respect. He is compelled to say: "I really have an upright servant." If the servant is unfaithful, the master says: "I would be willing to have any kind of servant except a Christian." Thus the saving doctrine is besmirched. This is what Paul intends when he says (v. 5): "Be careful that the Word may not be discredited." Here he indicates a distinction between the Word and our life. "The Word has glorified you and us. Now live a good life, and thus the Word will be glorified." We are to show a certain gratitude toward the Word that in turn it may be well heard and glorified in the sight of men, in the sight of God and of the holy angels.

---

15 A reference to the shrine of St. James at Santiago de Compostela in Spain, which Luther mentions frequently as a place of pilgrimage; see, for example, *Luther's Works,* 22, p. 250, n. 36.

It is glorified in the sight of men not only through a good life; nevertheless, that glory does not take place simply for the sake of the Word, but that others may be converted. Therefore we are to live a good life, not in order to attain salvation, but in order that more people may be converted. Those who are responsible for the Word's being discredited will have to give an account. Paul has expressed it well here, *that they may adorn*, that they may make it joyous, glorious, not contemptible, because it is *the doctrine of God our Savior*. Here, where he is speaking about slaves, he uses magnificent words which he does not use elsewhere, because the slaves' kind of life is a mean one and needs to be brought up with more impressive words than others do. Gentlemen and ladies can be brought up to some extent by shaming them; slaves can barely be brought up with blows. Therefore since this is a very mean way of life and yet one that is truly magnificent, it is necessary for us to educate the heathen by attracting them with grand words. The clergy despised marriage and thought it unworthy of them to live in this way of life; therefore they fell into filth. So it is with servants who do not think that their service is pleasing to God. Therefore God punishes their ingratitude as though they were masters. They ought to be willing to give a hundred thousand groschen to know that they have a way of life which they are certain is pleasing to God. But because its works, its duties, and their persons are so mean, they do not believe this. Yet God speaks with His own mouth: "Your service is an office by which you serve Me." To forsake one's wife and to serve God is to serve the devil. This is not, he says, an obvious doctrine. It is one which not man but God has put forth—He who is our Savior, whose intentions for us are good, who has done everything that you might be saved. If it does not impress you that you have enough to eat, then let it impress you that Christ pays attention to you as slaves. "Enter into joy." (Matt. 25:21)

11. *For [the grace of God] has appeared.* Since he has just referred to "the doctrine of our Savior," it is altogether consistent for him to move into this fine excursus. We have often heard that the coming of Christ into the world is set forth for a double reason: first, as an example; secondly, as a gift. We have the doctrine of salvation and of piety which teaches us how to act. God Himself set forth both of these by teaching such things and by demonstrating such things in practice: first, when He explains that Christ

taught such things; secondly, when He demonstrated such things by His own gift, "who gave Himself" (v. 14). If these fires do not stir you, you are colder than cold. *Has appeared* through the Gospel; that is, it is revealed through the Gospel throughout the world. *For salvation;* that is, it saves us. *Of all men,* men of every station — the old, matrons, husbands, wives, slaves, freemen. All of these are admonished to do good works. For the Gospel has been disclosed throughout the world, as the last chapter of Mark says (Mark 16:15). No one is excused. 12. *Training* [*us*]; that is, it teaches us. This grace sets forth a doctrine and chastises us, as one disciplines and punishes young children, if we live otherwise. It is an outstanding doctrine. [*To renounce*] *irreligion,* that is, unfaithfulness to God. Secondly, *worldly* [*passions*]. These are the two parts of life: irreligion in the spirit and worldly passions in the flesh. It is the tree with its fruits which is the root of all evils. Passions follow irreligion. That is, if you are unbelieving, it follows that you desire riches, popularity, and power. Those desires themselves are to be denied, not only the works. These two vices, irreligion and passions, continually war against Christians. We should learn to believe, but unbelief battles against us daily, and therefore daily [we must resist it]. Thus our desires are not yet dead, as Rom. 7:23 points out. The flesh always craves the flattery of the world and fears the harshness of the world, death, and the cross. Against such things, we must fight by dealing with them in a *sober* way, σωφρόνως, in a sensible, moderate, and decent way. First we ought to control our own person modestly; then we ought to show love to our neighbor, render obedience to the magistrate, and give tribute, that is, not defraud anyone. This is *upright. Godly,* that God may be served. When someone thinks as follows: "I am serving the government not for his own sake but for God's," this is godliness. I serve the brother not for his own sake but for God's. I love my wife, my family, and do everything I do for His sake. This is what it means to be *godly.* "And to Him alone," for godliness means rendering all our service to God.

In this world, because he had said earlier (v. 5) that they should not bring discredit [upon the Word]. 13. *Awaiting* [*our blessed hope*]. Our life ought to be one of such modesty in relation to ourselves, to our neighbor, and to God that we can confidently expect the appearing of our Lord. Is this not the most ample comfort? If a slave believes in Christ and obeys his master, he can confidently expect the appearing of Christ. If a husband does his duty, if a wife loves her husband and takes care of the house, they can be confident too; for they know that they are most certainly pleasing to God. Thus a preacher who pays attention to his office is confident; for he is completely sure that he serves God and does what God wishes, even though Satan certainly attacks him. A cleric cannot feel this way. Then we can expect the appearing of Christ with confidence, because we believe in Christ and adorn His doctrine despite any priest or monk. Such a one can say: "I have prayed seven hours." But he cannot add: "I await a blessed hope," because he cannot say: "I am sure that these works [are pleasing to God]." A servant girl can say this: "I have washed the pots, lit the fire in the oven, and made the beds." She confidently expects the appearing of Christ because she has done these works in Christ, and they are certainly [pleasing to Him]. So it is with a son who is obedient to his father. If he is sent to do his lessons, he does them and thinks: "This is my father's command, and it is pleasing to God." It is unavoidable that Satan will attack you if you obey your brother or love your husband. But he wants the very opposite. Thus the doctrine of God is adorned by our life, but not in the sense that we are justified by this. It is a great thing that He is willing to grant eternal life for the washing of pots. No, but He does give it to those who have lived in this way. "Fear not, little flock" (Luke 12:32). The passion and death of Christ are to be magnified; they have infinite [worth] because we believe in this blood. Therefore, believing and living this way as an example for others, we confidently await through Christ. This is how a Christian waits. These are magnificent words, and this is not a temporal hope which crucifies instead of bringing blessing. Then He will be revealed in His glory and greatness and divine majesty. Christ is God; this is the first part. The second is that He has given and administered His gifts. Christ strengthens the conscience, lest it despair of eternal life.[16]

We began to expound the appearing of Christ in a twofold way. First it is an example, that the grace of God which brings salvation has appeared through the Gospel so that He might chas-

---

[16] This is the end of the ninth lecture, delivered on December 4, 1527, and the beginning of the tenth, delivered on December 9.

tise all men and so that we might imitate Him as He has gone before us with His example. Christ was serious and filled with good works; therefore we ought to live according to this example. Secondly, Paul presents the appearing of Christ as a gift of God, by which the suffering and works of Christ are not merely an example but a gift given to us. And this is why he says: 14. *Who gave [Himself for us]*. These are very important words. The example of Christ would be in vain, because no one could follow it unless we were transformed into new men. For whenever a good law is prescribed to the old man, he spits it out, even though he is more ready to accept the law than the Gospel because he supposes that he is able to keep it by his own powers; but when the Gospel announces to him that he cannot do this, he will not stand for it. As long as the old man remains, therefore, nothing follows, no matter how much you say. Therefore he says: He has not only preceded us as an example; but He has become our gift, so that His righteousness might be ours. To what end? It is one thing to precede and show an example, quite another [to give a gift]. He chastises us with His life and example; this we perform with our works. But the other thing we do not attain by our works, only by believing that Christ, according to 1 Cor. 1:30, [is our righteousness]; for we were captive to sin and death, and therefore it was vain for the Law to be required and for good works to be required, since one who is captive to sin cannot do anything.

To purify [for Himself a people of His own]. This is how the apostles translate the Hebrew word סְגֻלָּה, private property, His own. In Exodus (Ex. 19:5): "You shall be peculiar to Me, a peculiar people." We say "My own," and Peter says (1 Peter 2:9) "a people for His possession." Vergil speaks of the *peculium*.[17] That is, this is a people which is the property of Christ, in whose midst He dwells, which is devoted to Him, which He looks after as He would a flock, to which He has given life. Not only has He rescued it, but He purifies it every day if there is any filth left. Likewise, *who are zealous [for good deeds]*, who with rivalry, zeal, and competition strive to do good works. Here he returns to the first point. We have been redeemed, and we are purified daily in order that we may live in good works. He was zealous. Then we shall be as we have been redeemed and purified. There

---

17 Probably a reference to Vergil, *Eclogues*, I, 33.

must be a careful distinction between the two. Thus Peter says (1 Peter 2:24): "He Himself bore [our sins]—that we might live to righteousness." Now that Christ has suffered in the flesh, it follows: "As He has done, so we ought to do." Thus John says (1 John 2:9): "He who says he is in the light." He is speaking of the imitation [of Christ]. But, on the other hand, he says (1 John 2:2): "not for our sins only but also for the sins of the whole world." Here he is referring to the gift. Therefore you must carefully consider these two things. Heretofore we have taught in the schools that Christ is an example and a lawgiver. But about the other part, how He has been given for us, they taught nothing at all. And yet this is the most important part and the summary of what ought to be taught and known in Christ; if this is not taught, faith perishes, because righteousness is not based on the teaching of the first part.

15. *Declare these.* The emphasis is on the pronoun "these." He is referring to his earlier statement about myths (1:14), where he said: "Do not give heed to those, but to these." Those myths ought to remain silent. In these two things, the teaching of faith in Christ as a gift, and in good works, we have difficulty enough. Satan persuades them that it is an easy thing to teach these two. Certainly the apostles did not regard it as an easy thing. If all of us together were to compose a sermon, we could not compose such a text as has been composed by Paul here. I say that faith and love cannot be taught enough. When these are being dealt with, Satan strains every power to make this doctrine contemptible, as 1 Cor. 8:2 says: "If anyone imagines that he is saying something, etc." That is, teach in such a way that other myths are despised. There are two kinds of doctrine. Christian doctrine must always be taught, because there are always listeners, and children grow up who need to be instructed in the things of which they are ignorant. One must exhort the same thing and constantly repeat, inculcate, and listen to one and the same thing. This they despise, and they find doctrines which have never been heard of before, as, for example, "whether original sin is a defect." [18] But one must set forth the same doctrine in the same form. They think that the devil is dead, and they do not know their domestic enemy, who goes about. Therefore the flesh snores daily. It has new laws, con-

[18] See p. 8, n. 4.

trary to faith and love. Therefore one must not stop teaching and exhorting with the same Word, because Satan harasses us every day with his flaming darts (Eph. 6:16). Those who are not harassed are possessed. Therefore every Christian has trials every day. His faith, his hope, and his chastity [19] are tried. What are we to do? Let us teach, let us expound, let us inculcate the Word, let us exhort. Holy Scripture has this grace, that it does not teach in vain. If only one opens the Book attentively, it does not depart without fruit but sets a man straight, purges away his evil thoughts, and brings in good ones. If the evil thoughts return, let him open the Book again. Therefore Scripture is called a book of patience (cf. Rom. 15:4). Therefore they do not hasten to pray the Our Father, even though you know that it is the nature of this Word to cleanse the heart and set it on fire. Since, therefore, we are always in trials from the world and from Satan, it is profitable for us to teach this way. "Therefore," he says, "teach these things which are good and useful."

Reprove [*with all authority*]. Does he want Titus to be domineering, contrary to what is said in the fifth chapter of Peter (1 Peter 5:3) and in 2 Cor. 4:5? To the Corinthians it is said (2 Cor. 1:24): "Not that we lord it over your faith"; and again (1 Cor. 4:8): "Would that you did reign!" But this authority means that he ought to inculcate his doctrine with authority. Not that he ought to seek authority for himself, but that he ought to seek authority for his doctrine. That is, you ought to speak in such a way that your doctrine holds authority, that you so urge and inculcate it that they accept it with reverence and hold it in authority, despising other myths. You ought to gain authority and reverence for your own doctrine and deprive the contrary doctrine of authority, so that it is without power. *With all authority,* that your doctrine may be authoritative and worthy of reverence. *Let no one* [*disregard you*], that is, someone who wants to instruct the proud and the powerful. Above (1:7) he used the word αὐθάδης. "So conduct yourself that you have a word that cannot be censured. Follow the four types indicated above." False prophets certainly despise this and walk in the clouds. They have φιλαυτία, "self-love"; but other teachers are righteous and learned. But he wants his doc-

---

[19] The text reads *castitas,* and we have translated accordingly; but in the context, *caritas,* "love," might be intended.

trine to be taught and imprinted in a way that will keep the adversaries from despising it; and if they do despise it, they will be caught in their pride. That is, let no one despise you by teaching and exhortation, as Matt. 10:14 says. In short, be powerful and diligent in your teaching. The good apostle saw that good preachers were needed to preserve his word in the church.

CHAPTER THREE

1. *Remind them.* Here at last he explains good works. So far he has been describing the summary of the Christian life, especially how Christians are to live with one another and in opposition to the false prophets, who make it a practice always to plant tares but do not come to places that are not prepared. In like manner our people ought to attack the pope in his own dominion. Now he also instructs them in the good works which they ought to perform, not to those of their own household but to those on the outside and especially to magistrates. For Christians ought to live in such a way that those who are on the outside are forced to give a good testimony about us and then that they may be brought to the faith, as Peter says about Christian wives (1 Peter 3:1). The magistrate ought to be honored in order that he may realize that this doctrine is sound. This is a noteworthy passage which ought to shake up the disobedient clerics so that they are not subject to Christian magistrates in external jurisdiction,[1] even though Paul subjects himself and all Christians to profane magistrates. When they brought it about that they were not subject to the laws of the emperor, a good part of Christian life perished. It is a great accomplishment to know that one is doing something that is pleasing to God, no matter how ordinary it is. Even if the command came from magistrates who are foolish and cruel and I did not obey it, I would be sinning; I would certainly obey it just as if it came from an angel. Then they chose for themselves their own forms of obedience concerning which they do not have a Word. Therefore all men should be taught to be quick to obey. The reason is that they should be sure they are not obeying men but God. If even a wicked master commands a peasant, he can joyfully carry the wood and be better when he does this than a monk with his works, because all he has to care about is the will

[1] Luther is referring to the legal exemption known as "benefit of clergy"; cf. *Luther's Works,* 30, p. 183, n. 9.

of God and what pleases Him. Among the clerics there is no such work. Instead, there is contempt of God, one's own choice, and obedience to the devil. These things should be inculcated in the peasants and servants, so that they may know what are good works. Otherwise they think that they are rendering service the way cattle and donkeys work, and so they become impatient and grumble, and do not serve with a pure heart. The teachers are at fault. But if a peasant knew that he is serving God, then many would be found who would understand this and would serve willingly. Then one would stir up another and instruct others. Therefore this is a precious work, which is pleasing in heaven and in the sight of the holy angels. Secondly, before this doctrine emerged, I knew many princes who thought that they were carrying on a profane office. When they acknowledged that the government is a divine ordinance, they acquired a good conscience and administered their office well. Otherwise one is presumptuous and becomes nothing but a tyrant, or he despairs and does nothing. Frederick had a monk at his court who held back from all the offices of the prince, especially from judgments, so that he did nothing but hear Masses and vigils.[2] But if he is taught: "You are in an office which is most pleasing to God, namely, [to protect] widows and orphans, as Rom. 13:3 says, to be a god established in this world (Ps. 82:5)," he can have a good conscience and then can become kind, pious, and firm according to necessity. If one's conscience is good, he can administer well, or at least carry out his office with clemency. Thus they would be of benefit to the common people. These things, I say, should be inculcated. That would be valuable. This Word gives and commends this office, and therefore all the works that are carried on in it are most acceptable to God and holy. A monk cannot say this: "This is a rule instituted by God." Therefore he ruins his life.

To rulers means to all powers of whatever kind, as, for example, to the magistrates in the cities. They are subject to the rulers. Here you have a divine sign: when you are subject to a ruler, you are subject to Christ, your Lord and God, who for you was obedient even [unto death], as Phil. 2:8 says. Should you not accept this with thanks? You are sure that he is a prince, that his work has

---

[2] It is not clear whether this refers to Frederick's court before or after Luther's emergence as Reformer, for many pre-Reformation practices had persisted there long after 1517.

been ordained by God, and that my obedience has been ordained
by God. Therefore you are subject to him freely. These things
ought to be taught. The Lord ought to convert the clerics who
have elevated their own works and despised those works. *Submissive,* that is, let them be ready, let them always remain in
subjection, let them not stir up sects. [*To be obedient*] *to a command,* so that if any command comes, they obey it. When a command comes from a ruler or a magistrate, I get right to work,
whether in peace or in war. If he commands me to go and dig
a mound, I go securely. Let the clerics go too! Formerly it used
to be said: "While you are planting, digging, and farming, we
pray God for you. You are not able to do so, since you have other
duties." When you work in your craft,[3] you are doing a better
work than I, unless I do my teaching and praying faithfully. The
works are different and greater, but the work is diverse. This is
how the murderers of bad consciences are to be instructed. A monk
ought to instruct a good, honest citizen to take someone along who
would bring about a good conscience. He should say: "Gracious
prince, you have entrusted this to me because it is an honorable
work, a work of majesty." It used to be that students, even children, gave themselves over to fornication and rascality.[4] If I kill
in war, it is a work of God. And when a judge sitting in court
passes sentence, why is it not a good work to kill with the hand
by the authority of the prince? For after all, that criminal was
killed even before the sword was used. We have taught vain things,
myths, and foolishness rather than such things. Thus all the works
of the government ought to be carried out by honorable persons
and those who have a good conscience. And it is good for such
a person to accept a reward. An executioner or a jailer is a better
man than a prior or an abbot, for this function has been entrusted
by God. Likewise, [*to be ready*] *for* [*any honest work*]. He explains what it means to be obedient. I want you to obey the government, but to the extent that it commands you to do good things;
for it happens that some men administer the government unjustly.
A Christian distinguishes between a good and a bad command
of a prince, as in the case of the legion which Aurelian commanded

[3] The text reads *incerte,* "unsurely," which does not make sense; we have
followed the suggestion of the Weimar editors and have read *in arte.*

[4] The original reads, in a mixture of German and Latin: "Olim fecit studentes
die sie haben verhurt und verbubt et pueros."

to kill the Christians. But they replied: "This far we are willing to go, because we are battling against the enemies of your kingdom. But no farther." [5] There they were ready for a good work, because one ought to obey God more (Acts 5:29). All these things are good, whatever they may be. *To speak evil [of no one].* These are the vices of the ignorant common people. Or you do not know that these works pertain to the government? Would that thunder and lightning would set house and home on fire, so that they get the plague! For they are ignorant beasts of the field. They suppose that serving God means to speak evil of the commands of the government. Paul does not want this; he wants them to give thanks and to praise God that we are worthy of being found in these works. This is how it would be if this were taught. It is a characteristic vice of the common people to speak evil of the government. *To avoid quarreling;* that is, let them be free of fighting, not rebellious, not seditious. Let them be obedient to the magistrates. Let them take care that everywhere the command of the prince is obeyed. They set him against the government. And if they could gather an army and kill, as the peasants did, that is forbidden.[6] The two vices are to curse and to rebel. But they should be ἐπιεικεῖς. This important word occurs frequently in Greek. Erasmus says that it refers to gentleness or equity.[7] In their own language and according to their own usage lawyers define it as equity.[8] But this is not enough in other fields. From the examples one should take 2 Cor. 10:1, [where Paul mentions] "the meekness and epieikeia" [of Christ]. And Tertullus (Acts 24:4) [mentions] "your epieikeia," that is, kindness, humaneness, gentleness.[9]

We began to treat this word ἐπιεικής, gentle. This term is quite famous among the Greeks but not so famous among the Latins. I have pointed out an example from Acts, where Tertullus says

---

[5] Luther is referring to an incident said by legend to have happened under Maximian, not Aurelian, the story of the so-called "Theban Legion," recounted in Eucherius of Lyons, *Passio Agaunensium martyrum, Patrologia, Series Latina,* L, 827—832.

[6] A reference to the Peasants' War of 1525.

[7] The Latin words suggested by Erasmus were *mansuetudo* and *equitas.*

[8] Cf. Cicero, *De Oratore,* I, 56, 240.

[9] This is the end of the tenth lecture, delivered on December 9, 1527, and the beginning of the eleventh, delivered on December 10.

"to hear us." Jurists define it as equity, when on account of an intervening case they soften the rigor of the law. Aristotle says in the fifth book of his *Ethics* that when a legislator sets down a law, he makes a distinction: The law is impossible, because moral questions concern themselves with the person.[10] Therefore the law can deal only with the general situation. The head of a household decides that his family should get up at the third hour. This is a general law. But a special case arises if someone in his family has a headache and cannot do this. If he is foolish, he pushes his way through and does not observe epieikeia. He does not soften the rigor of the law. This is what is meant by equity in moral laws. Carthusians have the law that they are not to eat meat. Here a wise moderator ought to say: "Here the rule should be given up. The rule is laid down for those who are tough, not for those who are weak." Another instance (Phil. 4:4-5): "Rejoice in the Lord," that is, "Be forbearing," ἐπιεικεῖς. The significance of the word is to be gathered from a comparison of passages, as, for example, 2 Cor. 10:1. And earlier, in chapter 2, verse 2, he spoke of wisdom, whose virtue it is that a Christian be gentle, flexible, kind and yielding to the evil, the weak, and to all cases of misfortune. In summary, whenever we Christians abide in the world, in the kingdom of the devil, it is necessary that certain things be decided upon; but when what is decided upon is carried out imperfectly, one must be courageous and sing: "So what!" I will not grieve myself to death, as new rulers sometimes do. One must dissemble a great deal, ignore and not see, which is a necessary virtue. Whoever does not know how to dissemble does not know how to rule; he does not know how to live with people. Thus Emperor Frederick III did not have epieikeia.[11] This virtue is related to gentleness and kindness; yet these latter do not depend on our dissembling a great deal whether our brother has done us injury of one kind or another, so that I torture myself but put the best construction on it. Therefore this virtue is praised most of all and is the treasure which the Lord entrusts in consequence of epieikeia. A gentle person does not become angry.

[10] Aristotle, *Nicomachean Ethics,* Book V, ch. 10.

[11] Frederick III had been emperor of the Holy Roman Empire 1440—1493; Luther's evaluation of him is confirmed by a contemporary chronicler, who writes: "He was a useless emperor, and the nation during his long reign forgot that she had a king."

Then they are ἐπιεικεῖς, that is, they dissemble a great deal. What if God wanted to deal with us according to a strict [interpretation of the Law]? No matter how much He dissembles, He does not withdraw His hand. Or would He want to dissemble and let everything go? [*To show perfect*] *courtesy* [*to all men*], that is, this gentle behavior and dissembling. The whole book of Ecclesiastes teaches nothing but epieikeia.[12] We should be willing to give our counsel gladly and to help. This is dissembling, not only to bear with something but to put the best construction on it as though I did not see it. It consists mainly in these objects which I suffer, as patience or epieikeia proceeds to deal with the evil things which we see happening. Therefore it is a patience toward public evils as well as a patience and tolerance toward private evils. Whoever is able to be gentle in that area, to soften the rigor of the law and of justice, is ἐπιεικής. Therefore when those who have been placed under magistrates see many things in the public realm which offend us and which ought to be changed, you must, if you want to be a good example to the heathen, put up with them and let them go, even though they trouble and bother you. Yet there will always be many things that do not go as they should. Therefore this is a necessary virtue for those who want to live either in the midst of public affairs or among those who administer public affairs.

Courtesy. The former is a more eminent virtue than courtesy. *Toward* [*all men*] I ought to show courtesy. Πραΰτης is that noblest of virtues which does not become angry. And here he sets it down as absolute and perfect, not bound to any time or case but in place at all times and toward all men. It is not an outstanding virtue to show courtesy toward one's friends, but [it is to do so] if you are irritated by a hostile or heathen person or if you have the occasion to become angry with me or with a friend. This virtue is to be counted among those that pertain to administrators, because in the public realm offenses which insult people are unavoidable. Besides, we are distrustful and weak. Someone suffers an insult or commits one. Such things cannot all be prevented and restrained even if there were a government official on every corner. Since therefore Satan does not stop with his insults, etc., do not try to repress these by force or check the vigor of the law.

---

[12] Luther had lectured on the Book of Ecclesiastes just a year earlier, from July 30 to November 7, 1526 (cf. *Luther's Works*, 15).

Solomon was not able to achieve this. There will be peace only if you are ἐπιεικής and courteous, if you do not take things personally, if you do not become exercised even when something bad happens to you, if anger does not bite you. Some people pine away with envy, will be consumed with the most evil thoughts, and are their own worst cross. Clerics have an advantage, since they do not deal with public affairs. 3. *For we ourselves were.* Here he sets some vices over against the virtues so that on the basis of these you might understand what he means by epieikeia and courtesy. We should, he says, bear the malicious acts of others. Why? Look behind you. If you see how your envy is tolerated and how those who are compelled to put up with your envy behave, you should act the same way toward that of others.

Once, before Christ. *Foolish.* You will find such men in the government. Do not be offended. Have epieikeia, and think to yourself: "That prince is crazy. I remember the time when I was too." Ἀπειθής, faithless. In the public realm or in the household you will see some who do not willingly obey the government or their parents or masters. Then you will become angry, but time was when you did not obey willingly either and did not know that the government is a divine ordinance. If you were to find such people now, you must bear with them. Take out the record book, and you will find that you, too, have been disobedient to parents as well as to magistrates. Under Maximilian the princes would have been willing to be without obedience; [13] then it was not a sin until the peasants came; they [threw out the baby with] the bath water. Now the nobles forget their nobility and do not do penance. *Led astray,* ignorant of those things which belong to faith, all wrapped up in various opinions. They worshiped Jupiter; nor is there any one of us who did not err in faith, because apart from Christ there is error. "All we [like sheep have gone astray]," as Isaiah says (Is. 53:6). *Slaves [to various passions and pleasures].* We, too, were such "good children," and yet to ourselves we seem to be holy and wise. To serve pleasure and to fulfill our pleasure and lust is not to hate them but to become enslaved to them. Nevertheless, it is praiseworthy to battle against them.

[*Passing our days*] *in malice* [*and envy*], spending our entire

---

[13] Cf. *Luther's Works,* 12, pp. 214—215.

life in malice. He who pursues pleasure and desires also comes to malice and envy, because Satan does not permit him to enjoy his delights without arousing rivalry. Then two dogs fight over one bone. Then it is "Hands off!" Malice means that I wish to do harm to someone else; and to wish this even where malice cannot be exercised is envy, which is a spiteful attitude that wants to do harm even when it cannot, and when it cannot, becomes disgusted and does harm to itself. What follows are the fruits which follow envy, what Solomon calls a rotting of the bones (Prov. 14:30). Hatred follows envy, so that it says and does what will harm the neighbor. It is directed especially against magistrates; when they can harm someone, they do so. God says (Ex. 23:9): "You were strangers in Egypt, therefore do good to the stranger." So we say: "Remember." The example of Christ and of ourselves is a powerful one. *Hated* [*by men*]: "He has a grudge against us, and so we have a grudge in return." If he says one word, a person responds with ten. Once more he sets forth the example of Christ, because our example is worthless.

4. *When* [*the goodness and loving-kindness of God our Savior appeared*]. This is a beautiful text. Because Paul is "a chosen instrument" (Acts 9:15) in preference to the other apostles, he enjoys setting forth this doctrine about the gift of Christ, how He was given, how He has been made our righteousness. No one sets forth this doctrine so copiously. Formerly, when I was a younger theologian, Paul seemed to me to be indulging in empty talk in the first part of his epistles; for I did not know that these were the principles of Christian doctrine with which he introduced his paraenetic epistles. I did not see that the doctrine about how Christ has been given for us is far more important in this epistle. Χρηστότης, as in Phil. 4:4-5. Χρηστότης is a sweetness of life, not only goodness but also kindness. A man is kind or sweet when he is friendly and well-disposed, easily approachable, not harsh, but pleasant and joyful. He makes an effort to have people enjoy being about him. They are glad to hear him speak. He is companionable, affable, and easy for everyone to get along with. He is a brother to every man you can think of. This is a sweet manner. This text sets forth Christ as one who had χρηστότης, the sweetness of golden virtue and of deity. God dwelt in Christ, He was in Christ. The "words of life" (John 6:69), that is, "Thou dost speak

in such a fine way and dost say such words." Whenever [Peter] remembered the sweetness of Christ he cried so much that his face was disfigured.[14]

Goodness, that most gracious treatment of us and attitude toward us in Christ. Whoever was with Him preferred His company to that of the Pharisees. Φιλανθρωπία is not to be understood as referring to the substance of human nature, as they have explained it, applying it to the incarnation.[15] Here he is speaking about Christ's activity. It means loving-kindness toward human beings; that is, He lived among us in the sweetest of ways, offended no one, and tolerated everyone. With this sweetness He did not serve Himself but sought to show love and the effects of love toward blind men by giving them sight, as Matt. 11:5 says; for this was the purpose and effect of His φιλανθρωπία, that He was eager to serve men out of generosity and friendliness. These virtues we see in Christ and in God. That kindness and φιλανθρωπία is not dead but is still in evidence and is revealed through the Gospel and then through its effects, that Christ is χρηστότης and φιλανθρωπία, and that God is so disposed in Christ, He who treats us sweetly, who does everything to help us, who gives His gifts, who gives teachers to teach the brethren and to help and strengthen us in bearing evils, who is present at death to receive our souls—in short, who wants to love people. *Of God our Savior.* Therefore you should not refer this only to the humanity of Christ but to God, who dwelt in Christ. 5. *He saved* [us]. What shall we say against this text? What we say is this: "God, who is merciful and kind, did not save us; but [our works did]." As he does to the Philippians (Phil. 3:9), so here he points to the works of the Law, which are the works of righteousness. These are Paul's qualities, and yet he rejects them all. The works of righteousness were present in us; yet we were not saved by these, but *in virtue of* [*His own mercy*]. This is an example which provokes us to epieikeia. You want the government to have everything so right and proper that nothing bothers you. Just remember and look behind you [at what you were]. He sets up an opposition between mercy on the one

14 An allusion to the story of Peter in the *Legenda aurea* of Jacobus de Vora-gine; cf. *Luther's Works,* 24, pp. 178—179.

15 See, for example, Pseudo-Primasius (Cassiodorus), *In epistolam ad Titum commentaria, Patrologia, Series Latina,* LXVIII, 683.

hand and righteousness and all merit on the other hand. If it is grace, it is not righteousness and our merit.[16]

We said above that this passage deals with redemption or righteousness. Paul enjoys dealing with this and often inculcates it, because this doctrine is the one and only necessary one. He does this, however, for the sake of the scornful and frivolous saints who are caught up in their own speculations and who pursue some sort of great spirits but in the meanwhile lose that trust in which they ought to persist. If you read Jerome, Origen, and Chrysostom and see certain games and allegories, your conscience is not made steadfast by their games and is not instructed or armed. Thus when I am cast into prison and see the jailer coming, I do not know why. Where there is an allegory, there is not a single verse in Jerome [to help] someone struggling with this. But if someone is .agitated, he should know that Jesus Christ is King, who [forgives] sins; such people stand firm. John Hus forgot every allegorical figure except Jesus Christ, the living Word of God. He took hold of the principal doctrine of the New Testament. Even among our brethren those who observe this doctrine of redemption are very rare; they follow our own speculations. Paul is exceedingly fond of dealing with this theme. See to it, therefore, that you meditate on and read such passages. Do not grow tired of them, for one day the hour will come when you will know that you did well to study them and that no one can do full justice to the full treatment of such passages. If God had not protected me from such speculations, which used to give me very great pleasure, I would have become the champion of the world. It is necessary to teach the uninstructed and young theologians not to follow allegory. This made a great impression on Jerome and on Origen. Our theologians used to think that Jerome and Origen were the very best, but we have a way of telling the difference. No matter how trite and commonplace things are [in Scripture], they are never easy enough to anyone; even when they are most common, they are completely hidden, because this matter is grasped by a profound experience of life, not of speculation. "Hallowed be Thy name" (Matt. 6:9) is a very common statement, and it can be expounded in a sufficiently learned way; but one can never expound it with ardent feeling and grasp it most ardently in one-

[16] This is the end of the eleventh lecture, delivered on December 10, 1527, and the beginning of the twelfth, delivered on December 11.

self. Other expositors are mere babblers, as Paul will warn later
on (vv. 9-11). Our heart catches fire, and it builds its knowledge
and faith in God the Savior on a solid rock which stands firm in
anguish, in the hour of death, in prison, and in judgment. Then
one could say: "Jesus is my Savior, and He is kind," so that one's
heart does not fear and is not confounded in His presence. So
Stephen stood in the Sanhedrin with a face "like the face of an
angel" (Acts 6:15), but someone else will not stand. These things
stand; and if they are not insisted on, we are cold in our treatment
of them. The gift of God is not merit by which we are saved, but
we are saved through mercy, which stands before our eyes, while
the wrath, rage, and examples of the wrath of God are far removed.
I ought to feel nothing in my heart except the sense of the mercy
of God, and when our heart is filled with that awareness and feeling of mercy, that is enough for it to fight against sin, hell, the
wrath of God, the warnings of the Flood,[17] Satan, and the power
of sin. It is the weakness of sin that battles against the spirit.
Countless darts (cf. Eph. 6:16) are directed against this feeling.
Therefore do not neglect it and give yourself over to speculation.

   *Not because of deeds [done by us in righteousness but in virtue
of His own mercy by] the washing [of regeneration and renewal
in the Holy Spirit]*. You have here a commendation of Baptism
such as I can hardly find anywhere else in the New Testament.
The enemies of the grace of God, under the pretext of love, have
preceded us and distorted all those other passages.[18] Therefore
this passage summarizes those. *By mercy,* he says, *we are saved.*
But by what road does mercy come to us? *By washing.* They say:
"Washing can refer to the Word, the Gospel, the Holy Spirit,
namely, that we are baptized in the Spirit. If He is conferred,
then Baptism is a washing of regeneration, that is, it is a sign of
those who are regenerated. In other words, the washing of regeneration is bestowed on those who have already been regenerated through the Holy Spirit." If we say: "By what authority
do you establish this as the meaning?" there is no one at home.
Therefore they say that no outward thing justifies or profits a per-

---

[17] From such passages as *Luther's Works,* 26, pp. 42—43, it is clear that reflection on the Flood was a frequent element in Luther's *Anfechtungen.*

[18] Cf. the treatise *Concerning Rebaptism* (*Luther's Works,* 40, pp. 229—262),
which Luther was writing at this very time in response to the Anabaptist interpretation of various New Testament passages on Baptism.

son. But Baptism with water is such a thing; and therefore wherever it is said of Baptism that it justifies, they add a gloss, as, for example, in the passage from Peter (1 Peter 3:21), which they take to mean: "You have had a seal impressed upon you by which it is declared that you have been baptized through the Holy Spirit." I can practice this art too, and better than they, but I ask them to prove it. Therefore I could say: "The blood of Christ does not profit us, because it is an outward thing. Christ was conceived [by the Holy Spirit], as we pray; therefore He does not profit us." This is their foolishness. We, too, say that an outward thing is nothing, if it is by itself; then it is utterly [without profit]. But if it is joined to the very will of God, then it does profit because of the will that has been attached to it. One cannot convince the sectarians of this, and to this argument they do not answer a word except to stick to their refrain about "an outward thing." Why do they teach this? We know. But if God binds His Word to a tree, it now becomes not only an outward thing, but through the Word there is the presence, will, and mercy of God. Thus in Baptism there is not only mere water, because there is present here the name, or all the divine power joined through the Word in Baptism, and God Himself is the One who baptizes. Take note of this. But they do not listen, but stubbornly harp on the words: "An outward thing does not [do it]." Beware of their madness, because when an outward thing is grasped through the Word of God, it is a saving thing. If the humanity of Christ were without the Word, it would be a vain thing. But now we are saved through His blood and His body, because the Word is joined to it. Thus Baptism bears the Word of God by which the water is sanctified, and we are sanctified in the water.

If you prove this, that an outward thing does not profit of itself but through conjunction with the Word and will of God, you have also destroyed both their argument and their gloss. This is the same spirit that Münzer had.[19] He thought that one should go off in a corner by oneself, not to read Scripture, not to listen to the outward Word, but to gaze into heaven and to receive the Holy Spirit from there. Then one should look at the book. Then one could [listen]. They want to receive the Holy Spirit directly, with-

---

[19] Thomas Münzer had been executed in May 1525, during the Peasants' War; cf. *Luther's Works,* 40, pp. 49—59.

out means, so that God speaks with them apart from the Word and Baptism. This is the source of those sects, the followers of Münzer nowadays, because they want to have the Holy Spirit through that solitude which they expect to come into the heart. And yet they do not expect anything outward, and therefore I warn everyone against them. Those miserable men are obliged to admit that they have never heard anything about Christ or about the sacraments except through the Word, and that they never could have thought of these things except through the Word. But we see what they have received through their spirit: they deny the humanity of Christ.[20] But we do not come to God except through Christ as the means. He it is whom God sent into the world to be our salvation, as Isaiah says (Is. 62:11). If we had been able to enter heaven without an outward thing, there would be no necessity for God to send Him. But God did place Him in the flesh and in the manger. Then, when He had abolished sin and death, God presented Him through His Word in Baptism and in the Sacrament, so that thus we might be assured of the certainty of the coming of His Spirit through this Word. Do not seek the Spirit through solitude or through prayer, but read Scripture. When a man feels that what he is reading is pleasing to him, let him give thanks; for these are the first fruits of the Spirit. It cannot be pleasing to you unless the Holy Spirit has had an effect on you. Someone who enjoys hearing is a different person; he has this from the Holy Spirit, and then it is time to pray: "Lord Jesus, Thou hast given me knowledge of Thyself and enjoyment. Increase, preserve, and strengthen it." Therefore so that we do not permit [a neglect of the doctrine] that we have been saved by mercy, it is hidden; but it comes to us through the washing. This washing is a bath that regenerates and renews. Yet we do not feel this, at least not perfectly, because of the weaknesses of the flesh. The first does not matter. Nevertheless, in faith I feel that my attitude has been changed toward the Lord Jesus and that I love the Word. If He imposes some cross upon me, I bear it with thanksgiving and praise, even though the flesh grumbles. Therefore the washing of regeneration is good because it brings about a new birth, in that one acquires a new sense, namely, that one says: "Although I formerly hated the Law, God, and Christ, now I am

[20] Apparently an attack on Caspar Schwenckfeld, whose treatise on the Eucharist Luther had received earlier in 1527; cf. *Luther's Works,* 37, pp. 288 ff.

beginning to love them. Formerly I regarded it as evil to love one God, but now I think of the commandments of God as very good, righteous, and holy, and I despise wickedness, lust, theft, and adultery." For where there is this new sense and feeling which guards such things as good and would want a perfect conscience, it resists the flesh, as Rom. 7 describes.

It also rejoices and takes pleasure in the cross, as Rom. 5:3 describes. We used to seek our own (1 Cor. 13:5) and to be afraid of such things. But now he includes one thing in the other, and a new man is created and begins to be renewed. These words are directed against the righteousness of works. If you enter a monastery, there is a novelty of dress, of habit, and of manner, so that you put on a crown, a change of food and of external works. None of this touches our essence, there is no regeneration of the spirit. Here there is not that kind of novelty. There is rather a being regenerated, changing your nature so that you are a new creature. Formerly you were inclined to lust and could not be continent for five days, but now you despise it. You were not able to forgive the offense caused by a brother; but now if you are aggrieved, you forgive it and treat it with a gentle heart. Formerly you thought of Christ as a judge and called upon Mary, but now your feeling is sweet toward Christ, who is your Mediator, Bishop, and Advocate, who speaks very good things on your behalf and offers His blood for you. This is a transformed feeling and a renewed heart, which no works can achieve. A monastic cowl cannot accomplish this. You can be puffed up so that you think that you are holier than those who are married. Nevertheless, change in relation to God and your neighbor does not take place but is obscured. In [this washing] one washes oneself, but in such a way that a man becomes a new man, not in such a way as a table is washed. This is a washing *of the Holy Spirit*. He is the one who bathes you in this washing. It is a glorious commendation that He is present in Baptism, but this is also the warmth that transforms the heart, the anointing, the heat of the fire, and the renewal which renews in such a way. These are very simple words. Our opponents call it a dog's bath,[21] and they blaspheme that outstanding renewal, where the Holy Spirit is present. According to them, those who have been regenerated by the Holy Spirit have such a symbol

---

[21] See *Luther's Works*, 30, p. 315, n. 11.

[in Baptism]. But the text is clear. It refers to everyone, that is, to renewing. You will not prove your glosses until you can prove such foolish ones as "Outward things do not profit." The Holy Spirit has His proper name because He makes people spiritual and holy, because by His activity He inspires them so that what formerly used to please them according to the world now becomes distasteful and unpleasant, so that I despise the flesh and the works of the flesh.

6. [*Which*] *He poured* [*upon us richly through Jesus Christ our Savior*]. How excellent Paul is here, and how excellently he is able to speak! He adds the word *richly.* How is that? Why did he add this word, that the Holy Spirit is not only poured out, but poured out richly, even though we do not feel this? It is faith [that does it]. The Holy Spirit grants Himself without measure; His gifts are felt, but one does not feel it when the Holy Spirit Himself is poured out richly. This is mercy, grace, eternal grace, and everything that is in the Holy Spirit; and all these things are without measure and beyond estimation, things that are incredible if we do not have the Holy Spirit. Through faith you accept these things, as Rom. 8:32 says: "If He gave His Son, then He will give everything." His gifts indeed are seen and felt in any case. But when the Holy Spirit Himself is given, He is given without measure; that is, all the things that are innumerable and inestimable are simply given, so that the righteousness of works is altogether abolished. And the works of the Law are a mere pittance, because they can scarcely even manage to restrain people from committing adultery. Here there is a richness of eternal and ineffable things, but only in faith, for only there will all of this become true. We do not attain this by any works, for he says that it has been *poured out.* Through whom? *Through Jesus,* who stands in the presence of the Father and mediates for us and speaks good things. If we hear and believe Him, He is poured out into us with these rich things. Such passages simply refute the righteousness of man. They come together in Christ and prove that we have everything through Him. 7. *So that we might be justified* [*by His grace and become heirs in hope of eternal life*]. By each word he commends Him. *Heirs.* This is richness and the fullness of all wealth, first of all, that we are justified without the merits of works, and then, that being redeemed in such a way from sin, we are finally set free from death because we are heirs.

Heirs of what? *Of eternal life.* We are this now; for those who believe in Christ are alive now, but in hope, as Rom. 8:24 says. The richness by which we are justified and saved is not visible; it must be believed. I must believe that as a child of mercy I have no sin whatever, even though I sense sin, death, and contrary feelings. In opposition to these the Word abides in your heart and does battle, and in the dark night of faith I am so gay. This richness is hidden under a contrary appearance: I am supposed to have eternal life and eternal salvation, but what appears is death and damnation. Therefore these things are not apprehended otherwise than solely by the Word and by faith. If this is preserved, then it remains in the Word and you have it through the words; you possess it, and you will be preserved. The Word says: "I am here"; the Word will consume all those sins and pretenses as the sun consumes the clouds. These topics cannot be expounded and inculcated seriously enough. Just experience them, and then you will understand them better than you would on the basis of the allegory of Origen about the trees in Paradise.[22] He who has been well trained in these things is the better able to sit in prison and in the peril of death. Such men are victors in the Word, even before death. 8. [*The saying is*] *sure.* This is most certainly true. This is a confirmation and testimony of Paul's faith, as though he were saying: "Why should one bother oneself with other sayings? This is a sure, good and firm saying. You can stand on it, you can stick to it; for it will preserve you in all anguish and tribulation." It has saved us. [*I desire you to insist*] *on these things:* This is what one ought to preach, and I want you to be concerned for these things, so concerned that you insist on them. Paul is speaking seriously: "I want you to insist on these things in such a way that you make them firm in yourself and in others." He does not say: "I want you simply to do and to say." No, he says: "Insist, as one pounds a post into the ground; that is, keep harping on it, so that you make it sure, firm, a matter of persuasion in the heart." We do indeed teach such things, but they only skim along the surface. "Be urgent in season and out of season" (2 Tim. 4:2), because it is not enough to have taught or read this just once. It is still loose; it has not yet gone deep enough to be made altogether firm. If some people grow sick of it, let them. We who

[22] Cf. *Luther's Works,* 1, p. 90, n. 16.

desire salvation enjoy listening to it and having it repeated every day, lest we do lose faith in a time of trial.

So that [those who have believed in God] may be careful to apply themselves to good deeds. Just as someone who is superior to others is preeminent and excels, so I wish that they might be most certain in the doctrine of Christ. Moreover, they excel others in works when they are, as it were, superior to others in good works, when they gladly do and endure everything. And those who excel over all others are those who are outstanding in good works. The more deeply rooted they are in faith, the greater are their good works. Therefore the works of those who grow sick of bearing [the burden] are not good. That is why he has joined these two things: that you make those who hear firm, and that they apply themselves to excelling in good works. *These are excellent;* these are good and useful. They are good and pleasant in the sight of God *and profitable to men.* No one knows this in the papacy. Instead, one is supposed to read the writers of *Sentences* who, like bees, have sucked the best things from the Bible.[23] It was the devil who spoke this way, to keep us from reading Holy Scripture.[24]

We have heard how the apostle completed his instruction of the true Christians, especially in that doctrine which pertains to heretics. It is unavoidable that Satan stir up sects in the church of God, because he is always present among the sons of God (cf. Job 1:6); therefore a Christian *should admonish once or twice.* If he sees that he succeeds, let him give thanks to God; if he does not succeed, let him *have nothing more to do with him.* Now there follow certain private commandments dealing with private matters. He commands Titus to send Zenas. There are similar things in Timothy, where he commands Timothy about parchments (2 Tim. 4:13). These completely domestic matters do not pertain to the common welfare of the church, but let us give thanks to the Holy Spirit that through the apostles He has also spoken about private and domestic matters, so that they might be written for the general reading of Scripture. These private matters are useful

---

[23] The *Sentences* of Peter Lombard were the textbook on the basis of which professors and students of theology, including Luther in 1510—1511, had studied and expounded theology.

[24] This is the end of the twelfth lecture, delivered on December 11, 1527, and the beginning of the thirteenth, delivered on December 13.

in commendation of the duties which we also exercise privately toward one another. The monks and the priests think that there are no other good works than to pray, etc. But here by this example Paul commends it even when I start a fire in the stove. These seem to be works of no value; but regardless of how private and domestic they are, they are outstanding if they are done on the basis of faith. A religious man does not speak about a parchment; therefore the Holy Spirit regards such mean and everyday works as precious. Thus all human life and all human works are done in the name of the Lord. A child may be filthy, scabby, and infected with lice; yet he is an altogether precious thing. Thus when a Christian does works that are good, moral, and theological, they are as good as bringing parchments. According to the theologians of Paris,[25] it is a neutral work to come to Nicopolis; but according to Christians, it is a positive work. Therefore these things are esteemed less than the common works of love.

12. *When I send [Artemas or Tychicus to you do your best to come to me at Nicopolis, for I have decided to spend the winter there].* He is warning him ahead of time, so that he may be ready to come when he is called. Tychicus was in Corinth. Nicopolis is in Ambracia in Illyricum, where Augustus defeated Antony.[26] 13. *[Do your best to speed] Zenas [the lawyer and Apollos on their way; see that they lack nothing].* That impoverished apostle, who did not have anything, who says in 1 Corinthians (4:11): "We still thirst," nevertheless does have something and is concerned that it be taken care of. If a brother converses with a brother or does any kind of work, this is an act of love in the sight of God which is not without value. 14. *[And let our people] learn [to apply themselves].* This is a prolepsis. Paul says to Timothy: "I am concerned, lest those whom I am to send to you be in need. And where am I to get a purse? It is empty." Christians are lukewarm in their generosity. He replies: *Our people,* that is, those of the household, the brethren, not only the common brethren of the church. To excel or to be preeminent is a word for going beyond the habitual. *[So as to help cases of] urgent need.* An urgent need for generosity is the reason for sending Artemas. Although these

---

[25] On "neutral works," cf. *Luther's Works,* 26, p. 267, n. 70.

[26] Augustus defeated Antony at the Gulf of Actium, near the city of Ambracia; the name "Nicopolis" was given to several different cities near which victories had been won.

are domestic matters, nevertheless they are urgent to me. Therefore inform people of the coming of these men, so that they may
be willing to contribute in cases of urgent need. Nevertheless,
I do not want to trouble the brethren where there is no need; but
where there is a need, the word *urgent* is added. *Urgent,* that is,
that only as much be given as is needed for use, not to be laid
by; then for *urgent need,* that is, they are not to be troubled for
superfluous use. *And not be [unfruitful].* If they have neglected
to help cases of urgent need, they are completely unfruitful. Then
the devil will arise at some time or other, so that they will give
superabundantly. When we refused to give for charity, the pope
came along so that we gave for St. Peter's church. This has lasted
ever since the time of Hus, for 115 years until now.[27] The pope
and the pontiffs used the pretext of a war against the Turks for
wicked purposes. What one refuses to give to God is devoured
by the devil; what is withheld from honor is reserved for shame.

15. *In the faith.* This is a gibe. Since the entire epistle was
written to preserve godly [28] Christians against ravenous wolves
(Matt. 7:15), he at least makes some distinction. Everyone, he
says, loves us, but deceitfully and only in words. We do not want
to be loved by those who despise Jesus, in whom and for the sake
of whom we want to be loved, regardless of how much the heretics
may flatter and pretend [29] love, as the fanatics do. I do not want their
love. In fact, of course, they do not love, but hate most ardently.
Therefore we do not care, because they tread our Lord underfoot;
He ought to be loved first of all, then we in Christ and for His
sake. We have this epistle, which is brief but is filled with very
good instruction and admonitions, so that there is almost nothing
in the church that is not treated here. Let everyone see to it that
he abides in the Christian message [30] that Christ has been given
for us, and in [works of] love that are not vain. Peter says (2 Peter
1:15, 13): "I will see to it that after my departure you may be

---

[27] The Weimar editors suggest that "115" should be read "1415" (the year
of the execution of Hus), so that the passage would be translated: "This has lasted
ever since the time of Hus, from 1415 until now." The sense, of course, is the
same either way.

[28] The text read *impiis;* but in the context it should almost certainly read
piis, and we have translated accordingly.

[29] The original has *fugant,* which some manuscripts have changed to *fugiant;*
but we have conjectured the reading *fingunt,* which seems to fit the context better.

[30] The Latin phrase is *in summa Christiana.*

able at any time to recall these things. As long as I am in this body, I will arouse you by way of reminder." And Christ, when He had instituted the Supper, said (1 Cor. 11:23): "Do this in remembrance of Me," so that He might be well established and preached [among them]. Galatians [4:19]: "with whom I am in travail." Because we have this trial, of which 1 Peter 5:8 speaks, and our flesh and reason, which of themselves are inclined to vanity, tempt us to turn away from Christ, we are more than ready to follow our own ideas. And through our reason Satan battles against us. In summary, tyrants do not accomplish this except by force, which does not harm a Christian, so that even if some deny their faith, this is still not sincere. You do not see a single epistle written against tyrants, but only against false teachers; the same thing is true of the warnings of Christ. In the case of tyrants exhortation is enough; but in the case of false teachers there is need for instruction and warning.

Satan, our reason, and his fanatics. He who wants to be a good Christian must urge that Christ be preached in all purity. After the feast [31] we shall add, at the end, an epistle of love.

[31] The "feast" is apparently Sunday, December 15; see Introduction, p. x.

LECTURES ON PHILEMON

Translated by
JAROSLAV PELIKAN

THIS epistle is indeed a purely private and domestic one. Never-theless, Paul cannot refrain from inculcating the general doctrine concerning Christ even here in treating a private matter. "In the faith" (Titus 3:15). This is how he urges and insists in order to preserve this doctrine in the church.[1] He reconciles a slave to his master in such a way that it seems that he will not accom-plish anything. But you will see the outstanding doctrines, which Cicero did not see. We shall set these forth diligently in order to see that one can say nothing so ordinary that Christ is not present.[2]

The argument of this epistle is that Paul reconciles Onesimus, the slave of Philemon, to his master. Perhaps Onesimus had stolen something from him, or at least by running away he had broken off his service to his master. Perhaps he wanted to abuse the Christian liberty which he had heard proclaimed and, falling into a carnal attitude, did not want to serve his master any longer. Or if there was some other cause, this is still the argument of the epistle. He attacks Philemon in so many passages that even if he were made of stone, he would have to melt, so that if anyone is looking for an example [he can find it in this epistle]. He goes after him both with arguments that are generally applicable and with arguments that pertain to him individually, so that he is compelled to accept Onesimus as a free man. This is a supreme art and an example for us to consider here, for we see how brethren are to be handled if they fall. Knowing that we are pleasing to Christ, we have the confidence to strengthen them, bear with them, and reconcile them, thus destroying the works of the devil (cf. 1 John 3:8) and restoring the works of Christ. Thus no one ought to despair about anyone else. In church history there is

[1] The word we have translated "doctrine" is *locus;* a more literal translation would be "topic."

[2] This is the end of the thirteenth lecture, delivered on December 13, 1527, and the beginning of the fourteenth, delivered (probably) on December 16; cf. Introduction, p. x.

the story of the bishop's son who became a thief, and John went into the desert.[3] These are eminently Christian accounts, which contain a great deal of consolation. Therefore Paul here refers to his "bowels" (v. 7) and to what he feels for this thief and unfaithful slave. On the basis of this example we should not despair either about ourselves or about our brethren. It is our duty to encourage them this way in the church.

1. *Paul a prisoner.* In the first place, by the very greeting he claims the authority to make this appeal. *A prisoner.* He introduces, as it were, an epistle of mercy, so that Philemon is forced to say: "Even if he were free, you would have to yield to him; much more now that he is a prisoner." *Of Jesus,* that is, for the sake of the name of Jesus. This is a Hebraism; we say "for the Lord Jesus." Surely he refers to Him so that he does not seem to be alone in his request. We are so constituted that we are unwilling to put up with tyranny and the prayers which it makes necessary. As we say in German, we should be armed when the princes are unreliable.[4] The prayers do indeed obtain their results by force, but against our resistance. But where [someone else] bears embarrassment, this allures and melts one so that he is ashamed to say no. Thus Paul adds embarrassment when he adds the name of *Timothy.* I would be profoundly ashamed if someone pleaded with me as Paul does here. All of this happens for the sake of an example, for we ought to act humbly. Φίλῳ: But this is a dissimulation, for it seems to me that he wants to flatter him.

Paul associates Philemon with himself in the same grace. Συνεργῷ: "You who minister to the saints, you yourself teach." He was his disciple. Indeed, this refers to all his fellow workers who cooperate in the Gospel, whether they grant hospitality or saintly support or charity or assistance. First of all, his speech provokes pardon, and then embarrassment. He not only commands Philemon but associates his own flesh with him. This is really what you call arousing goodwill. He takes advantage of acute embarrassment wherever he can as a person of low estate and

[3] We have been unable to identify the source of this report in the church histories used by Luther.

[4] The Weimar editors conjecture that *zwancke* here means "unreliable" and suggest that Luther is alluding to a German proverb; it would appear to be the one cited in *Luther's Works,* 13, p. 180, and quoted in full in *Luther's Works,* 14, p. 232.

a stranger. He says *beloved;* the very words are fire and flame.
2. *Archippus.* In Colossians (4:17) he calls him the bishop of the
city: "Say to Archippus," who was the bishop of the Colossians
and himself a citizen of Colossae. Use the proper title for each
person. He addresses Philemon as an entire company, because
he also adds the name of a bishop. The bishop is joined by his
wife, the church. Paul does not say "to my disciple," but he puts
Archippus on the same level as himself, not calling him a soldier
but *our fellow soldier:* "For you are the same as I, though no
greater, as one who is with us in the battle." He calls Philemon
a fellow worker because he is in the simple work of providing
for the saints and because he shows hospitality to the brethren,
but also because this pertains to the Gospel. He calls even a bishop,
who is a leader in the Word and who stands in the battle, *our fellow
soldier,* one who is appointed to battle against Satan, death, and
sin. The pope would never do this, especially if he were an apostle, to write to a bishop this way; he would not call him "our
fellow pope." This is a holy form of flattery. *And the church* [*in
your house*]. Here you have Archippus and the church. He was
most likely a rich townsman. But I believe that the house was
a place for prayer and preaching. He deserved to be called a fellow worker, since he supported an entire church. Undoubtedly
there were several churches, different houses in different cities,
where ten people who had someone like Archippus would gather.
Philemon, as well as Archippus, is surrounded by prayers, by
flaming words, and by fires. 3. *Grace* [*to you*]. Why should he
refer to this? Because it brings the forgiveness of sins. *And peace,*
which is the joy of consciences; but this does not come from the
world, but from *God our Father and* [*the Lord*] *Jesus* [*Christ*].
This salutation and signature would have been enough for Paul
to obtain grace for his friend Onesimus. But let us see how he
proceeds. 4. *I thank* [*my God always when I remember you in
my prayers*], 5. *because I hear* [*of your love and of the faith which
you have toward the Lord Jesus and all the saints*]. This is Paul's
general method of arranging his epistles, to begin with thanksgiving. But he adapts this rule to his purpose here, since he wants
to motivate Philemon to a good work. Look at the individual words.
I thank my [*God*] *always.* You know that these things are taught
by the feeling that comes from the Holy Spirit Himself. For Paul
had suffered from false prophets and had heard that many were

forsaking the faith and were stirring up heresies and sects, just as is happening to us. It is a rare thing to hear a preacher who is constant in the Word. But if we hear one, this is a cause for prayer and thanksgiving. The very nature of the Gospel or the Spirit produces this in us. So we are trained by hearing evil everywhere to give thanks when we hear something good. *I thank,* so that things may remain as I have heard. *Because I hear.* This seems a rare thing to me, because I hear that many act otherwise and persecute. He praises them very highly, but in Christ he attributes faith and love to them, as though he were saying: "I thank God that you have faith and love toward God and the saints."

The faith which you have toward the Lord. Hearing of this refreshes me and compels me to give thanks, because Satan is lying in wait for you as [he is for everyone]. I wish that the word *saint* could be used as generally among us as is the word "brother." If one is ashamed to use this word "saint," why not the word "brother," which means even more? For someone who calls another a Christian brother thereby uses a prouder name than the name "saint," because this name contains the word "Christian"; for if I call a brother "Christian," I am not emphasizing the flesh but the name of Christ. *Saints,* that is, of your own church and even strangers. You are a host who feeds even strangers and provides for them. 6. [*And I pray that*] *the sharing* [*of your faith may promote the knowledge*]. This is what he wants to say: "I give thanks and pray for the love and faith of which I hear, namely, that this faith and love may grow and become more effective from day to day, in that you acknowledge all the good that is in you in Christ Jesus." *The good,* that is, the universal faith which you and I have and which all those who are with you have, the same faith, the universal faith that is shared by all the saints who are in your church, the faith that is especially present in you. This *sharing* is not spiritual, as some say; [5] but it means that everyone has [what everyone else has], that he has the body which you have, which even I have. Here he speaks of faith, which is a thing distributed among many; that is, the body is something distributed in that bread which you and I have.[6] But such people are tropical,

---

[5] Cf. Jerome, *Commentaria in epistolam ad Philemonem, Patrologia, Series Latina,* XXVI, 646—647.

[6] Thus Luther's substitute for a "spiritual" interpretation of this "sharing" or "communion" is a eucharistic interpretation.

or, more precisely, topical, subverters.[7] *May promote:* that the faith I hear about in you may not grow lazy, but rather may become richer, more splendid, and more active. Why? Because I want to propose a good work to you. You have shown your love well. You must go on with your faith, so that it may *promote.* Soon he will turn to the specific good work about which he is writing in connection with Onesimus. *In [Christ],* that is, of all those good things: that you might obtain a full knowledge of all those good things which are yours in Christ Jesus. This is what I have often said, and it is a topic that deserves to be emphasized: that Christian doctrine is to be set forth often, because it is based upon knowledge, so that it is the most important thing among Christians that they grow in the knowledge of Jesus, as Peter also says (2 Peter 3:18). The fanatics suppose that once they have heard the Word, they know everything, as though they were filled with the Holy Spirit. This is the most important thing we do and hear throughout our lives, because this knowledge is being opposed by sin, a weak conscience, and death; Satan frightens and persecutes it, and the heretics undermine it. It must stand alone, doing battle against all these enemies. One has to grow up into this knowledge. *Promote:* In what sense? That your knowledge and sure conviction are confirmed by doctrine, that you may stand undefeated in every battle. This is what it means to become firm, that is, that you take good possession of the treasure of all the benefits and innumerable graces which are yours in Jesus. *That is yours:* You have the treasure of all wisdom, knowledge, life, and salvation. Now you must act in such a way that this treasure is grasped and held firmly. We are earthen vessels (2 Cor. 4:7) and carry the treasure in earthen vessels. It slips away quickly, and therefore [we must take care].[8]

Yesterday we dealt with the topic which Paul is fond of setting forth everywhere, so that he is not able to keep silence about it even in an epistle written about private matters. "Out of the abundance of the heart [the mouth speaks]" (Matt. 12:34). His heart

[7] *Tropici* would be exegetes who distorted, or "subverted," a "trope," or figure of speech (cf. *Luther the Expositor,* pp. 150—154), while *topici* would appear to be exegetes who, in the process, managed also to "subvert" the subject matter or content itself.

[8] This is the end of the fourteenth lecture, delivered (probably) on December 16, 1527, and the beginning of the fifteenth, delivered on December 17.

is filled, and therefore he always speaks and writes about Christ. We do not find such things in the theologians after the apostles; nor do we find them among the other apostles. Our concern and entire life ought to be concentrated on this, that this knowledge may become firm. For this we need the Holy Spirit, to know what has been given to us, namely, salvation, righteousness, redemption from every evil, life eternal, a status as a brother of Christ, as a fellow heir of Christ, an heir of God (Rom. 8:17). These things are expressed in short words; therefore the Holy Spirit is needed to make the knowledge grow. He always instructs about faith and redemption. 7. *For [I have derived much] joy [and comfort from your love, my brother].* Until now he has referred to many topics and used ardent words to move Philemon; now he sets forth this topic on the basis of his own example and from himself: "I am about to write to you concerning a certain work; for I am sure that you will hear me out because I am sure that you are listening as you did before, so that [your love] will be revived. On what account? Because I have recognized your love, as I said earlier (v. 4)." *[Because] the bowels [of the saints are refreshed through you].* You have done many favors for Christians who were poor, afflicted, feeble, and suffering from many evil things; you refresh them. *Bowels* is a Hebraism. We use the word "heart," [9] saying, "It touches my heart." In the German language, "the heart is open wide." When someone loves a particular thing or a girl or glory, we say that he has a heart for it, that money or glory is his heart, that he is completely devoted to it. *Bowels* means feelings: "You have refreshed the heart of the beloved saints; that is, they have become aware of your love and of your generous intentions toward them, and this has benefited them cordially." He sets forth to him the example of his own action, for which he is commended by the other saints. "I am armed with all these topics and arguments. Your faith, your love, and your possession of all the things and graces which you have in Christ have made it possible for me to presume to command you with the full assurance that you will accept my command." Such a presumption of friendship and love brings pleasure to the human heart, if a friend believes a friend and you trust me so much. On the other hand, we take pleasure in the honor that people trust us. This is good flattery; but it is holy,

[9] Elsewhere, too, Luther had proposed that the Latin *adfectus* be rendered in German as *hertz.*

because it proceeds as in Christ. Whomever I praise, I praise as a Christian; therefore I neither flatter him nor am disappointed in him, because it is impossible to praise Christ enough. If I flatter a Christian man, I do so not for his sake but for the sake of Christ, who dwells in him; and Him a Christian should honor.

8. *Accordingly, though I am bold enough.* Why? In you? No, but *in Christ.* He takes hold of Philemon in Christ as follows: "that I might enjoy," or "let them marry," but "in the Lord" (1 Cor. 7:39). Thus one person should trust another, but Christ must be between them. I should like to command you, and I am bold enough so far as this matter is concerned, because this is not a frivolous or unnecessary matter, but a useful one. Therefore I am bold enough to command you with the certainty that you will obey. But I would rather admonish you for the sake of love.

I do not want this to be a matter of obligation, but of entreaty. But I have also experienced how laws usually take away desires. A man is more easily drawn than pushed, and compulsion brings with it a rebellious will. A Christian, however, does not act that way. Nevertheless, Paul flatters him in such a sweet manner that even in addressing a Christian he avoids a domineering tone. To be sure, there is not this danger among Christians, for the matter proceeds in love and there is pure love in you, not compulsion. Therefore it is my wish that you do this out of love, not out of compulsion. I want to beseech you on the basis of love. "I can command," he says, "for I am an old man. There is a twofold ground: You are younger than I, who am an old man; and I am a prisoner for Christ. I have been commissioned with the authority of the Gospel, and you are my disciple. Nevertheless, I shall refrain from invoking the reverence that is owed to age and the authority of my apostolic office, and I shall deal with you as brother with brother." When did the pope and the other officials act this way, when do they humble themselves this way, as Paul becomes a young man with the young, an equal with equals? You see what the state of Paul's heart is. "I shall not use either [my age or my apostolate], although I would have a perfect right to do so, and you would obey." Spoken this way, it is expressed even more vigorously. This petition is a veritable oven! "I am not asking you on behalf of some heathen or stranger or scoundrel, nor even on behalf of a simple brother." There is great ardor in the word *my child.* When Philemon hears this, he should be frightened. What was he to do? And this is the kind of child who ought to stir your feelings even more, [one who had been born] when the Word was shut up in that need and captivity, as though he were saying: "He is beloved all the more because [he was born] in my imprisonment." And this is proper, for he had been an upright slave, who in his flight came to Paul and sought to be reconciled. He also remains a slave in accordance with the custom of the heathen. Nor does Paul release him from his servitude or ask Philemon to do so; indeed, he confirms the servitude. And beyond this he calls him a son, and his slave a brother: "You have a slave, I have a son. Should you not pay more attention to him because he is my son? Besides, I do not take him away from you but restore him to you." And he was the kind of son *whose father I have become.* Onesimus means "useful." [10] By citing his name he presents an argument from the word "Onesimus." He has done a work to live up to his name." Paul takes upon himself the sin of Onesimus against Philemon. He justifies him to Philemon and concedes to Philemon his full right over his slave and over his slave's crime. This again is a powerful passage concerning the confession which easily placates one who has been offended. "There is reason for the offense, we confess. You, Philemon, are our man, to whom I and we confess it." I would not stand for it to have someone test my faith this way. This was written as an example, so that we might see what the love of a Christian is. *Formerly he was useless to you,* without any use, but only abuse. This is a different word from [ἄχρηστος]; [11] it refers to stealing, to deserting his duty and the servitude which he owed you. But his running away has been fortunate; for it has proved beneficial and useful to produce a twofold usefulness, one to me and the other to you, so that from a single evil a double good has issued, and from a single injustice a double justice. What a passage this is! Paul confesses the sin in such a way as to boast that from the one single sin there has come a double justice, namely, toward God and toward Paul. This is indeed an impressive passage, and now he proceeds. 12. *I am sending him back.* This is the [point of] the epistle. He is doing this to reconcile the slave to his master. He says: "I am simply

[10] It seems clear that, in this case at least, a play on words noted by Luther was intended by the Biblical writer as well.

[11] At the suggestion of the Weimar editors, we have supplied this word where there is a lacuna in the text.

sending him back. I do not ask that you grant him his freedom,
but that he might return to the original servitude, so that he might
serve you twice as well as he did before." You see that slavery
is not being abrogated here. *You therefore [receive him]*; now
the entreaty and the reconciliation proceeds. *As my bowels.* The
Book of Kings says (1 Kings 3:26): "Her bowels yearned"; not
the intestines, but the heart has pity and is stirred. She was affected
to the bottom of her heart. A German thinks only of the bowels
of swine [when he hears this phrase]. "As my very heart." That
is certainly a precious recommendation. This carries a great force
of persuasion. If he had recommended his very heart to me,
I would have said: "Be free." I would want to open everything
in the house to Paul's heart. It was impossible for Philemon not
to accept him. 13. *I [would have been glad to keep] him [with me].*
Such emotion! How that man can speak! *But you receive him;*
that is, he is my very heart. This is a new emotion and another
topic. I have a claim upon Onesimus, because in my imprisonment I have become his father. He will be my son, and besides
you ought to minister to me in my need. Now I could make use
of him on the basis of a twofold right, keeping him as my servant
in your stead and as my own son. Thus I renounce my right as you
ought to renounce yours, and I set him forth as my example so
that you may be confounded if you do not do the same. In addition,
*[in order that he might serve me on your behalf] during my im-
prisonment of the Gospel.* Such fine words! Is the Gospel imprisoned? As though Christ and the Gospel were imprisoned.
A Christian boasts and is aware of this, that I am not imprisoned
for my own sake; for it will redound to the glory of the Gospel,
for its expansion and dissemination. These are pure Hebraisms.
Rejoice [12] when Christ binds or has commanded to be bound. I am
referring to imprisonment "for" or to the praise of the Gospel.
I need a ministry in the bonds of the Gospel, through which you
have been saved; therefore those bonds are precious in the sight
of the Lord. I have a twofold obligation, you see. So do you, who
are likewise in a most precious ministry, namely, in the cause
of the Gospel. Christ would have been satisfied with this. Therefore you should be also. Nevertheless, I yield to you. 14. *[But
I preferred to do nothing] without your consent.* But I did not

---

[12] The text reads *latare*, but it seems to make more sense to read *laetare*.

undertake anything without your agreement. Therefore I submit
myself to you and obey you. If you want to send him to me, well
and good; if not, [that is well and good also]. *In order that* [*your
goodness might not be by compulsion but of your own free will*].
In Christian matters nothing should be done by compulsion, but
there should be free will. It is a remarkable statement when 2 Cor.
9:7 uses the words "not under compulsion." [13] This was written
for the instruction of the entire church. God is not pleased with
compulsory acts of service. Children have to be trained to serve
under compulsion, but of adults a voluntary spirit is required.
He was not afraid that this would happen to Philemon, but that
this would be set up as a rule among Christians; [he was con-
cerned] that no one should do anything by compulsion. As Malachi
says (Mal. 1:10): "[O that there were one among you] who [would
shut] the doors!" Therefore the monks do not merit anything,
for they act out of compulsion. The pope has an entire church of
this sort which he compels to do things by his commandments.
Therefore his church is not of Christ, although he is seated in it
(cf. 2 Thess. 2:4); it is a synagog. He forces men by sheer commandments; and anyone who obeys him does so not voluntarily
but out of necessity or convenience, and such people do not belong to the church but to the Law and to the synagog. From this
passage you should conclude that such people do not please God,
because He "loves a cheerful giver," one who does not give "reluctantly" (2 Cor. 9:7). "He who does acts of mercy, [let him do
it with cheerfulness]," as Rom. 12:8 says, because God does not
regard those who sacrifice reluctantly and sadly.

15. *Perhaps this is* [*why he was parted from you for a while*].
Here again there is an excuse for the sin which he previously
denounced, confessed, and called a double convenience. Here
he expresses and acknowledges that it was truly a sin for Onesimus to run away, but he vigorously extenuates the sin. It is the
work of the Holy Spirit to do this. On the other hand, it is the
work of the devil to make the sin worse. He makes laughter
a mortal sin. Contrary to this, the Holy Spirit extenuates the sin,
because there is forgiveness of sins, and He takes them away
completely. Thus Paul calls it *a while*. Paul was imprisoned in
Rome. Those who are in Phrygia and in Rome are far apart, and
this is an extenuation of the sin. [*That you might have him back*]

13 The original has "2 Cor. 8."

forever. From this sin there will come unlimited and manifold fruit. From one evil hour there comes an eternal time, that is, for always. He does not want to free him from his servitude. 16. *No longer as a slave.* Consider. Previously he was an unbeliever, and he fled from his master as an unbeliever. He hears the Gospel, but he does not believe it. Now he shares in all the good things which he has in Christ. He believes and is a beloved brother. Now he will serve with the spontaneous obedience of love, and therefore you will benefit from his having run away. Formerly he looked for opportunities, any opportunities, [to run away]; but now he will serve you steadfastly. The Gospel has taught him that this ought to be done, and nothing has been omitted that would impress even a heathen, more so a Christian. If he is very dear to you on account of the Gospel of Christ, he is dear most of all to me. If he is dear most of all to me, how much more should he be very dear to you! He should be very dear to you on a double basis, according to the flesh and according to the Lord. He should be more to you [than to me], because he is in the flesh; that is, by Gentile law [as well as by the Gospel] he is subject to you according to the ordinance and the government. *Both in the flesh* [*and in the Lord*] he should be very dear to you, because he is a slave who has truly been born in the Lord, because he is your brother in the Lord and one who will serve you in a brotherly way. He does not deny that he belongs to you. You have him as a good [brother]. These are very powerful statements about how one ought to accept the heart of another.[14]

17. [*So if you consider me your partner,*] *receive him* [*as you would receive me*]. This is a final statement which urges what the words "my bowels" (v. 12) had said. He repeats the same thing now, saying *as you would receive me.* And he says this with a kind of oath. The words *if* [*you consider me your partner*] he puts between Philemon and Onesimus, as though he wanted what was owed him by Philemon the free man [to be paid back] by his accepting [Onesimus]. If I am worthy to be your partner, receive him. On the other hand, there is still the issue between them. 18. [*If he has wronged you at all, or owes you*] *anything,* [*charge that to my account*]. If his guilt is not to be remitted completely without the payment of a price, so be it. But before this is allowed

[14] This is the end of the fifteenth lecture, delivered on December 17, 1527, and the beginning of the sixteenth, delivered on December 18.

to pass, I want to deal with you in accordance with your full right and to return to you [what belongs to you]." Thus Paul tried to do everything by mercy. This was the highest law of love. In the end, it was also a law. Thus in the world we usually conclude that if one cannot dispose of a thing, the law disposes of it for us and makes an account of it. He had sinned by stealing and by neglect, and he had neglected his duty by his absence. "Let this be my guilt, and regard me as your debtor." 19. *I [Paul write this with my own hand, I will repay it—to say nothing of your owing me even your own self]*. What an exaggeration! This is how intensely Christian hearts feel. This is to be a special memorandum, and I want to put my seal upon it, so that you may have a testimony. Because we want to proceed in a completely legal manner, you ought to give me a free Onesimus to pay your debt. Nevertheless, you owe me your own self. If you demand your rights, I will do the same. You do not owe me your house, but yourself. My brother, let me enjoy you. Augustine says that a creature is not meant to be enjoyed but to be used.[15] This is the supreme argument. I want to find my consolation in you, that is, in you as a Christian, not in you as Philemon.

A Christian man cannot flatter, because he does not regard a brother as flesh and blood but as a believer in Christ. But I shall enjoy you in such a way that there is enjoyment in the Lord. I shall not cling to you, that is, my heart, that is, Onesimus himself; but in Christ he is my bowels. Therefore if you accept him, you will refresh my bowels. Now there follow words of excuse for attacking Philemon with so many arguments and topics. 21. *[Confident of your obedience, I write to you, knowing that you will do even more than I say.]* I would not have written unless I had been full of confidence about your obedience. I know that you are a Christian, and therefore [I have written] looking to your faith, only so that you might recognize that I am seriously supporting the cause of Onesimus. Again, this is an argument by which one would flatter another. Paul is confident that Philemon will do more than he asks; in this he is surely overcome.

22. *[At the same time] prepare a guest room for me, [for I am hoping through your prayers to be granted to you]*. Here again

---

[15] Augustine, *De doctrina Christiana*, Book I, chs. 22—23, pars. 20—23, *Corpus Christianorum, Series Latina*, XXXII, 16—19, on the distinction between things to be used and things to be enjoyed.

you see that although Paul is a saint and "a chosen instrument" (Acts 9:15), nevertheless he everywhere requests prayers and support for himself and asks that others stand by him in battle. Thus every one of us needs the prayer of others even more, we who are conscious of being in the same Christ, but are far inferior to him. "Not only am I sending Onesimus, but you will have me as well." Now there follow greetings. [23. *Epaphras, my fellow prisoner in Christ Jesus, sends greetings to you.*] *Epaphras* is the one who had established and given birth to the Colossians. Consult that epistle (Col. 1:7; 4:12). He was certainly a pious person, one who receives great praise from Paul. [24. *And so do Mark, Aristarchus, Demas, and Luke, my fellow workers.*] *Mark*, whom he once wanted to take along as a companion on his journey (Col. 4:10). *Demas* is still a man of sincere faith (cf. 2 Tim. 4:10), because he mentions Luke after him. This must have been shortly before [the apostasy of Demas], because Paul is already in prison. He was a great man, since he is mentioned before Luke, that is, a great man in preaching, expounding, and writing the Gospel. As long as the Roman Empire stood, there was completely free passage throughout the world. Therefore he had many such with him, to see to it that nothing evil [befell the Gospel]. They were his messengers and visitors. Timothy, Titus, Crescens, and Luke had to run in order to resist the false prophets everywhere and to see Philemon and Archippus. Thus we have a private epistle from which much should be learned how brethren are to be commended, that is, that an example might be provided to the church how we ought to take care of those who fall and restore those who err; for the kingdom of Christ is a kingdom of mercy and grace, while the kingdom of Satan is a kingdom of murder, error, darkness, and lies.

LECTURES ON HEBREWS

Translated by
WALTER A. HANSEN

CHAPTER ONE

1. *In multifarious and many ways* [*God spoke formerly to our fathers by the prophets*].

THE difference between "in multifarious ways" and "in many ways" seems to be that "in multifarious ways" looks at the distributions of the gift of prophecy among many, as we read in Num. 11:17: "I will take some of the spirit which is upon you and put it upon them," and in Acts 2:17: "I will pour out My Spirit upon all flesh." "In many ways," on the other hand, looks at the various and repeated use of the same gift by any prophet, namely, so that he has either impressed the same prophecy time and again or has presented it in ever-changing visions. The meaning, therefore, is that God formerly distributed the gift of prophecy among many and through this distribution caused Christ to be foretold in various ways, so that not only one herald of Christ is commissioned but many, and not only many but also every one of them is commissioned in many ways. For this is the way even Paul cites many prophets and the same one, such as Isaiah or David, in many ways. This difference seems to be borne out by the Greek text, which reads: πολυμερῶς καὶ πολυτρόπως, that is, when transliterated, *polumeros kai polutropos*. For *polu* means "many," and *meros* means "a part." Therefore *polumeros* is an adverb like "in many parts," which our Latin text has expressed with "in multifarious ways." *Tropos*, on the other hand, means "way" or "manner." Therefore the correct meaning of *polutropos* is "variously" or "in many ways."

Therefore the apostle presents a most powerful argument from the lesser to the greater, as one says, namely, that if the Word of the prophets has been received, the Gospel of Christ should be received all the more, since it is not a prophet who is speaking but the Lord of the prophets, not a slave but a son, not an angel but God, not to the fathers but to us, namely, in order to exclude every reason for unbelief, which they had in a very high degree because they received the Word through the angels, through Moses and the prophets, as they said in John 9:28-29: "We are disciples of Moses. We know that God has spoken to Moses, but as for this man, we do not know where he comes from." And thus the apostle brings this argument to a conclusion in the second chapter (Heb. 2:1), where he says: "Therefore we must pay closer attention [to what we have heard, lest we drift away from it]."

2. [*But in these last days He has spoken to us by His Son, whom He appointed the Heir of all things*], *through whom He made the worlds* [*also*].

He describes the same Christ as the Son of Man and the Son of God. For the words "He was appointed the Heir of all things" are properly applicable to Him because of His humanity, but the words "the worlds were made through Him" apply to Him because of His divinity. With these words, however, and with those that follow up to the end of the chapter he deals copiously with what he touched on briefly in the prolog to Romans (1:4), when he said: "Who was predestined to be the Son of God in power." For there he does not explain but only relates that He was "declared the Son of God." Here, however, he says this very thing and explains it both in his own words and on the basis of authoritative statements of Scripture, of which he introduces six in particular. Moreover, he says "the worlds also," in the plural, although there seems to be only one world. Perhaps it is his purpose to show that Christ is the Author of all worlds, that is, of all times. And so "world" can properly be taken to mean 100 years, as one says; [1] but it is better understood as having designated two ages, namely, the present and the future, about which Christ says in Matt. 12:32: "Whoever speaks against the Holy Spirit will not be forgiven, either in this age or in the age to come." And in Eph. 1:21 the apostle says: "Above every name that is named, not only in this age but also in that which is to come." But the created angels are in the future age. And so man, according to the body of this life, is in the present age. According to his soul, however, he is in the future age. For he embraces, and participates in, both.

---

[1] The Latin word *saeculum* was used both for "century" and more generally for "age"; it is frequently translated as "world."

One should also note that he mentions the humanity of Christ before he mentions His divinity, in order that in this way he may establish the well-known rule that one learns to know God in faith. For the humanity is that holy ladder of ours, mentioned in Gen. 28:12, by which we ascend to the knowledge of God. Therefore John 14:6[2] also says: "No one comes to the Father but by Me." And again: "I am the Door" (John 10:7). Therefore he who wants to ascend advantageously to the love and knowledge of God should abandon the human metaphysical rules concerning knowledge of the divinity and apply himself first to the humanity of Christ. For it is exceedingly godless temerity that, where God has humiliated Himself in order to become recognizable, man seeks for himself another way by following the counsels of his own natural capacity.

3. *He is the brightness [of His glory and the figure of His substance].*

He says the same thing in Col. 1:15: "He is the image of the invisible God," that is, of the God who is not seen. And in Wisd. of Sol. 7:26 we read: "[Wisdom] is a reflection of eternal light, a spotless mirror of God's majesty and an image of His goodness." For the brightness or brilliance of God is called the image of God's glory; for the similitude of God's glory, in which the Father recognizes Himself, shines, not for us but for God Himself. But what follows, "and the figure of His substance," is a tautology; that is, it repeats the same thing. Nor is the distinction of Persons necessarily expressed, as some think,[3] by "the brightness of His glory," and the unity of substance by "the figure of His substance." For both have both meanings. And one should note that the Greek does not have τύπος here, that is, "form," which really means "figure," or οὐσία, which means "essence" or "substance." But this is what it has: χαρακτὴρ τῆς ὑποστάσεως αὐτοῦ, that is, the "sign," "mark," or "form" "of His reality" or "of His substance," the figure of God's substance, not for us but for God Himself, so that God alone recognizes His own form in Himself. Thus he has not

2 The original has "John 6," perhaps in an allusion to John 6:44; but it is John 14:6 that is quoted.

3 Peter Lombard, *Collectanea in epistolam ad Hebraeos, Patrologia, Series Latina,* CXCII, 402—403.

spoken simply of "His brightness and His figure" — for both angels and men are images of God's brightness, signs of His majesty — but he speaks of "the brightness of His glory and the figure of His substance," in order that in this way we might understand the inmost and proper figure of God. For we are the images of God for ourselves rather than for God, because God does not know Himself through us, but we know God through ourselves.

Upholding all things by the Word of power.

This participle, "upholding," has special emphasis and is a Hebrew idiom with which neither the Greek nor the Latin expression is sufficiently in agreement. For the apostle employs a Hebraism. What we call "to preserve" the Hebrews state more suitably with "to uphold," which expresses a certain tender and, so to speak, motherly care for the things which He created and which should be cherished, as in Deut. 32:11: [4] "He spread His wings to receive him and bore him up on His shoulders." And in Isaiah 46:3-4 we read: "Hearken to Me, O house of Jacob, and all the remnant of the house of Israel, who are carried by My bowels, who are borne by My womb. Even to your old age I am He, and to gray hairs I will carry you. I have made, and I will bear; I will carry and will save." Likewise in Num. 11:12: "Did I conceive all this people, that Thou shouldst say to me: 'Carry them in your bosom, as the nurse is wont to carry the sucking child'?"

When He made purification for sins, [He sat down at the right hand of the Majesty on high].

With this brief word he makes useless absolutely all the righteousnesses and deeds of penitence of men. But he praises the exceedingly great mercy of God, namely, that "He made purification for sins," not through us but through Himself, not for the sins of others but for our sins. Therefore we should despair of our penitence, of our purification from sins; for before we repent, our sins have already been forgiven. Indeed, first His very purification, on the contrary, also produces penitence in us, just as His righteousness produces our righteousness. This is what Is. 53:6

---

[4] The original has "Deut. 22."

says: "All we like sheep have gone astray, we have turned everyone to his own way, and the Lord has laid on Him the iniquity
of us all."

5. [*For to what angel did God ever say*]: *Thou art My Son. Today
I have begotten Thee?*

One may understand the words "today I have begotten Thee"
to refer to both births of Christ. St. Augustine understands it as
referring to the divine birth.[5] Therefore he explains that "today"
means "in eternity." So does the first book of the Master of the
Sentences.[6] But it is not improper to understand it as referring
to the human birth, because, in the first place, the divine birth
is described nowhere else in Scripture as occurring in time or
with the word "today." Indeed, it is described as occurring before the times, as in Ps. 72:17: "Before the sun His name remains,"
which Burgensis explains in this way: "Before the sun His name
will be brought forth as a Son,"[7] or, as other Hebrew commentators say: "Filiation took place before the sun," or "He was
named a Son."[8] And again in Prov. 8:25: "Before all the hills
I was brought forth."

Secondly, because the Hebrew idiom expresses a definite and,
so to speak, a special time with the word "today," as their articles
usually do among the Greeks. For in the Hebrew it has this meaning: "I on this day," or "on the first day" (namely, on some special
and single day), "I have begotten Thee." This certainly was the
day of Christ's nativity. Thirdly, it agrees with Is. 8:2-3: "And
I got reliable witnesses, Uriah the priest, and Zechariah the son
of Jeberechiah, to attest for me. And I went to the prophetess,
and she conceived and bore a son." Nicholas of Lyra proves with
sufficient learning that these words are spoken not with reference
to the person Isaiah but to the Person of God Himself, in par-

[5] Augustine, *Enarrationes in Psalmos*, II, 6, *Corpus Christianorum, Series
Latina*, XXXVIII, 5.

[6] Peter Lombard, *Sententiae*, Book I, Dist. 2, ch. 6, *Patrologia, Series Latina*,
CXCII, 528.

[7] Nicolaus de Lyra, *Postilla super Psalterium*, with the *Additiones* of Paulus
Burgensis (Mantua, 1477), *Additio* III on Ps. 71:17; hereafter referred to as *Postilla super Psalterium*.

[8] Cf. Paul of Burgos, *Scrutinium Scripturarum* (Mantua, 1475), Dist. 9, ch.
10, dealing with rabbinic exegesis of the words: "His name shall be forever."

ticular from the fact that Zechariah and Uriah (but Isaiah calls them "witnesses") lived long after Isaiah.[9] Therefore the Lord "went to the prophetess," that is, to the Virgin Mary; for she submitted to no other man than God. And thus "she conceived and bore the Son" of God, not from the flesh (which God does not have) but from the Holy Spirit, through whom "He came to her." Concerning Him He now says: "Today I have begotten Thee," which means: "Even as man Thou art My Son, but a Son born of the Virgin."

> [*Or again*]: *I will be to Him a Father* [*and He shall be to Me a Son*]?

We do not deny that word for word this text (2 Sam. 7:14) can be understood as referring both to Solomon and to Christ. Nevertheless, as one can gather from the text itself, then from the prophets, who repeat the same text so often and proclaim it with the greatest diligence, especially in the Psalms, it can be abundantly shown that it has been stated as well as understood concerning Christ alone. For He says to David (2 Sam. 7:11-12): "Moreover, the Lord declares to you that the Lord will make you a house. And when your days are fulfilled and you lie down with your fathers, I will raise up your son after you, who shall come forth from your body, and I will establish his kingdom." This is proclaimed in Ps. 132:11: "One of the sons of your body I will set on your throne." It is clear, however, that before the days of David were fulfilled, his son Solomon was raised up and went forth from his body, yes, was established in the kingdom. Therefore Christ is understood here — Christ, who is "the fruit of the womb" of David, that is, of the Virgin Mary, who was born from the seed of David. For this reason her womb is also called the womb of David. This is not extraordinary in Scripture, since in Job 40:16 both "the belly" and "the loins" of man are called the devil's: "his strength in his loins and his power in the navel of his belly." Therefore it is proper for us, along with David and the other prophets, to understand this promise as referring to Christ. Hence Is. 55:3 says: "I will give to you the faithful mercies of David," or, as Luke has translated it in Acts 13:34: [10] "I will give to you the holy and

---

[9] Nicolaus de Lyra, *Postillae, Biblia Latina* (Basel, 1498), *ad* Is. 8; hereafter referred to as *Postillae*.

[10] The original has "Acts 15."

sure blessings of David," that is, sanctifying grace, the eternal grace promised to David out of mercy. Likewise in Ps. 89:1: "I will sing of the mercies of the Lord forever," or better, "the eternal mercies of the Lord."

6. [*And again, when He brings the Firstborn into the world, He says*]: *And let all God's angels worship Him.*

Although we read that the angels were worshiped by Moses, by Lot and Abraham, and by Joshua and other prophets,[11] yes, that even kings were worshiped, as David was by Nathan and Bathsheba, according to 1 Kings 1:16, 23, yet nowhere do we read that angels worshiped any angel or man. Therefore there is firm proof that the man Christ is true God, because it is recorded that He is worshiped by the angels, not only by some but by every one of them. But although the authority of the apostle would be sufficient here, yet almost every word of the psalm that is quoted confirms the same thing, namely, that this psalm refers to Christ, the incarnate God, for the sake of the kingdom of the present church. For when the psalmist says (97:1): "The Lord reigns, let the earth and the islands rejoice, etc.," he undoubtedly means the people on earth and on the islands; for in the kingdom of God it is rather the heavens that should rejoice and the angels who should be glad. Therefore because the kingdom of heaven does not have "clouds and darkness round about" (Ps. 97:2) but has the most brilliant splendor, we shall surely see Him as He is (1 John 3:2). The kingdom of Christ, on the other hand, is in the cloud and enigma of faith, as we read in Ezek. 32:7: [12] "I will cover the sun with a cloud"; that is, "I will take captive the wisdom of men by faith." Besides, in the kingdom of Christ His throne "is set straight by justice and judgment" (cf. Ps. 97:2). In heaven, however, there will be no place for setting straight or for judgment or any cross, but it is a place of peace and perfect well-being. Nor "shall fire go before Him to burn up His adversaries round about" (Ps. 97:3), since only friends are there. Nor "will the heavens proclaim His righteousness" (Ps. 97:6) then, for tongues will cease (1 Cor. 13:8). Nor will there be need of the exhortation

11 Cf. Ex. 3:2-5; Gen. 19:1; Gen. 18:21, Joshua 5:14.
12 The original has "Is. 61."

"You who love the Lord, hate evil" (cf. Ps. 97:10), for there everything is good.

7. [*Of the angels He says*]: *Who makes His angels spirits* [*and His servants flames of fire*].

The Master of the Sentences and many others [13] construe and
understand this verse by hypallage,[14] namely, that God made the
spirits angels and not the angels spirits, since they think that this
verse describes, not what the angels are, but what they do. Yet
one has good reason to disagree with them. In the first place, the
apostle certainly understands and uses this word "makes" with
reference to the creation of angels, as if he were saying: "He
makes," that is, creates, angels so that they have a spiritual existence. In the second place, their reasoning, namely, that the word
"angel" does not state what the nature of the angels is but describes their office,[15] lacks sufficient validity. On the contrary,
it does refer to their nature, though the name has been given because of the office and because of its proper meaning, just as one
reads many things in Scripture that are called by the names of
future happenings, like the tree of the knowledge of good and
evil, likewise the tree of life, etc. The third reason for disagree-
ment is that it will be difficult to invert the other part of the verse
in the same manner, namely, to be "who makes flames of fire
His servants." After all, the Holy Spirit, if He wanted to do so,
could have said plainly: "Who makes spirits His angels and flames
of fire His servants." Therefore it is not rash on our part to understand this verse to mean that God makes those who are and are
called angels to be spirits, and those who serve Him to be a flame
of fire. With these words he praises their substance metaphor-
ically, namely, that they are neither flesh nor body but "spirit"
or wind, that is, of a most refined and exceedingly swift nature.
Therefore Ps. 104:3 [16] says of them: "Who walkest on the wings
of the winds," that is, of the spirits or angels. Moreover, they are

[13] Peter Lombard, *Collectanea in epistolam ad Hebraeos, Patrologia, Series
Latina,* CXCII, 409—410.

[14] Cf. Quintilian, *Institutiones Oratoriae,* Book VIII, ch. 6, par. 23.

[15] Cf. Peter Lombard, *Collectanea in epistolam ad Hebraeos, Patrologia,
Series Latina,* CXCII, 410, apparently quoting Isidore of Seville.

[16] The original has "Ps. 53."

of the clearest and brightest nature, like the resplendence or the red glow of fire, as was evident in the case of the angel who was sitting at the tomb of Christ—the angel whose "appearance was like lightning" (Matt. 28:3). For what is called "a flame of fire" here is, according to St. Jerome, called "a burning fire" in the Hebrew. Johannes Reuchlin speaks of it as "a glittering and sparkling fire," [17] just as a polished sword or a concave mirror glitters and sparkles against the sun. This certainly points out that the angels are fiery and mobile, like twinkling stars; for they rejoice and exult in praise and honor of God, as is stated in Job 38:7: "When the morning stars praised Me, and all the sons of God shouted for joy."

8. [*But of the Son He says*]: *Thy throne, O God, is forever and ever.*

It is well known that "throne" in Greek is the same as "seat" in Latin. This throne, however, is heaven itself, that is, a spiritual people whose "commonwealth is in heaven" (Phil. 3:20). As in Is. 66:1: "Heaven is My throne." And in Ps. 19:4: "In them He has set a tent for the sun," as it is in the Hebrew. And Ps. 114:1-2: "When Israel went forth from Egypt, the house of Jacob from a barbarous people, Judah became His sanctuary, Israel His dominion." This means that Judah became a priesthood and Israel a dominion or kingdom, in order that He Himself might be King and Priest, and His people a priestly kingdom or a royal priesthood, as we read in 1 Peter 2:9: "But you are a chosen race, a royal priesthood, a holy nation." And Moses says in Ex. 19:5-6: "All the earth is Mine, and you shall be to Me a priestly kingdom, a holy nation." But everything that is said in this verse is so inconsistent with all understanding that those who want to grasp the truth of these things have need of an exceedingly robust faith. For if considered according to the outward appearance, nothing is more unlike a throne and the throne of God than the people of Christ, since it does not seem to be a kingdom but a place of exile, or to be living but to be constantly dying, or to be in glory but to be in disgrace, or to dwell in wealth but to dwell in extreme poverty, as everyone who wants to share in this kingdom is compelled to experience in himself. The ornaments of Chris-

[17] See Johannes Reuchlin, *De rudimentis hebraicis* (Pforzheim, 1506), p. 263.

tians are poverty, tribulations, afflictions. This is the way God's throne, which is man, should be adorned.

A staff of justice, or of guidance [is the staff of Thy kingdom].

According to the Hebrew idiom, this "staff" means a royal scepter, as in Gen. 47:31 [18] and Heb. 11:21: "He bowed in worship over the head of his staff," which Jerome has translated with "he turned toward the head of his bed." In Greek it is called a scepter; in Latin it is called a staff. Thus in Esther 5:2: "He held out the golden staff which he held in his hand, and Esther approached and kissed the top of the staff." This is the "rod of iron" with which Christ rules us and "dashes in pieces like a potter's vessel" the carnal and old man (Ps. 2:9). Concerning this staff Ps. 110:2 also states: "The Lord will send forth from Zion Thy mighty staff. Rule in the midst, etc." Is. 2:3 and Micah 4:2 interpret this in the following way: "Out of Zion shall go forth the Law, and the Word of the Lord from Jerusalem." And in Rom. 1:16 the apostle says: "For I am not ashamed of the Gospel, for it is the power of God for salvation to everyone who has faith." Therefore although others interpret this staff to mean inflexible power,[19] as it seems to be, actually, however, it is nothing else than the same Gospel, namely, the Gospel itself or the Word of God. For Christ rules the church with no other power than the Word, as it is written (Ps. 33:6): "By the Word of the Lord the heavens were made." But it is called "a staff of justice," that is, of rectitude, or, what is the same thing according to the Hebrew idiom, "of just guidance," which in Latin would be called *virga equa, recta, directa,* etc., as when Ps. 21:3 says, "with blessings of goodness." In Latin we would say *in benedicionibus dulcibus.* Therefore it is called "the staff of Thy kingdom" to distinguish it from all other kingdoms, even from the kingdom of the synagog, though this kingdom had the Law of God. Their staffs are crooked and unjust. But only Thy staff is "a staff of rectitude." For absolutely no doctrine, be it civil, ecclesiastical, or philosophical and in any way human, can direct man and make him upright, since it leads only so far that it establishes good behavior, while man remains as he has been of old. And so of necessity it makes nothing but

---

[18] The original has "Gen. 49."

[19] A reference to the *Glossa interlinearis* on Heb. 1:8.

pretenders and hypocrites; for those dregs of the heart and that bilge water of the old man, namely, love of himself, remain. Therefore it deserves to be called an evil doctrine, since it is not able to offer rectitude. But the Gospel says: "Unless one is born again of water and the Spirit, he cannot enter the kingdom of heaven" (John 3:5). And thus the Gospel preserves nothing of the old man but destroys him completely and makes him new, until hatred of himself utterly roots out love of himself through faith in Christ. Therefore all boasting of erudition, wisdom, and knowledge is useless; for no one is made better by these, no matter what good and laudable gifts of God they are. Indeed, besides the fact that they do not make a man good, they become a covering for wickedness and a veil over the disease of nature, so that those who are pleased with themselves because of them and seem to themselves to be good and sound are incurable.

9. *Thou hast loved [righteousness and hated lawlessness].*

This text aptly follows the expression "a staff of guidance," for the staff itself brings about this love of righteousness and this hatred of lawlessness. Therefore this verse fits no one but Christ, because no one but Christ alone loves righteousness; all others love money, pleasure, or honor, or, if they despise these, at least love glory. Or if they are the best of all, they love themselves more than they love righteousness. Therefore Micah 7:2, 4 says: "The godly man has perished from the earth, and there is none upright among men. . . . The best of them is like a brier, and the upright of them a thorn hedge." And the reason follows in the same place: "The evil of their hands they call good" (cf. Micah 7:3). Therefore since love of himself remains, it is utterly impossible for man to love, speak, or do righteousness, even though he can feign all this. The result is that the virtues of all the philosophers, yes, of all men, be they jurists or theologians, are virtues in outward appearance but vices in reality.

Yet one must know that this righteousness means the righteousness of God, not the righteousness of man. For the righteousness of man always remains incomplete, since it renders to everyone what is his,[20] namely, in money, possessions, honors, etc.,

---

[20] One definition of *justitia* in the first section of Book I of the *Institutes* of Justinian; cf. *Luther's Works,* 36, p. 357, n. 17.

but does not give to others their own things and at least covets the things of others for itself. Then, what is worst, it never renders glory to God. The righteousness of God, however, renders and gives itself and everything it has to God and to men. Therefore it is the nature of Christ alone to love righteousness and to hate lawlessness, but it is the nature of man to love lawlessness and to hate righteousness. It is the nature of a Christian man, however, to begin to hate lawlessness and to love righteousness. And he does not love it except through Christ, that is, because Christ, who loves righteousness, completes our incipient love with His love. Therefore Job 15:16 speaks of "one who is abominable and unprofitable, a man who drinks iniquity like water." Likewise Ps. 116:11: "Every man is a liar." But concerning the Christian man James 1:18 says: "That we should be a kind of first fruits of His creatures."

12. [*Like a mantle Thou wilt roll them up*] *and they will be changed.*

He says properly that "they will be changed," not that "they will perish," but that "they will be changed," like clothing. For this is why they are called changes of raiment, just as in 2 Kings 5:22-23 Naaman gave two changes of raiment to the servant of Elisha. Likewise in Zech. 3:4: "Behold, I have clothed you with a change of garments." Therefore Christ did not say in Matt. 24:35 that "heaven and earth will perish," but that they "will pass away"; that is, they will pass over or be changed from their old and present form to a new and better form and in a measure will themselves also have their own passover.

13. [*But to what angel has He ever said: Sit*] *at My right hand* [*till I make Thy enemies a stool for Thy feet*]?

Many interpret the phrase "at the right hand of God" to mean "preferable blessings." [21] Although we do not disapprove of this, yet it seems that with these words dominion that is universal and completely on a par with God's dominion is expressed, as the apostle says in 1 Cor. 15:27, which is taken from Ps. 8:6: "He has put all things in subjection under His feet." Certainly "He is excepted who put all things under Him." Therefore the meaning

[21] Lyra, *Postilla super Psalterium, ad* Ps. 110:1.

seems to be this: "Sit at My right hand," that is, "Reign over as many as I myself reign over and as widely as I myself reign, except that Thou shouldst be subject to Me alone." Then a beautiful admonition to mildness is commended when He says: *Till I make,* not "till Thou makest," in order that we may learn to leave vengeance to God; for even Christ, Lord of all, left it to God, as Deut. 32:35 states: "Vengeance is Mine." Therefore it belongs to no one else.

14. [*Are they not all ministering spirits*] *sent forth to serve, for the sake of those who are to obtain the inheritance?*

It is a much-discussed question whether all the angels are sent.[22] St. Dionysius says that the higher hosts are never sent.[23] Here, however, the text states clearly that "all are sent forth to serve." Daniel, who distinguishes between the angels who stand by and the angels who serve, certainly gives support to Dionysius when he says in ch. 7:10: [24] "A thousand thousands served Him, and ten thousand times a hundred thousand stood before him." Therefore a very small part of the angels is in service. On the other hand, Luke 2:13 [25] seems to agree with this apostle. There we read: "And there was with the angel a multitude of the heavenly host." There it seems that all the angels were present with the angel who made the announcement, as he also said above (v. 6): "Let all His angels worship Him." Therefore the answer is that Dionysius is speaking about the visible sending, for not all are sent in this way; but the apostle is speaking about the invisible sending, and all are sent in this way. Bonaventure speaks more extensively about this in Book II, Question 2, Distinction 10.[26]

[22] Peter Lombard, *Sententiae,* Book II, Dist. 10, *Patrologia, Series Latina,* CXCII, 672.

[23] Dionysius the Areopagite, *De coelesti hierarchia,* Book XIII, chs. 1 ff., *Patrologia, Series Graeca,* III, 300 ff.

[24] The original has "Dan. 9."

[25] The original has "Luke 1."

[26] Bonaventure, *In quatuor libros Sententiarum expositio,* Book II, Dist. 10, art. 1, q. 2, *Opera omnia,* ed. A. C. Peltier (Paris, 1864), II, 489.

2. *For if the message declared by angels was valid, [and every transgression and disobedience received a just retribution].*

SCRIPTURE has an idiom of its own when it says that the Law or the message is "valid" or "invalid." For to be "valid" means to be fulfilled; but to be "invalid" means not to be fulfilled, as Rom. 8:3 says: "For what the Law could not do, in that it was weakened because of the flesh," that is, was not fulfilled but was rather neglected. In the same way the Law is said to be established and ratified, and, on the other hand, to be destroyed and to become invalid, as below in ch. 10:28, where "a man making void the Law of Moses" is mentioned. And in Rom. 3:31 [1] we read: "Do we, then, overthrow the Law? By no means! On the contrary, we uphold the Law." But the question is asked how it is true that the message declared by angels was valid in spite of the fact that Paul teaches everywhere that the Law is invalid rather than valid, as has already been stated, and that through it sin abounded, as he contends at great length in the Epistle to the Romans (5:20). The answer is that to explain what he meant by this validity he went on to say: "And every transgression and disobedience [received a just retribution]." This indicates clearly that he is speaking of the external punishments which the Law imposed, as below in ch. 10:28, where "a man making invalid, etc.," is mentioned. But if he is speaking of external punishment, it is clear that he is also speaking of external transgression, likewise of external fulfillment or validity. Therefore just as they were punished externally for an external transgression, so they were rewarded externally for an external observance. The result was that they fulfilled the Law only out of fear of punishment or out of love of reward. But to fulfill the Law in this way is to practice pure hypocrisy. What is more, it weakens the Law, for the will of the heart has

---

[1] The original has "Rom. 4."

regard for something far different from the Law, namely, for punishment or reward. Therefore in 1 Kings (18:21) Elijah accuses
the people of limping in two directions and doing one thing in
their hearts and feigning something else in their work. This is
true of every man who is outside Christ. Therefore "every man
is a liar" (Ps. 116:11), and "every man living is altogether vanity"
(cf. Ps. 39:5). Man is consumed only by the pride of his mind.[2]

3. [*How shall we escape*] *if we neglect such a great salvation?*

The Law and the Gospel also differ for this reason, that in the
Law there are very many works – they are all external – but in the
Gospel there is only one work – it is internal – which is faith. Therefore the works of the Law bring about external righteousness; the
works of faith bring about righteousness that is hidden in God.
Consequently, when the Jews asked in John 6:28: "What must
we do, to be doing the works of God?" Christ draws them away
from a large number of works and reduces the works to one. He
says: "This is the work of God, that you believe in Him whom
He has sent" (John 6:29). Therefore the whole substance of the
new law and its righteousness is that one and only faith in Christ.
Yet it is not so one-and-only and so sterile as human opinions
are; for Christ lives, and not only lives but works, and not only
works but also reigns.[3] Therefore it is impossible for faith in Him
to be idle; for it is alive, and it itself works and triumphs, and
in this way works flow forth spontaneously from faith. For in this
way our patience flows from the patience of Christ, and our humility from His, and the other good works in like manner, provided that we believe firmly that He has done all these things for
us, and not only for us but also before our eyes, that is, as St. Augustine is wont to say, not only as a sacrament but also as an example.[4]
Therefore St. Peter says in 1 Peter 2:21 [5] that Christ suffered for
us (this insofar as it is a sacrament), "leaving you an example."
The sacrament of Christ's Passion is His death and the remission

[2] Cf. Cicero, *Epistolae ad familiares,* Book XIII, ep. 15, par. 2.

[3] The connection of "lives" and "reigns" is an echo of the "mediation" or
"oblation" in the collects of the Mass: "through Jesus Christ our Lord, who lives
and reigns."

[4] Apparently a reference to Augustine, *De Trinitate,* Book IV, ch. 3, par. 6,
Patrologia, Series Latina, XLII, 891—892; see also p. 225, n. 4.

[5] The original has "1 Peter 4."

of sins. The example, on the other hand, is the imitation of His punishments. Therefore he who wants to imitate Christ insofar as He is an example must first believe with a firm faith that Christ suffered and died for him insofar as this was a sacrament. Consequently, those who contrive to blot out sins first by means of works and labors of penance err greatly, since they begin with the example, when they should begin with the sacrament. Therefore the Gospel is neglected through unbelief of the heart, but the Law is neglected through the disobedience of the works.

4. [*It was declared at first by the Lord, and it was attested to us by those who heard Him, while*] *God also bore witness by signs* [*and wonders and various miracles and by gifts of the Holy Spirit distributed according to His own will*].

It is difficult to establish how these words differ, especially since Scripture uses them all without making distinctions. For the things God did in Egypt in times past it sometimes calls "signs," sometimes "marvels," likewise "miracles," "portents," "terrible deeds," "mighty deeds," etc. Therefore Ps. 78:43 says: "As He wrought His signs in Egypt and His miracles." And in the same psalm (v. 12) we read: "In the sight of their fathers He wrought marvels." And Deut. 29:3 mentions "the great trials and portents which your eyes saw." And Ps. 145:6 says: "And men shall proclaim the might of Thy terrible acts." Therefore on the basis of all these passages it seems likely that just as the Word of God, though it is the same, nevertheless has very many names, such as "Law," "declaration," "message," "precept," "command," "testimony," etc., as is clear in Ps. 119, so the work of God, even though it is the same, also has many names, and rightly so. Hence it is called "strength," because it happens with might and power, a "sign," because it shows divine power, wisdom, etc., a "portent," from its effect, also "terrible deeds," "marvelous works," etc. But Paul opposes this in 1 Cor. 12:29-30, where he distinguishes between "gifts," "ministries," and "workings," and also between "the gift of healing" and "the working of miracles." He says: "Are all apostles? Are all prophets? Are all teachers? Do all work miracles? Do all possess the gift of healing?" Therefore it is necessary to understand "various miracles" in this place — if we follow Paul — as meaning the workings of mighty deeds, that is, of miracles that do not pertain to healings or the restoring of health. Here the miracles are the moving of mountains, trees, water, air, fire, rain, and the like. But the "signs" must be understood as meaning healings and the restoring of health, as in Mark 16:17-18: "These signs will accompany those who believe: in My name they will cast out demons . . . they will lay their hands on the sick." And so "portents" refer either to the same "signs" and "miracles" or to those that cause great astonishment and admiration, like resurrections of the dead and terrors caused by celestial bodies.

According to His own will.

It seems that Christ teaches the opposite, namely, that we receive according to our will; for He says (Matt. 7:7-8): "Ask, and it will be given you; seek, and you will find; knock, and it will be opened to you. For everyone who, etc." But this is easily explained; for this very wishing and asking, seeking or knocking, is the gift of prevenient grace, not of our eliciting will.[6] Therefore He also "distributes" our petitions "according to His own will." Or one may say that He distributes our wishes according to His own wishes, as John 3:27 states: "No one can receive anything except what is given him from heaven."

7. *Thou didst make him a little lower [than the angels, Thou hast crowned him with glory and honor].*

Many have worked hard to expound this verse. A great number of teachers, especially Jerome and, at different times, Augustine, Ambrose, and Chrysostom, seem to understand it as referring to mankind alone.[7] But we state briefly that though it is possible to understand this verse in an improper sense as referring to man, just as if someone were to understand the statement in Ps. 72:8

---

[6] Cf. Peter Lombard, *Sententiae,* Book II, Dist. 26, ch. 4, *Patrologia, Series Latina,* CXCII, 711.

[7] Jerome, *Breviarium in Psalmos,* VIII, 6, *Patrologia, Series Latina,* XXVI, 888; Augustine, *Enarrationes in Psalmos,* VIII, 10, *Corpus Christianorum, Series Latina,* XXXVIII, 53—54; Ambrose, as quoted in Peter Lombard, *Collectanea in epistolam ad Hebraeos, Patrologia, Series Latina,* CXCII, 416—417; Chrysostom, *Homiliae in epistolam ad Hebraeos,* IV, 2, *Patrologia, Series Graeca,* LXIII, 38 (Greek) and 263 (Latin translation of Mutianus). Hereafter we shall cite Chrysostom simply as *Homiliae,* adding the number of the homily and of the paragraph, then the column numbers of the Greek text and (in parentheses) of the Mutianus translation, which presumably was what Luther used.

that "He will rule from sea to sea" in an improper sense as referring to the emperor, whereas it refers to Christ alone, or the statement in Ps. 128:3 that "your children will be like olive shoots" were to be taken as referring to some father of a household, whereas it refers to the children of the church, yet in the proper sense this verse can be understood only as referring to Christ.[8] Otherwise it is necessary to force the words that precede and those that follow into that meaning by means of extraordinary twistings and turnings. Therefore those who think that this verse refers to the dignity of human nature, which is very close to that of the angels, follow an improper understanding, which is the death of true understanding. Others understand this verse as referring to Christ, namely, that He is lower than the angels, not according to His soul but according to His body, which is capable of suffering.[9] But even this interpretation is inadequate, since He was not only made lower than the angels. Indeed, He Himself says in Ps. 22:6: "I am a worm, and no man." Thirdly, Faber says that the Hebrew text reads: "Thou didst make him a little lower than אֱלֹהִים," which means God, and not "than מַלְאָכִים," which means angels.[10] But Erasmus, on the other hand, opposes this,[11] in the first place, because Christ was made lower not only than God but also "the lowest[12] of men," as was said above. Therefore he should not have said that He was made "a little lower" but rather that He was made much lower by far than God. In the second place, the Hebrew word אֱלֹהִים means not only God but also angels, yes, judges and any who hold a position of power. Thus Ex. 21:6 says concerning a servant for life: "His master shall bring him to the gods," namely, to אֱלֹהִים in the Hebrew, that is, to the judges and priests. Add this, that although Faber is motivated by the greatest piety, he does not establish what he intended, namely, that the

---

[8] The Latin terms are *abusive* and *proprie.*

[9] Thomas Aquinas, *Super epistolam S. Pauli apostoli ad Hebraeos expositio,* Chapter 2, Lection 2, *In omnes S. Pauli apostoli epistolas commentaria* (2 vols.; Turin, 1929), II, 314.

[10] Faber Stapulensis (Le Fèvre d'Étaples), *Epistolae beatissimi Pauli* (Paris, 1512), f. 232 B.

[11] Desiderius Erasmus, *In Novum Testamentum Annotationes* (3d ed.; Basel, 1522), pp. 562—569, in a lengthy polemic against Faber.

[12] The Weimar text reads *novissimus virorum,* and we have translated accordingly; but the contrast with *Deo,* "than God," suggests the reading *novissimis virorum,* "than the lowest of men."

apostle wrote this epistle in Hebrew and that for this reason the Greek translator did not render the word אֱלֹהִים faithfully.[13] In the first place, the apostle very rarely quotes the Bible according to the Hebrew, as is clear in Rom. 3:10 ff. and in many other places. In the second place,[14] it is more likely that this epistle was written in Greek, not in Hebrew, since the apostle is writing to those converts to Christ who were scattered among the Gentiles and used the Septuagint translation. Thirdly and finally, Erasmus thinks that "a little lower" does not refer to the measure of the diminished dignity but refers to the brief time during which Christ was made lower, as the *Glossa ordinaria* and Chrysostom say.[15] But the difficulty still remains, namely, that in that short time Christ was nevertheless made a great deal lower "than the angels." Speaking without rashness, therefore, it seems that this verse says nothing about the dignity of our nature but is an explanation of the preceding verse, namely, of that wonderful memory and visitation of God, who is most mindful when He forgets and who visits most when He abandons. For He exalted Christ above all things when He cast Him down below all things. For His very Passion was a "passover," that is, a passing over to the highest glory. The reason for this lack of knowledge is the translation of this verb "Thou didst make lower." For the Hebrew word חָסֵר in this place means "to fail," "to be wanting," etc. Therefore the meaning is this: Thou madest Him to be forsaken and deserted by God or the angels, and not for a long time but for a little while, yes, less than a little while, that is, for a very short time, namely, for three days, because Thou didst deliver Him over into the hands of sinners. Therefore it makes no difference whether in this place אֱלֹהִים refers to God, angels, judges, or any persons in high positions, though it would be more proper to take it as referring to "God." For God caused Him to be forsaken not only by His divinity but also by the protection of angels and all the power there is in the world. One concludes, therefore, that the verse "Thou didst make Him for a little while lower than the angels, Thou hast crowned Him with glory and honor" has the same meaning as

[13] Faber, *Epistolae,* f. 230 B.

[14] We have followed the conjectural emendation suggested by the Weimar editor and have read "In the second place" here and "Thirdly" in the next sentence. Apparently something is missing from the manuscript.

[15] *Glossa ordinaria, ad* Heb. 2:7; Chrysostom, *Homiliae,* IV, 2, col. 39 (264).

Is. 54:7-8: "For a brief moment I forsook you, but with great compassion I will gather you. And in a moment of indignation I hid My face a little while from you, but with everlasting mercy I have had compassion on you." Furthermore, the verse "What is man, etc.?" because of the interrogative "what," seems rather to sound as though man were unworthy beyond measure of God's visitation. But in Hebrew it reads: מָה־אֱנוֹשׁ כִּי־תִזְכְּרֶנּוּ, which can be translated literally with "What is man, that Thou art mindful of him?" But it is better to translate it as an expression of wonder, namely, "What a man, that Thou art mindful of him!" For Burgensis says in his comment on Is. 38:22 [16] that the Hebrew word מָה is taken sometimes interrogatively and sometimes as an expression of wonder, as in Ps. 84:1: "How lovely is Thy dwelling place!" Therefore he finds fault in the same place with our rendering, which reads: "Hezekiah also said: 'What will be the sign that I shall go up to the house of the Lord?'" although it should have been translated with "What a sign!" that is, "What a wonderful sign this is, that I shall go up to the house of the Lord!" Thus it seems that here, too, one should say: "What a man He is!" instead of "What is man?" The meaning is this: "What a wonderful man, that Thou art mindful of Him whom Thou seemest to have completely forgotten!" Therefore the meaning is similar to what is stated in Ps. 118:22-23: "The stone which Thou hast rejected has become the chief cornerstone. This is the Lord's doing; it is marvelous in our eyes."

In Hebrew there are three names for human nature: אִישׁ, אֱנוֹשׁ, and אָדָם. Therefore our text says: "What is אֱנוֹשׁ that Thou art mindful of him, and the son of אָדָם, etc.?" Eusebius says in his Praeparatio evangelica, Book XI, Chapter 4, that man is called אֱנוֹשׁ because of the verb meaning "to forget." [17] But in my judgment it is better to say that it comes from the word "affliction." For according to Johannes Reuchlin, אָנַשׁ points out that he "felt sorrow," "bore with grief," etc.[18] Accordingly, man is called אֱנוֹשׁ so far as his soul is concerned. His life, as Solomon says, is nothing but affliction of the spirit (cf. Eccles. 1:13). He is called אָדָם so far as his body, which was made from the earth, is concerned. For

---

[16] Paul of Burgos, Additio III on Is. 38:22.

[17] Eusebius, Praeparatio evangelica, Book XI, ch. 6 (ch. 4 in the Latin translation of Georgius Trapezuntius), Patrologia, Series Graeca, XXI, 856—857.

[18] Reuchlin, Lexicon hebraicum.

אֲדָמָה means "earth," especially somewhat reddish earth. For אָדֹם means "reddish" or "ruddy." From it come "Edom" and "Edom-ites." And perhaps from it comes the popular saying that "Adam was created in a Damascene field" [19] — certainly not from the field near Damascus, the city of Syria, but from the adjective "Dam-ascene," that is, red, from אָדָם, or from דָּם, which means "blood." Josephus also writes that Adam was made from red earth; for, as he says, this is the color of virgin earth in its unspoiled and true nature.[20] Hence the male body also has a greater tendency to be red than the female body has, just as the female body has a greater tendency to be white, as if both bodies represented their sub-stance even by their color; for the female body was taken from bones, but the male body was taken from red earth. But man is called אִישׁ relatively either with reference to sex — as in Gen. 2:23: "She shall be called אִשָּׁה, because she was taken out of אִישׁ; that is "She shall be called *vira* (if one may speak this way), because she was taken out of *vir* — or אִישׁ may refer to power and dominion, as in Judg. 7:14: "This is no other than the sword of Gideon . . . a man of Israel," that is, a hero, a leader, of Israel.

9. *But [we see] Jesus, who for a little while was made lower than the angels.*

This text has been corrupted either by a translator or by a scribe, since not one iota makes it mean that Christ was made a little lower than the angels. In fact, in the Greek text the words are identical with those used above (v. 7), namely, "Thou didst make Him for a short time lower than the angels." Therefore the text can be understood to have been arranged as follows: "But Him who was made lower than the angels for less than a short time" (for this is what *paulominus* means). Here the Holy Spirit con-soles us, in order that in the time of suffering we may have patience and hope; for tribulation lasts for a little while, but the consola-tion is eternal, as is stated in 1 Peter 5:10: "And after you have suffered a little while, the God of all grace . . . will Himself perfect, etc." And in Ps. 2:12: "For His wrath is quickly kindled. Blessed are all who trust in Him." For the same Hebrew word that is translated in our text with "for a little while" is translated with

[19] Cf. Luther's comments of almost two decades later on this idea, *Luther's Works*, 1, p. 91.

[20] Josephus, *Antiquities of the Jews*, Book I, ch. 2.

"quickly" in this psalm. Indeed, the same verse could be translated literally as follows: "Since He will be angry for a little while, blessed are all who trust in Him"; that is, since it is necessary that He be angry and scourge, blessed are they who endure, "lest when He is angry in this way, you perish from the way" (cf. Ps. 2:12). The wrath of God is necessary because of "the body of sin" spoken of in Rom. 6:6 and because of "the law of my members" (Rom. 7:23). For it is necessary that "the body of sin" and the law of the flesh or the members "be destroyed" (Rom. 6:6), since it is impossible for "anything unclean to enter the kingdom of heaven" (cf. Rev. 21:27). But such destruction comes about through crosses, sufferings, deaths, and disgraces. Therefore God kills in order to make alive; He humiliates in order to exalt, etc. And this is what the apostle glories in when he says that he knows nothing except Jesus Christ, and Him not glorified but crucified (cf. 1 Cor. 2:2). He bears on his body the marks of his Lord (cf. Gal. 6:17). For to bear Christ crucified in oneself is to live a life full of trials and sufferings, and for this reason He becomes for carnal men "a sign that is spoken against" (Luke 2:34). Therefore one should resolve to receive with open arms every trial, even death itself, with praise and joy, just as one should receive Christ Himself. For it is true that Christ always comes in the form He assumed when He "emptied Himself" of the form of God (cf. Phil. 2:7). Thus James 1:2 says: "Count it all joy, my brethren, when you meet various trials." And in Is. 48:9 we read: "For the sake of My praise I restrain it for you, that I may not cut you off." And in Ps. 18:3: "I will call upon the Lord, and I will be saved from my enemies."

So that by the grace of God He might taste death for everyone.

This conjunction "so that" states the consequence of the knowledge. It should be connected with the participle "made lower" and not with the participle "crowned," lest the sense be absurd, as if He had been crowned so that He might taste death, when it is rather the case that He tasted death so that He might be crowned. Or it surely should be referred to everything that precedes as well as to the text in its entirety, as the apostle says in Gal. 2:2: "I laid before them the Gospel . . . lest somehow I should be running in vain or had run in vain," that is, so that as a result of this discussion it might be established among you that actually "I did not run in vain." For this is the way St. Jerome interprets the same passage.[21] Thus also in Rom. 4:18: "Abraham believed God, so that he should become the father of many nations," not that he sought to become the father by believing, but that this was the result of his faith. Likewise here: "He was made lower and crowned with glory," so that it is clear that He tasted death by the grace of God, not out of necessity. This is what others mean when they say that the conjunction "so that" is understood in a consecutive sense but not causally.[22] This use occurs frequently in Scripture. But the emphasis is on this verb "to taste." For the apostle did not say "so that he might die" but "so that he might taste death." As Chrysostom says: "For in fact, as one who tastes, so He spends a short interval of time in death and has immediately arisen. . . . Just as a physician who does not need to taste of the food prepared for the sick man yet in his care for him tastes first of his food to persuade the sick man to take that food more readily, so also — because all men feared death — the Lord, persuading them to approach death confidently, also tasted death Himself, though it was not necessary for Him to do so. 'For the ruler of this world is coming,' He says, 'and He has no power over Me' (John 14:30)." [23]

10. [*For it was fitting that He, for whom and through whom all things exist, in bringing many sons to glory, should make*] *the Author of their salvation* [*perfect through suffering*].

Ambrose prefers "the Leader of salvation" to "the Author of salvation." [24] Others prefer "the Prince and Head of salvation," namely, so that it is interpreted as referring to Christ the man, who, in saving His children, was appointed Leader by the authority of the Father. For authority rather than obedience befits God. Christ the man renders obedience. Chrysostom,[25] however, understands "the Leader of salvation" to be identical in meaning with "the Cause of salvation," as in Heb. 5:9: "He became the Source of eternal salvation to all who obey Him." Here it is beau-

21 Jerome, *Commentaria in epistolam ad Galatas*, Book I, ch. 2, *Patrologia, Series Latina*, XXVI, 358.

22 Faber, *Epistolae*, f. 233 A.

23 Chrysostom, *Homiliae*, IV, 2, cols. 39—40 (264).

24 Apparently taken from Erasmus, *Annotationes*, p. 570.

25 Chrysostom, *Homiliae*, IV, 3, col. 40 (265).

tifully shown how we are saved, namely, through Christ as the
Idea and Exemplar, to whose image all who are saved are con-
formed.[26] For God the Father made Christ to be the Sign and
Idea, in order that those who adhere to Him by faith might be
transformed into the same image (2 Cor. 3:18) and thus be drawn
away from the images of the world. Therefore Is. 11:12 says: "The
Lord will raise an Ensign for the nations, and will assemble the
outcasts of Israel." Likewise in the same chapter (v. 10): "The
Root of Jesse which stands as an Ensign to the peoples; Him shall
the nations seek." This gathering together of the sons of God is
similar to what happens when the government arranges a spectacle
to which the citizens flock. They leave their work and their homes
and fix their attention on it alone. Thus through the Gospel as
through a spectacle exhibited to the whole world (cf. 2 Cor. 4:9)
Christ attracts all men by the knowledge and contemplation of
Himself and draws them away from the things to which they have
clung in the world. This is the meaning of the statement that they
are transformed and become like Him. In this way he says that
Christ is the Cause and Leader of salvation, for He draws and
leads His sons to glory through Him. One would commonly say
that Christ is the Instrument and the Means by which God leads
His sons. Therefore since He has determined to draw His sons
through Christ, the text says correctly that "it was fitting that He
should make Christ perfect through suffering," that is, that He
should make Him the most perfect and the complete Example
through which to inspire and draw His sons. For God does not
compel men to salvation by force and fear, but by this pleasing
spectacle of His mercy and love He moves and draws through
love all whom He will save.

Make [the Author of their salvation] perfect through suffering.

The text of those who have "to be made perfect through suffering" should be corrected. For the Greek has "sufferings," in
the plural, and "to make perfect," in the active voice. Then this
phrase, "through sufferings," or in Hebrew, "in sufferings," should
be changed to the way of speaking by which we express it in Latin,
namely, without a preposition. Then we should have *passionibus.*

[26] On these terms, cf. Dionysius the Areopagite, *De divinis nominibus,* ch. V,
par. 8, *Patrologia, Series Graeca,* III, 848.

Thus in Ps. 33:6 — "By the Word of the Lord the heavens were made" — [no preposition is used in the Latin text with "the Word"], whereas the Hebrew has "in the Word of the Lord" and the Greek has "through the Word of the Lord." Thus here — "It was fitting to make perfect through sufferings" — [the preposition "through" signifies] "by means of," so that the sense is that it was fitting for God to make Christ the perfect Author of salvation and, in order to accomplish this, to make use of sufferings. The reason is that without sufferings the perfection of the example would have been lacking — the example by which He would move and draw us even to the point of loving death and suffering.

11. *For He who sanctifies and* [*those who are sanctified have all one origin. That is why He is not ashamed to call them brethren,*

12. *saying: I will proclaim Thy name to My brethren, in the midst of the congregation I will praise Thee.*

13. *And again: I will put My trust in Him. And again: Behold, I and My children, whom God has given Me*].

These two references (Ps. 22:22 and Is. 8:17-18) are quoted by the apostle in an obscure manner, except as much as one can take from the preceding words, namely, that he wants to prove that "He who sanctifies and those who are sanctified have one origin." For this reason Chrysostom also says that with these words He points to the Father, just as with the words "I will proclaim Thy name, etc.," He points to the brethren.[27] And thus those two quotations prove that He who sanctifies is from God. But that those who have been sanctified have the same origin is proved by the words "I will proclaim Thy name to My brethren." In fact, the words "I and My children, whom God has given Me" prove this with greater clarity. It seems, however, that both quotations have been taken from the eighth chapter of Isaiah, where we read: "I will wait for the Lord (for this means to trust in the Lord) who is hiding His face from the house of Jacob, and I will look for Him. Behold, I and My children whom the Lord has given Me are signs and wonders in Israel from the Lord of hosts." But apart from the apostle's reference in this passage, it is also evident from the preceding words in Is. 8 that this is being spoken in the Person

27 Chrysostom, *Homiliae*, IV, 3, col. 41 (266).

of Christ. There we read: "Bind up the testimony, seal the Law among My disciples. I will wait for the Lord," as above (Is. 8:16 ff.).

14. *Since therefore the children share in flesh and blood,* [*He Himself likewise partook of the same nature*].

Here the apostle distinguishes the brotherhood between us and the angels from that between Christ and us. He praises the abundance of God's love, namely, that He made Christ our brother not only according to the spirit but also according to the flesh, so that at the same time the very same Christ is higher than the angels, like us, and nearer to us than the angels. Therefore He also calls Himself alone our neighbor in the parable of the Samaritan in Luke 10:30-37. But it is characteristic of Scripture to use the expression "flesh and blood" to refer to man, especially after the Fall, as in Gen. 6:3: [28] "My Spirit shall not abide in man forever, for he is flesh." Indeed, the apostle calls even the apostles themselves "flesh and blood" in Gal. 1:16 when he says: "I did not confer with flesh and blood"; that is, "I did not discuss the Gospel with the other apostles." Sometimes, however, it is taken in a bad sense for the vices of nature or for vitiated nature, as in 1 Cor. 15:50: "Flesh and blood cannot possess the kingdom of God" and in Eph. 6:12: "We are not contending against flesh and blood." The reason for this twofold meaning is that man is called what he is and also what he loves. For he really is flesh and blood; he also loves flesh and blood. For in this way he is also called righteous, wise, and good when he loves righteousness, wisdom, and goodness. Therefore here the apostle did not want to state without emphasis that the children were flesh and blood, but rather that "they share in flesh and blood," in order to show that they are not flesh and blood pure and simple, but that they only share in flesh and blood through Christ, who also shares in flesh and blood.

[*He Himself likewise partook of the same nature*], *that through death He might destroy* [*him who has the power of death, that is, the devil*].

CONCERNING THE CONTEMPT OF DEATH

Scripture attributes death to the devil. Wisd. of Sol. 2:24 says: "By the envy of the devil death came into the world." And in

[28] The original has "Gen. 8."

Wisd. of Sol. 1:13-14 we read: "For God did not make death, neither has He pleasure in the destruction of the living. For He created all things that they might exist." It is as if he were saying: "Death is not listed among the works of God at the beginning of Genesis." Likewise in Ezek. 18:32: [29] "'I desire not the death of him who dies,' says the Lord." In Ezek. 33:11 we read: "'As I live,' says the Lord, 'I desire not the death of the wicked.'" And Ps. 30:5 says: "For wrath is in His indignation, and life in His will"; that is, death and wrath are displeasing to Him, and life is pleasing to Him. Hos. 13:14: "O death, I will be your death." For if death were the work of God, He would not destroy it. Now, however, as 1 John 3:8 says, "The reason the Son of God appeared was to destroy the works of the devil"; that is, as John 10:10 states, "I came that they may have life, and have it more abundantly." It remains, then, that death as well as sin are the works of the devil. Therefore in Rev. 9:11 the devil is called "the angel of the bottomless pit." In Hebrew the name is אֲבַדּוֹן. In Greek it is Ἀπολλύων. In Latin it is *Exterminans*. God's proper work,[30] on the other hand, is "life, peace, joy," and the other fruits of the Spirit in Gal. 5:22. Yet in this the Lord "exalted His holy One" (Ps. 4:3) and is "wonderful among all His saints" (Ps. 68:35) that He destroyed the devil, not by a work of God but by a work of the devil himself. For this is the most glorious kind of victory, namely, to pierce the adversary with his own weapon and to slay him with his own sword, as we sing: "He fell prostrate on his own darts." [31] For in this way God promotes and completes His work by means of an alien deed, and by His wonderful wisdom He compels the devil to work through death nothing else than life, so that in this way, while he acts most of all against the work of God, he acts for the work of God and against his own work with his own deed. For thus he worked death in Christ, but Christ completely swallowed up death in Himself through the immortality of His divinity and rose again in glory. God is called the "arm" (Ps. 89:10). Therefore He promises this victory most joyfully in Job 40:24 (cf. also 41:1-7): "Can one take him with hooks, or pierce his nose with

[29] The original has "Ezek. 8."

[30] On the distinction between the "alien" and the "proper" work of God, based on Is. 28:21, cf. *Luther's Works,* 13, p. 79, note 9.

[31] An allusion to the Christmas hymn, included in the sequences of St. Notker, "Eia recolamus laudibus piis digna."

a snare? Can you draw out Leviathan with a fishhook, or press down his tongue with a cord? Can you put a rope in his nose, or pierce his jaw with a hook? . . . Will you play with him as with a bird, or will you put him on leash for your maidens? . . . Can you fill his skin with harpoons, or his head with fishing spears? Will traders bargain over him? Will they divide him up among the merchants?" Concerning this passage see Gregory in his *Moralia.*[32]

Therefore just as in "the Author of salvation," in "the Holy of Holies," in Christ, our Head, death and all the works of the devil have been destroyed, so it will have to happen in each of His members. For just as Christ was at once a mortal and an immortal Person, He was indeed subject to death by reason of His humanity; but because His whole Person could not be slain, it happened that death failed, and the devil succumbed in slaying Him; and thus death was swallowed up and devoured in life.[33] In this way the curse was swallowed up and conquered in the blessing, sorrow in joy, and the other evils in the highest good. Thus now, too, it pleases our most gracious God to destroy death and the works of the devil in us through Christ. We Christians should learn, in order that we may die joyfully. For just as it is impossible for Christ, the Victor over death, to die again (cf. Rom. 6:9), so it is impossible for one who believes in Him to die; as Christ says in John 11:26, 25:[34] "He who believes in Me shall never die. And though he dies, he shall live." Whatever becomes alive with God is immortal. Also Ps. 23:4: "Even though I walk in the valley" — that is, in the midst of the shadow of death — "I shall fear no evil, for Thou art with me." For just as Christ, by reason of His union with immortal divinity, overcame death by dying, so the Christian, by reason of his union with the immortal Christ — which comes about through faith in Him — also overcomes death by dying. And in this way God destroys the devil through the devil himself and accomplishes His own work by means of an alien work. This is what the world does not grasp, as Hab. 1:5 says: "Behold, I am doing a work in your days which no man will believe when it is told." Therefore Chrysostom says on this pas-

---

[32] Gregory the Great, *Moralia,* Book XXXIII, ch. 7—17, *Patrologia, Series Latina,* LXXVI, 680—695.

[33] An allusion to the third stanza of the Easter sequence of Wipo, "Victimae paschali laudes."

[34] The original has "John 6," apparently thinking of John 6:51.

sage: "Here he points out something wonderful, namely, that the devil was overcome by that through which he had power. The weapons—that is, death—which were his strength against the world, through these weapons Christ smote him. Thus you see what a great blessing death has wrought. Why do you tremble? Why do you fear death? It is no longer terrible, but it has been trodden underfoot; it has been despised." [35] And further on he says: "For death is no longer bitter, because it does not differ from sleep." [36] Therefore the apostle Paul also proclaims the resurrection of Christ everywhere with great joy, because through it the Law, sin, death, hell, the devil, the world, and the flesh have all been overcome for all who believe in Him and call upon Him. Thus 1 Cor. 15:57 states: "But thanks be to God, who gave us the victory through our Lord Jesus Christ." "Gave us," he says. He did not keep it for Himself alone. And 1 Thess. 4:13-14 says: "We would not have you ignorant concerning those who are asleep, that you may not grieve as others do who have no hope. For if we believe that Jesus died and rose again, even so, through Jesus, God will bring with Him those who have fallen asleep." And in Hos. 13:14 we read: "I will deliver them out of the hand of death. I will redeem them from death. O death, I will be your death. O hell, I will be your bite." The next verse tells how He does this: "The Lord will bring a burning wind from the desert, and it shall dry up his springs and shall make his fountain desolate." For Hosea is alluding to Ex. 14:21, when the Lord brought a mighty and burning wind throughout the night and dried up the Red Sea. This represents the drying up of the veins of death, that is, of sins, because death rules in consequence of sin. That wind, however, is the Holy Spirit, who has been brought and given from the desert, that is, from Jesus Christ, who was crucified.

COROLLARY

He who fears death or is unwilling to die is not a Christian to a sufficient degree; for those who fear death still lack faith in the resurrection, since they love this life more than they love the life to come. Properly speaking, they are those about whom Ps. 106:24 [37]

---

[35] Chrysostom, *Homiliae*, IV, 4, col. 41 (266).

[36] Chrysostom, *Homiliae*, IV, 5, col. 44 (268).

[37] The original has "Ps. 77 [78]."

says: "They despised the pleasant land." He who does not die willingly should not be called a Christian. Therefore Chrysostom, with reference to this passage, censures those who mourn the dead. He says: "Those who truly deserve to be mourned are those who still fear death and shudder, who still do not believe in the resurrection." [38] Therefore when such people pray "Thy kingdom come," they either do not pray at all or they pray against themselves; that is, they mock both God and themselves, and they have been baptized in vain, since, according to what the apostle says in Rom. 6:3-4, as many of us as are baptized into the death of Christ are certainly baptized to accept death quickly and to attain to the image of Christ more quickly. But you might say: "I do not fear death, but I do fear an evil death, because 'the death of sinners is the worst, and evils shall destroy the unrighteous man'" (cf. Ps. 34:22). But he who says this proves clearly that he is deficient in faith in Christ, for he does not believe that Christ is "the Lamb of God who takes away his sins" (cf. John 1:29). For the less firmly this is believed, the more death is feared; and the more firmly it is believed, the more confidently death is despised. For it is true that only the awareness of sin makes death dreadful, because "sin is the sting of death" (1 Cor. 15:56). But only faith in Christ removes the awareness of sin; for "the victory has been given to us through Jesus Christ," as stated above (cf. 1 Cor. 15:57). For God makes death, judgment, and hell manifest in order to show the power of faith in Christ, so that a Christian may overcome these through faith. For those dreadful things are nothing else than exercises through which faith should become "strong as death and hard as hell" (cf. Song of Sol. 8:6), although they try vigorously with might and violence to separate the heart from trust in Christ. Therefore when Christ had foretold dreadful signs in Luke 21:28, He immediately added the following words for the strengthening of faith: "Now when these things begin to take place, look up, and raise your heads," in order that these things might be overcome through faith. For if death is feared on account of sin, it should be desired much more on account of sins, because death alone puts an end to sin and slays it. Therefore death, the murderer of sin, should be loved as much as sin is feared. For this reason St. Cyprian says in his work on immortality: "The battle we fight is with greed, with lewdness, with

[38] Chrysostom, *Homiliae,* IV, 5, col. 43 (268).

anger, with ambition. There is a perpetual and troublesome struggle with carnal vices, with worldly allurements. The mind of man, besieged and surrounded as it is on all sides by the assaults of the devil, barely opposes and resists one of these." And Cyprian concludes that death comes to our aid. And later he says: "The soul suffers so many persecutions every day, the heart is beset by so many dangers and delights in lingering long here amid the devil's swords, when one should rather desire and wish to hasten to Christ with the aid of a speedier arrival of death." [39] That is what Cyprian says. The consolation of death. Yet those who fear death should not despair; but they should be encouraged and exhorted as people who are weak in faith, who, as the apostle enjoins in Rom. 14:1,[40] should be welcomed. For that contempt for death and the gratitude for it, proclaimed by the apostle and the saints, is the goal and perfection toward which the whole life of Christians should strive, even though very few are so perfect. Thus in the Epistle to the Romans Paul also calls Christians righteous, holy, and free from sin, not because they are, but because they have begun to be and should become people of this kind by making constant progress. For even saintly men have been frightened by death and the judgments of God. Their voice is heard in Ps. 55:4: "The fear of death has fallen upon me." And again in Ps. 55:5: "Fear and trembling have come upon me." And elsewhere (Ps. 39:10-11): "By the strength of Thy hand I am spent with rebukes." In Ps. 116:3 we read: "The sorrows of death encompassed me, and the perils of hell came upon me." Likewise in Ps. 88:3: "My soul is surfeited with troubles, and my life has drawn near to hell."

Therefore such people should be consoled and encouraged, first through Christ Himself, who, in order to omit nothing that one could desire from the most pious priest, not only underwent death for us to overcome it for us and to make it deserving of our contempt but also, for the sake of the weak in faith, took upon Himself, overcame, and sanctified the very fear of death, lest such fear be scorned to our damnation. Otherwise it is truly a sin to be unwilling to die and to fear death. Therefore consider. What more should the most merciful Savior have done but did not do? He

[39] Cyprian, *De mortalitate*, chs. 4—5, *Corpus scriptorum ecclesiasticorum Latinorum*, III-1, 299; Luther here calls it *De immortalitate*.

[40] The original has "Rom. 15."

took sin completely away. He left death, but He left it conquered. Besides, He made the fear of death harmless — the fear one has even though death has been conquered and should not be feared. Secondly, such people should be consoled and encouraged with that with which He Himself consoles us, with what He says in Matt. 10:28: "Do not fear those who kill the body." And in Is. 10:24 we read: "My people, do not be afraid of the Assyrians." For the Lord does not will death. And although He uses the devil and evil in the slaying and suffering of His saints — as Job 40:19 says: "Let Him who made him bring near His sword" and, as we read in Is. 10:5: "Woe to the Assyrian, the rod and staff of My anger, My indignation is in their hands!" — yet He does this very thing with a completely friendly and calm heart, as Job 41:1 (Vulgate) says: "Not as one who is cruel will I stir him up." Finally He reproves and rebukes those who have done more than He has commanded, as we read in Zech. 1:14-15: "I am exceedingly jealous for Zion, and I am very angry with the wealthy nations; for I was angry a little, but they furthered the evil." Indeed, God is more wonderful in this, that He smites and bruises His saints in order to incite others to compassion and in order that they may intercede before God on their behalf, as Ezek. 13:5 says: "You have not gone up to face the enemy, nor have you built up a wall for the house of Israel, to stand in battle in the day of the Lord." And in Ezek. 22:30 [41] we read: "And I sought among them for a man who might set up a hedge and stand in the gap before Me for the land, lest I destroy it; and I found none." This is the reason for the statement in Job 19:21: "Have pity on me, have pity on me, at least you my friends." Therefore Moses is also praised in Ps. 106:23 [42] because "he stood in the breach before God, lest He destroy Israel." In Ps. 69:26,[43] on the other hand, God severely rebukes those who "have added to the pain of the wounds, because they have persecuted Him whom Thou hast smitten."

15. *[That through death he might deliver all those]* who through fear of death were subject to lifelong bondage.

Chrysostom understands this in a threefold way: ["It means] either that he who fears death is a slave and endures everything,

[41] The original has "Ezek. 24."

[42] The original has "Ps. 77 [78]."

[43] The original has "Ps. 108 [109]."

lest he die; or that all men were slaves of death and, because they had not yet been released, were held in its power; or that men lived in continual fear, always expecting to die, and, since this fear remained with them, could have no feeling of pleasure." [44] It seems, however, that these three meanings all flow together into one explanation of the words of Paul. For Paul himself points out the contrast. Because he had said that the devil is the lord of death, some must have been subjected to his lordship. Thus the second meaning is the true one, namely, that all were slaves of death and subject to the prince of death. Then the first and third express the miseries accompanying the same subjection. The first points out that those who are subjected in this way are assailed by fear and uncertainty, since they do not have true peace; as Isaiah (48:22) states: "There is no peace for the wicked, says the Lord." And in Deut. 28:65-67 we read: "The Lord will give you a trembling heart . . . and your life shall hang in doubt before you. . . . In the morning you shall say: 'Would it were evening!' And at evening you shall say: 'Would it were morning!'" But the third interpretation points out that the fear of death makes men slaves of sin. For this is "the spirit of slavery" (Rom. 8:15), which always makes men worse, because it leads them to a greater hatred of the Law and righteousness. Therefore when Christ took away the fear of death, He set us free from slavery to sin and by this same act destroyed him to whom we were subject only through the fear of death. Yet he did not destroy him in such a way that he did not exist; but just as we are freed from the Law by the Spirit, not so that the Law does not exist, but so that the Law is not feared, so we are also freed from the devil, not so that he does not exist, but so that he is not feared, and from death, not so that it does not exist, but so that it is not feared, etc. I conclude, therefore, that for a Christian there is nothing more to fear either in this life or in the life to come, since for him both death and all evils have been changed into a blessing and a gain.

16. *For nowhere He takes hold of the angels [but He takes hold of the descendants of Abraham].*

Chrysostom notes the emphasis on the verb "to take hold of." [45]

---

[44] Chrysostom, *Homiliae*, IV, 4, col. 41 (266).

[45] Chrysostom, *Homiliae*, V, 1, cols. 45—46 (271).

For the apostle did not say that He received, but that "He took hold of," namely, from the figure of persons pursuing and doing everything to seize and take hold of those who are fleeing. For when human nature fled far away, He pursued, and took hold of it. He showed that He did this only out of mercy and grace and because of the care He has for us. This is what Chrysostom says. And this is clear in the Gospel from the parables of the lost sheep (Matt. 18:13) and the lost coin (Luke 15:8), which He sought and found, certainly not because of what they did, but out of compassion.

17. [*Therefore He had to be made like His brethren*] *so that He might become a merciful and faithful* [*High Priest in the service of God*].

The apostle commends the two things in Christ that should shine forth in every priest according to the example of Christ, namely, that he should be merciful to the people and faithful to God for the people. For through mercy he should empty himself and make all the evils of those who are under him his own, and should feel them in no other way than if he himself were in them. But through faithfulness he should share with them all his own good things. For thus, as Phil. 2:6-7 says, Christ "emptied Himself of the form of God and took the form of a servant"; that is, He considered the things that were ours, not those that were His. For His things were righteousness, wisdom, salvation, glory, peace, joy, etc.; ours were sin, foolishness, perdition, dishonor, the cross, sorrow, etc. Therefore He took these things of ours and acted as if He did not know His own. Therefore in the Law in Ex. 28:38 it is stated that "Aaron shall bear the iniquities of the things the Children of Israel brought as offerings." And Num. 18:1 states: "The Lord said to Aaron: 'You and your sons and your father's house with you shall bear iniquity in connection with the sanctuary; and you and your sons with you shall bear iniquity in connection with your priesthood.'"

CHAPTER THREE

1. *Therefore, holy brethren, who share in a heavenly call, [consider Jesus].*

SOFTLY and gently the apostle draws them to Christ by calling them "holy" and, as it were, flattering them. Here he teaches us that we should not preach Christ with fury or with a tempest of words. Indeed, Christ can be preached in no other way than peacefully and calmly. For roaring talk pertains to the Law, as has been pictured in Ex. 20:18, where the hearers were terrified by the sound of the trumpet, the darkness of the mountain, and the fire of the lightning. Likewise in 1 Kings 19:11 ff., where, after the wind, after the earthquake, and after the fire, there came "a still small voice," and there the Lord was. Therefore the Law should be revealed with thunderbolts to those who are foolish and stiff-necked, but the Gospel should be presented gently to those who are terrified and humbled. Therefore Is. 42:1, 3 says about Christ: "Behold, My Servant. . . . A bruised reed He will not break, and a dimly burning wick He will not quench"; that is, He will prefer to console the timid and the afflicted.

[Jesus, the Apostle and High Priest] of our confession.

A new way of speaking, but one that comes from a Hebrew idiom and expresses the matter with remarkable fitness, since our whole work is a confession, as Ps. 96:6 says: "Confession and beauty are before Him" (that is, in His church), "holiness and magnificence are in His sanctification." And Ps. 111:3: "Confession and magnificence are His work." The meaning of these verses is expressed in Ps. 145:5: "They will speak of the magnificence of the glory of Thy holiness, and will tell Thy wondrous works," which states that everything they say and do is praise, confession, magnificence, and sanctification, with which they praise, confess, glorify, and sanctify Thee. Yet all this is Thy work in them, as

[W, LVII-3, 137, 138]

Ps. 8:2 says: "Out of the mouth of infants and of sucklings Thou hast fashioned praise." Likewise Is. 43:21: [1] "This people I have formed for Myself; they will declare My praise." Therefore Christ has on the cross the title King of the Jews, that is, of the confessors.[2] This confession is understood as a confession not only of sins but also of praise. Indeed, the confession of sins and of praise is one and the same confession, unless it is the confession of those Jews who are named for Judas Iscariot, that is, the confession of those who are despaired of [שָׂכָר, that is, wages].[3] For that is the true confession with which a man gives the glory to God with regard to righteousness, wisdom, virtue, and all works but gives nothing to himself except sin, foolishness, and weakness, and that with a true mouth, heart, and work. And in this statement the apostle distinguishes confessions, yes, even possessions. For with respect to the world it would be appropriate to say that God is Lord or King of lands, rivers, cities, beasts, etc. For such possessions do not consist in confessions or words but in things. Furthermore, the synagog also had its own confession, namely, that of Moses, because it dealt with the physical wonders by which it was redeemed from the weakness, poverty, and toil of Egypt. Therefore the apostle speaks of "our," that is, a new confession, because we believe, declare, and confess other wonders, namely, redemption from spiritual weakness, toil, and poverty. Therefore Moses is the apostle of their confession, but Christ is the Apostle of our confession. Therefore Chrysostom interprets "of our confession" to mean "of our faith." [4] Yet in his interpretation there seems to be a metonymy, that is, the use of one thing for that of another associated with it, namely, of "faith" for its own work, which is confession, just as the grammarians take "Mars" as a term for war, "Minerva" as a term for the arts.[5]

---

[1] The original has "Is. 53."

[2] The source of this information is the interpretation, presumably based on Gen. 29:35, supplied by Jerome, *Liber interpretationis Hebraicorum nominum,* 1 Corinthians, "I," *Corpus Christianorum, Series Latina,* LXXII, 154.

[3] In distinction, that is, from the usual view, that the name was derived from Judah, the fourth son of Jacob.

[4] Chrysostom, *Homiliae,* V, 3, col. 50 (274).

[5] On "Mars," see Vergil, *Aeneid,* XII, 712; on "Minerva," see Horace, *De arte poetica,* line 385.

5. [*Now Moses was faithful in all God's house*] *as a servant, to*
testify to the things [*that were to be spoken later*].

Again one sees a Hebraic way of speaking. For in this way
God calls His Word and His preachers witnesses. Ps. 81:8 says:
"Hear, O My people, and I will call you to witness." The Latin
language cannot express this verb adequately with one word. But
the meaning is this, that in the future I will speak a Word in your
[singular] midst or among you [plural]. (For the Hebrew has "I will
call to witness in you.") This Word will not be a manifestation
of things at hand, but it will be a testimony of things not seen.
Therefore it is necessary for you to hear what you will not be able
to see or grasp. For thus Christ says in John 3:11: "Truly, I say
to you, we speak of what we know, and bear witness to what we
have seen; but you do not receive our testimony." For in this
passage (Ps. 81:8) both verbs, namely, "hear" and "I will call to
witness," are used independently. This means that you shall be
the hearer, and I will be the Preacher. For what Christ has said
about heaven and the life to come is grasped only by hearing,
since it transcends not only all understanding, be it ever so deep,
but also all capability of desiring, be it ever so extensive. Therefore the testimony of the Lord is the Word of faith, hidden wisdom; it is understood by children. Is. 53:1 also calls it something
that is heard. There we read: "Lord, who has believed what we
have heard?" This means the Word we cause to be heard by
preaching the Gospel.

And surely the Word of God is most appropriately called a testimony. For just as in legal disputes whatever judgment is passed
on the basis of the reports of witnesses is arrived at by hearing
alone and believed because of faith, since it cannot be known
in any other way, neither by perception nor by reason, so the
Gospel is received in no other way than by hearing. And for this
reason the apostles are called witnesses of Christ, as Is. 43:10
states: "Truly you are My witnesses, says the Lord, and My servant whom I have chosen, that you may know and believe Me,
and understand that I am He." Thus Ps. 122:4 also says: "To that
place did the tribes go up, the tribes of the Lord, Israel a testimony." In my opinion this ought to have been translated as
follows: "To that place did the tribes go up, the tribes of the
Lord as a testimony to Israel." For since the Hebrew has "to

Israel," or "for Israel," in the dative, and "testimony," in the ablative case, it should, according to our texts, be taken as "for a testimony," as Christ says in Matt. 10:18: "You will be brought before kings and governors for My sake, as a testimony before them and the Gentiles." The same thing is now true when the apostle says that Moses was "a servant to testify to the things that were to be spoken later," that is, to be a witness of God in the things that were spoken through the angels.

6. [*And we are His house*] *if we hold fast our confidence and the hope in which we glory to the end.*

Chrysostom says: "He who sorrows in tribulations, he who falls, does not glory; he who is ashamed, he who hides himself, has no confidence." [6] From this it is clear that "glory" is used here for glorying or boasting, which the Greek text also has, namely, καύχημα. For in Greek "glory" is called δόξα, which means opinion, renown, glory among us. Therefore κενοδοξία means "empty glory." Thus the Hebrew word כָּבוֹד means "glory," and פְּאֵר means "glorying." Thus Ps. 24:8 says: "Who is this King of glory," that is, כָּבוֹד. And in Ps. 89:17 we read: "For Thou art the glory (that is, פְּאֵר, or "glorying") of their strength," which means "Thou art their strength, of which they glory." But these words are confused in a strange manner, even though there is no small difference in the matter itself. For "glorying" is taken more in an active sense, but "glory" is taken in a passive sense. For "glory" is the opinion of us, that is, the opinion of others about us; but "glorying" is our opinion about ourselves. If it is in ourselves, it is empty; but if it is about us in Christ, it is genuine, as the apostle says in 2 Cor. 10:17: "Let him who glories, glory in the Lord." Therefore we accept Chrysostom's distinction between "confidence" and "glory" in our hope. According to him, "confidence" is characteristic of one who has the courage to take up the cross of Christ, just as diffidence is characteristic of one who flees from the cross of Christ and is ashamed of it. "Glory," on the other hand, is characteristic of one who makes progress and triumphs; but complaining or sadness is characteristic of one who fails and falls down. Thus Rom. 5:3 says: "We glory in tribulations." But the apostle says this here because he had called us

---

[6] Chrysostom, *Homiliae*, V, 3, col. 49 (273).

the house that Christ "builds" (Heb. 3:4, 6). The construction, however, is nothing else than tension, pressure, and in every way the cross and the sufferings that are in Christ. Therefore he wants us to know that if we are to be built and constructed, we need firm confidence and the glory of hope in Him, lest we fail and suffer worse destruction while the building takes place.

7. *Therefore, as the Holy Spirit says: Today if you hear His voice* *[do not harden your hearts].*

The most literal translation of the text from the Hebrew is as follows: "For He is our God, and we are the people of His pasture and the sheep of His hand. On that day, when you hear His voice, harden not your hearts as in the rebellion, as on the day of temptation in the wilderness, when your fathers tempted Me, tested Me, and also saw My work for 40 years. I loathed that generation and said: 'They are a people who err in their hearts.' And they do not know My ways. To them I swore in My anger: 'They shall not enter My rest'" (cf. Ps. 95:7-11). In the first place, it is clear from this text that the prophets knew that the future was prefigured in the history of the Children of Israel. Therefore it speaks figuratively,[7] saying: "Do not harden your hearts on the day on which you will hear His voice in the future as they hardened their hearts on the day on which they heard His voice in the past." Therefore the psalmist realized that another possession was meant by the Land of Promise, and he indicates this understanding of His with a special note when he says: "They shall not enter My rest." He does not say: "They shall not enter that land," as Num. 14:30 states: "You shall not enter the land over which I lifted up My hand." At the same time, therefore, he reminds us of that rest during which God rested from His works, as is stated in Gen. 2:2.[8] In the second place, by using the word "today" or the phrase "on that day" the text distinguishes clearly between another day and the day previously mentioned, as Heb. 4:8 states: "For if Jesus had given them rest, He would not speak later of another day." Accordingly, this is the day the prophets are wont to speak of when they use the phrase "on that day," namely, to indicate the time of fulfillment by syn-

---

[7] The Latin word is *comparative.*

[8] The original has "Gen. 1."

ecdoche, or collectively, instead of using the plural. "As on the day of temptation" corresponds to this.

But "when you hear in His voice" is a Hebraism. For the verb "you hear" is taken in a neutral sense, or rather as if it were a noun instead of what it is. Thus it means "when you will have become hearers" or "when you will have had the hearing," namely, "in His voice," that is, "through His voice." For the hearing comes through the Word of Christ, as Rom. 10:17 says. And it is stated more meaningfully as it is in the Hebrew than our translation has it. For there it sounds like the promise of the future hearing through the voice of Christ, as if he were saying: "When He Himself will speak and make you hear, do not harden, etc." In our translation, however, it sounds like an uncertain event.

One should note that this is the one, and the greatest, thing God requires of the Jews, yes, of all men, namely, that they hear His voice. Therefore Moses impresses so many times throughout Deuteronomy (Deut. 6:4): "Hear, O Israel." Likewise (cf. Deut. 5:25): "If you hear the voice of the Lord your God." He does so to such an extent that Jer. 7:21-23 says: "Add your burnt offerings to your sacrifices, and eat the flesh. For in the day that I brought them out of the land of Egypt, I did not speak to your fathers or command them concerning burnt offerings and sacrifices. But this command I gave them, saying: 'Hear My voice, and I will be your God, and you shall be My people.'" Indeed, nothing resounds in the prophets more frequently than "hear," "they did not hear," and "they were unwilling to hear." And rightly so, because without faith it is impossible for God to be with us (cf. Heb. 11:6) or to work, since He does everything through His Word alone. Thus no one is able to cooperate with Him unless he adheres to the Word. This takes place through faith, just as a tool does not cooperate with a workman unless it has been taken hold of with his hand. Therefore, it is perverse in the extreme for one to hasten to works before God works in us, that is, before we believe.

But human nature recoils violently from this hearing, because it must be reduced to nothing and to sheer darkness, as Ps. 73:22 [9] states: "I was made ignorant," as we also read (Ps. 116:11): "I said in my consternation: 'Every man is a liar.'" Thus when a potter

---

[9] The original has "Ps. 27," which may have been intended as "Ps. 72 [73]."

fashions a vessel out of clay, it is impossible for him to preserve the previous form of the clay and at the same time to fashion a vessel, since the previous form resists, and lacks the form of, a vessel, and, in general, as the philosophers say: "The evolvement of one thing is the destruction of another, and motion is from opposite to opposite." [10] And in this way nature with its own light is disposed toward the light of grace, just as darkness is disposed toward light and formlessness toward form. Therefore Jer. 18:6 gives a most beautiful example of the potter and the clay: "Behold, like the clay in the potter's hand, so are you in My hand, O house of Israel." Consequently, it is impossible for the natural state,[11] the wisdom, prudence, purpose, or good intention of that man with whom and in whom God works to remain as it is or to move forward. For all these are the raw material and the unformed clay, as it were, which gives place to the direct opposite when God has begun to work.

Here, therefore, those who rely on their own counsel and "do not wait for the counsel of the Lord" (cf. Ps. 106:13) harden their hearts to their own immeasurable harm and impede the work of God in themselves. For God works beyond strength, beyond perception, beyond intention, and beyond every thought, as Is. 55:9 says: "For as the heavens are higher than the earth, so are My ways higher than your ways, says the Lord." For He is the highest. Therefore His work is also the highest, as is clear from every example of the exodus of the Children of Israel. And from this one now understands who the people are who annoy, irritate, exasperate, and contradict, as Scripture rather frequently speaks of them, namely, the people who do not believe the Word of God and are impatient of the work of God, since, like a horse and a mule (cf. Ps. 32:9), they follow their master as long as they are aware of visible things to rely on. If these things fail, they fail too. Therefore faith in Christ is an exceedingly arduous thing, because it is a rapture and a removal from everything one experiences within and without to the things one experiences neither within nor without, namely, to the invisible, most high, and incomprehensible God.

[10] Cf. Gregorius Reisch, *Margarita philosophica nova* (1508), Book VIII, ch. 33: "De generatione et corruptione."

[11] The Latin word is *dictamen*, which had become a technical term.

9. *When your fathers tempted Me* [*and saw My works for forty years*].

This is said for the purpose of censuring such great unbelief. For although faith in God is truly the most difficult thing of all, yet it is greatly strengthened and made easier through preceding words and works of God. Therefore those who had so often experienced similar, yes, greater, things with the help of God are accused of not believing the promise of God when He promised the land of Canaan. For it was no less impossible to escape from the Egyptians through the Red Sea than it was to conquer the Canaanite nations. Nevertheless, they had seen this happen, as He also says here: "They saw My work." It is as if He were saying: "I would be less angry if they were forced to believe this on the strength of My Word alone, without having seen any similar work before," just as He was not angry when they crossed the sea, though they doubted even then. And from this the prophets and the saints take for themselves the doctrine which consoles them and strengthens their faith. Therefore Ps. 143:4-6 says: "My spirit is anxious within me, and my heart within me is troubled." What shall I do? Shall I be distrustful? By no means! But the psalmist goes on to say: "I remembered the days of old, I meditated on all that Thou hast done; I mused on what Thy hands have wrought. I stretched out my hands to Thee, my soul thirsted for Thee like a parched land." Likewise Ps. 77:11-12, where, after lamenting a similar affliction he had suffered, he says: "I remembered the works of the Lord, for I will remember Thy wonders from the beginning; and I will meditate on all Thy works and muse on Thy deeds." Hence that statement in Maccabees (1 Macc. 4:9): "Remember how our fathers were saved," namely, through faith, as Ps. 44 has shown more beautifully than any other: "We have heard with our ears, O God, etc.," and throughout the entire psalm. Therefore it happens that the faith of the fathers who preceded is gain and strength of faith for those who come later; and for this reason the more remarkable the faith of the ancient fathers was, the more it was strengthened by the support of fewer examples, and the worse the unbelief of those who came later, the more it is not strengthened by the support of more examples. But the unbelief of Christians who, because of what so many martyrs and saints have encountered, now shudder at the very

sad way of faith and refuse to take it is detestable in the highest
degree.

10. *For forty years I was very close to this generation [and said:*
    They always go astray in their hearts].

"For forty years I was very close," which is chanted in the
church, has been taken from the Roman Psalter, which alone has
this reading.[12] All the others — the Greek, the Hebrew, and the
Latin — differ and have "I was provoked" or "I was annoyed."
But if one wants a forced agreement, one can say that He was
"very close," namely, by reprimanding. For God draws near in
two ways: by being angry and by being merciful, as Ecclus. 5:7
says: "Mercy and wrath approach quickly from Him," and thus
"provoked" and "very close" will amount to the same thing. But
it is strange how the adverb "always" crept in here, since even
a child knows that עַם in Hebrew does not mean "always" but
means "people." For תָּמִיד means "always." It remains, therefore,
that the error came from the Greek. For λαοί means "peoples,"
in the plural; ἀεί means "always," and thus, perhaps with the
omission of the letter λ, αοί, the remaining letters, began to be
read as ἀεί. Perhaps it is for this reason that "the people err" was
written instead of "they always err." [13]

It is certain that the Hebrew words "I will loathe a generation"
(cf. Ps. 95:10) are in the future tense for the Hebrews, though
for both the Greeks and the Latins they are in the past tense.
Therefore it seems either that the future was used for the past,
which is often the case in the Old Testament, or rather that the
prophet meant that in the future there will be a similar people
which displeases God just as that people displeased God. For
by the very manner of speaking, these words, "I will loathe a generation," without the addition of "this" or "that," give expression
to the annoyance of the speaker, as if he disdained to point to a specific generation. For this is how people are accustomed to speak
about something that is very annoying.

---

[12] Cf. *Liber usualis*, p. 370.

[13] This conjecture appears to be Luther's own, although there were similar
ones on other passages in his authorities.

11. *To whom I swore in my anger: If they will enter [My rest]!*

"If they will enter," is also a Hebrew idiom. For this is the way God is accustomed to swear as by means of a certain breaking off—aposiopesis in Greek [14]—as if "Let Me be a liar," or "Let Me not live, if they will enter," were supplied. But because this should not be thought, much less spoken, about God, it is properly left unsaid. Thus He swears in Ps. 89:35: "Once I have sworn by My holiness: 'If I will lie to David.'" But others who swear call down upon themselves without breaking off, as Saul and David swear: "The Lord do so to me, and more also." (1 Sam. 14:44; 25:22; cf. 2 Sam. 3:9)

12. *Take care, brethren, lest there be in any of you an evil heart.*

The whole emphasis of this statement is on the word "heart." For he does not say: "Take care, lest there be in any of you a grasping hand, a deceitful eye, a lustful ear." For above all one must take care that the heart is good, pure, and holy, as Ps. 51:10 states: "Create in me a clean heart, O God, and renew a right spirit within me." It is as if he were saying that cleanness of the works of the body is nothing unless there first is cleanness of the heart. But this uncleanness of the heart is so deep that no human being is sufficiently aware of it, much less can purge it away by his own strength, as Jer. 17:9-10 says: "The heart of man is deceitful and inscrutable. Who will search it out? I the Lord search out the heart and the reins." Therefore the heart becomes pure and good only through faith in Christ, as we read in Acts 15:9: "He made no distinction between us and them, but purified their hearts by faith." For faith in the Word purifies, because just as the Word of God is completely pure and good, so it makes him who adheres to it pure and good like itself. Whatever it has and is able to do it shares with him who adheres to it and believes it. Ps. 19:7 says: "The Law of the Lord is unstained, changing the souls." And Christ says in John 15:3: "You are clean because of the Word which I have spoken to you." Thus also Ps. 51:4, in the Hebrew: "Against Thee alone have I sinned . . . so that Thou art justified in Thy sentence and blameless in Thy judgment." He who believes in the Word of God is righteous, wise, true, good, etc. Thus, on the contrary, he who is separated from the Word of God or de-

---

[14] Cf. Quintilian, *Institutiones Oratoriae,* Book IX, ch. 2, par. 54.

parts from it will necessarily remain in wickedness, in uncleanness, and in everything that is opposed to the Word of God. "He
who trusts in his own mind is a fool" (Prov. 28:26), which is a statement against his own confidence. Therefore the apostle says in
Titus 1:15: "To the impure nothing is pure, but their minds and
consciences are corrupted." This is what the apostle means here
when he speaks of "falling away from the living God." For one
falls away from the living God when one falls away from His Word,
which is alive and gives life to all things, yes, is God Himself.
Therefore they die. He who does not believe is dead. But falling
away comes about through unbelief. And thus it is clear what an
"evil heart" of unbelief is. It is a heart in which nothing is good,
but everything is evil, because it departs from everything that
is good.

13. *But exhort one another every day [as long as it is called today].*

Since we are in the midst of enemies and are continually at-
tracted by innumerable allurements, hindered by cares, and engaged in business affairs, through all of which we are withdrawn
from purity of heart, therefore there is only one thing left for us:
we must exhort ourselves with all zeal and, so to speak, stir up our
sluggish spirit by means of the Word of God, by meditating on it,
reading it, and continually listening to it, as the apostle admonishes
here. Just as we read about St. Cecilia that she "constantly bore
the Gospel of Christ in her heart and devoted herself day and
night to prayer and conversations with God." [15] If this did not
happen, we would certainly be swallowed up in the end by the
great number of those things, and acedia [16] and lukewarmness
of spirit, the greatest of all dangers, would overwhelm us. This
is what the Jews experienced in the wilderness when they became
sick of the manna. Thus Ps. 107:18 says: "They loathed any kind
of food, and they drew near to the gates of death." Indeed, the
psalmist, too, had this experience. In Ps. 119:28 he says: "My
soul melts away for sorrow; strengthen me according to Thy
words." And again (Ps. 102:4): "I am smitten like grass because
I forgot to eat my bread." For just as the body cannot do without
its bread—otherwise it is weakened—so the heart of man is not

[15] Jacobus de Voragine, *Legenda aurea*, n. 164.

[16] One of the seven deadly sins, acedia, was slothfulness, thought to afflict
monks especially; cf. Thomas Aquinas, *Summa Theologica*, II-II, Q. 35.

strengthened except by this bread of God's Word. For as often as we forget the Word of God, so often do we fall back into the love of things and are polluted. We are cleansed from this pollution only when we return to the Word. To illustrate this, Scripture often mentions earrings; for just as earrings always hang on the ears, so the Word of God should resound continually in the heart. By earrings the Word of God is always meant, as in Ex. 35:22.[17] It is for this reason that Christ has been so careful to commend the preaching of His Word.

[That none] of you [may be hardened] by the deceitfulness of sin.

Again, how appropriately and properly he speaks when he mentions "the deceitfulness of sin"! For unbelief arises in the following way: First one overlooks the Creator, takes pleasure in the creature, and clings to it as though it were good. Every man desires to know nature, but he does so in the wrong way. Next the habit of loving it is established, and thus the heart is hardened toward the Word of the Creator, who calls it back from affection for the creature. Then unbelief follows. Therefore he rightly calls this "the deceitfulness of sin," for it deceives under the appearance of being good. But this "deceitfulness of sin" must be understood in a very general manner as including even one's own righteousness and wisdom. For one's own righteousness and wisdom deceives most of all and hinders faith in Christ, since we love the flesh and the sensations of the flesh, likewise property and riches, in a similar way. But we love nothing more passionately than our own feeling, judgment, purpose, and will, especially when they have the appearance of being good. Therefore Christ declared in John 5:44 that it is impossible for such people to believe. He says: "How can you believe who receive glory from one another?" Christ heals a sick man. Why are they not able to believe? Because "the deceitfulness of sin," that is, the love of their own righteousness, blinds and hardens them, since they consider it good to glory in and to be pleased with their own righteousnesses, although this is the worst of all vices, the very opposite of faith, which takes pleasure and glories only in the righteousness of God, that is, in Christ.

---

[17] The original has "23. [Ex.]."

One should also note that here "hardening" means absolutely every thing that makes it difficult to believe. For just as the Hebrew language is wont to employ very beautiful metaphors, so "hardening" has the same meaning that "disinclination" or "ineptitude" has. The metaphor is taken from wax, which, when it is hard, does not take the figure of the seal but, when it is soft, is easily shaped into everything. Thus the heart of man stands at a place where four roads intersect. For when it clings to God, its nature melts through the Word, softens toward God, and hardens toward the creature. But when it clings to the creature, it hardens toward God and softens toward the creature. For continually the human heart is now hard, now soft with regard to different things. For this clinging is the very faith in the Word. Indeed, it is that tie of betrothal about which Hos. 2:20 says: "I will betroth you to Me in faithfulness," according to the well-known statement in 1 Cor. 6:17: [18] "He who clings to God is one spirit with Him." "The prisoner follows the lover." [19]

It follows as a corollary that faith in Christ is every virtue and that unbelief is every vice, as is sufficiently clear from what has been said. For through faith a man becomes like the Word of God, but the Word is the Son of God. In this way, however, it comes about that everyone who believes in God is a child of God, as John 1:12 says, and for this reason is without any sin and full of every virtue. On the other hand, he who does not believe is of necessity full of every vice and evil, namely, a child of the devil and of iniquity.

14. [*For we become partakers of Christ,*] *if only we hold the beginning of His substance* [*firm to the end*].

It is certain that in this place the shoes of philosophy should be removed from the feet of the faithful, for the word "substance" cannot be taken here as it is taken when qualities [20] are mentioned. Indeed, in Greek it is ὑπόστασις, not οὐσία. Therefore according to the usage of Scripture it means capability, or the possession of

---

[18] The original has "1 Cor. 7."

[19] Baptista Mantuanus, *Adulescentia* (Mantua, 1498), "Aegloga prima de honesto Amore & felici eius exitu," Aiiii (Fortunatus).

[20] The Latin term is *praedicamenta,* the ten categories of Aristotle's *Organon;* cf. *Luther's Works,* 4, p. 259, n. 35.

things, in this passage, as in Prov. 3:9: [21] "Honor the Lord with
your substance." And in Luke 8:43 we read about a woman who
"had spent all her substance on physicians." 1 John 3:17 states:
"If anyone has the substance of this world and sees his brother
in need, etc." In this statement the apostle John clearly points
out two kinds of substance: the one of this world, the other of the
life to come. Thus below, in ch. 10:34, the same thing is pointed
out: "You joyfully accepted the plundering of your property, since
you knew that you have a better substance and a lasting one."
And faith begins this, or faith is its beginning; for through faith
we begin to possess what we shall possess perfectly in sight.[22]
Thus below in ch. 11:1: "Now faith is the substance of things
hoped for," that is, the possession of future things. For in this
way St. Jerome explains Gal. 5:23, on the word "faith." [23] But
Chrysostom's understanding of *substantia* is different from Saint
Jerome's. He takes it to mean "essence" or "subsistence." For
he says in this place: "He calls the beginning of substance the faith
through which we have been born and subsist and—if I may speak
this way—have become essential." [24] This must be understood,
not of the natural subsistence but of the spiritual subsistence
in Christ, according to Eph. 2:10: "For we are His workmanship,
created . . . for good works." And John 3:5 says: "Unless one is
born again of water and the Spirit, he cannot enter the kingdom
of God." In Gal. 6:15 we read that in Christ "neither circumcision counts for anything, nor uncircumcision, but a new creature." James 1:18 says: "Of His own will He brought us forth by
the Word of truth, that we should be a kind of beginning of His
creation." Therefore we pray for "our daily bread." In Greek the
bread is called "supersubstantial," that is, the bread that transfers us into a new substance and creature in the Spirit.[25] To pray
is to speak well, elegantly, and distinctly. And even though this
interpretation of "substance" does not seem appropriate in the

[21] The original has "Prov. 5."

[22] An allusion to the distinction between faith and sight in 2 Cor. 5:7.

[23] Jerome, *Commentaria in epistolam ad Galatas*, Book III, ch. 5, *Patrologia, Series Latina*, XXVI, 420; cf. also *Luther's Works*, 27, p. 377.

[24] Chrysostom, *Homiliae*, VI, 2, col. 56 (279).

[25] An allusion to the Vulgate of Matt. 6:11: "Panem nostrum supersubstantialem da nobis hodie," where the Latin neologism "supersubstantialem" was
a literal transposition from the puzzling Greek term in the original.

commendation of faith below in ch. 11:1 — for there "of things hoped for" modifies substance — yet even in this passage it cannot seem inappropriate. Therefore let us unite both into one; for through faith Christ is called our "substance," that is, riches, and through the same faith we simultaneously become His "substance," that is, a new creature.

15. *Today, if you hear His voice, [do not harden your hearts as in the rebellion].*

St. Chrysostom [26] thinks that here there is a hyperbaton (that is, a transposition and disturbance of the order), namely, in such a way that the words "for some who heard" (v. 16) up to the words "for we shall enter" (4:3) have been inserted and thus interrupt the order, and that this is the order of the words: "Therefore . . . let us fear, etc.," up to "we shall enter"; then "for some who hear, etc.," should follow up to "Therefore . . . let us fear." Then "While it is heard: 'Today, if you hear His voice, etc.'" should follow. And this is the end of the hyperbaton. Then "for we shall enter, etc.," follows. And it is right in a teacher who is so highly learned in Greek.

16. *[For some who heard rebelled,] but not all those who came out [of Egypt under Moses].*

One should note that the exodus of the Children of Israel from Egypt was not only physical. Indeed, it was spiritual at the same time, as the apostle states clearly in 1 Cor. 10:1-4: "I want you to know, brethren, that our fathers were all under the cloud, and all passed through the sea, and all were baptized into Moses in the cloud and in the sea, and all ate the same spiritual food, and all drank the same spiritual drink." How, then, will these words stand, namely, that he says "all" there but "some" here, yes, that there he immediately adds: "But with many of them God was not pleased, for they were overthrown, etc."? The answer is that there as well as here the apostle is speaking to those who have attained "the beginning of the substance of Christ." To persuade them to persevere he sets before them the example of those who all made a good beginning but did not persevere. Therefore they did not arrive either. Consequently, in the same place the apostle — after

26 Chrysostom, *Homiliae*, VI, 2, 56 (279).

he had said that all had been baptized and yet that some had later been overthrown — concluded by saying: "Therefore let anyone who thinks that he stands take heed lest he fall" (1 Cor. 10:12). This means: "When you see what has happened to them, preserve with fear what you have begun, lest you fall in like manner." Here he gives an exhortation that is similar in all respects. "Since we have become sharers in Christ," he says, "and have the beginning of His substance" — that is, since we have begun happily, just as they had — let us fear, lest by defecting we abandon "the beginning of the substance," as they abandoned it and deserted. And according to my own idea, I think that the text "Some who heard rebelled, but not all" should be understood in the following way: Not all rebelled when they came out of Egypt, but all were believers at that time, as Ex. 12:50 says and as is stated above in 1 Cor. 10:2 that "all were baptized, etc." Accordingly, all began the exodus well through Moses, but later they failed to make progress; therefore He says: "For 40 years I was provoked." What is more by far, however, they did not arrive. Therefore he says that God swore to those defectors that they would not enter His rest.

CHAPTER FOUR

1. [*Therefore, while the promise of entering His rest remains*] *let us fear* [*lest anyone of you be judged to be found wanting*].

CHRYSOSTOM has "lest anyone of you," [1] although on the basis of what Faber says,[2] it seems that one should read "but anyone of us," because "let us fear" is spoken in the first person, and the text does not have "you should fear." Likewise below (v. 2), where the text has "for good news came to *us*," in the first person, not "to *you*." But his reason is not sufficiently impelling, since it is characteristic of the Holy Scriptures to change the persons, the tenses, the numbers, and the moods in various ways. In fact, 1 Peter 2:21 says: "Christ suffered for us that you may follow," not "that we may follow."

To be found wanting, etc.

Chrysostom interprets the expression "to be found wanting," Faber with "to be disregarded," Erasmus with "to have been disappointed," "not to have achieved," namely, that although others go forward and enter, they remain behind them. For this is what happened to those who were overthrown in the wilderness. And the words "remains" and "to be found wanting" are spoken for the sake of a beautiful antithesis. This means: "Let us fear, lest while we abandon the promise because of unbelief, God's rest also abandon us because of God's wrath." The other part of the contradictions is true, etc.[3]

2. *For good news also came to us* [*just as to them*].

The Greek text has "We, too, have been evangelized, just

---

[1] Chrysostom, *Homiliae*, VI, 2, col. 56 (279).

[2] The Sixtine text of the Vulgate was also to have the reading *nobis* rather than *vobis*.

[3] We have followed the Weimar editor and attached this "addition" to the preceding paragraph.

as they have been." For this is how it is stated in Latin: "We are taught" and "We have been taught." Therefore just as in this place, the translator has rightly changed the case and the verb, namely, the nominative to the dative and the passive verb to an impersonal verb, in this way he should have made "the poor are evangelized" in Matt. 11:5 to read "to the poor it has been evangelized" or "it is evangelized."

But the message which was heard did not profit them.

Chrysostom has it this way: "The message of the proclamation did not profit those who were not combined by faith in the things they had heard." Faber follows him and translates this way: "But the Word of hearing did not profit them, when those who heard were not united to the faith." For he, together with Chrysostom, does not read *admixtus* ("united"), in the singular, but *admixtis*, in the plural, so that it refers to the pronoun "those." Erasmus, however, has *admixtus*, in the singular, and translates as follows: "It did not profit them to have heard the message, because it had not been united by faith with those who had heard." Yet this is of little importance, for that uniting or combination of the Word and the hearts is reciprocal. For these three — faith, the Word, and the heart — become one. Faith is the glue or the bond. The Word is on one side; the heart is on the other side. But through faith they become one spirit, just as man and wife become "one flesh" (Gen. 2:24). Therefore it is true that the heart is combined with the Word through faith and that the Word is combined with the heart through the same faith.

3. [*For we who have believed shall enter into His rest, as He has said: As I swore in My wrath: They shall never enter My rest*], *and indeed from the works finished at the foundation of the world.*

This translation is obscure. But it seems that this was written by the apostle for the sake of explaining "My rest," which he had said, and of distinguishing that rest, so that if someone were to ask: "What is that rest of the Lord into which we shall enter?" the answer would be that it is that rest "from the works finished at the foundation of the world." Therefore Faber translates as follows: "As I swore in My wrath: they shall not enter into My rest, namely, from the works completed at the foundation of the world." According to this meaning, the text should be arranged and understood this way: We shall enter His rest, that is, the rest that is His from the works finished at the foundation of the world. Likewise the words "into My rest," that is, the rest that is Mine, namely, since the foundation of the world, etc.

But when our translation says "and indeed," one must understand something, that is, "As if I were calling that My rest which is Mine after the foundation of the world, etc." Therefore Chrysostom, who has "although," must be understood as follows: "We shall enter into His rest, although from the foundation of the world"; that is, although there has been rest since the beginning of the world, yet one shall not enter it. This is certainly the opposite of the rest of man, which is prepared after work. But this rest is prepared before our work.

4. *And God rested* [*on the seventh day from all His works*].

St. Augustine explains God's resting in a threefold way in the ninth chapter of the fourth book of his work on Genesis, *De Genesi ad litteram.*[4] First in this way: "Just as it is right to say that God does whatever we do when He works in us, so it is right to say that God rests when we rest because of His gift." But this is the tropological meaning, because it suggests God's effective rest, about which Is. 11:2 says: "And the Spirit of the Lord shall rest upon Him." And in the last chapter of the same book: "In whom My Spirit will rest, etc."

Therefore in the second place, below in chapter 12, he mentions another meaning when he says that "God rested from the making of new kinds of creatures," although John 5:17 states: "My Father is working still, and I am working." For this, says St. Augustine, refers to the management of the creatures, not to the act of creating them. In the third place, he has this to say in chapter 16: "To those who have the right understanding God's rest is the rest by reason of which He needs the blessing of no one and is blessed in Himself." And the text can be taken in the first and third way here, when He says: "They shall never enter My rest." The second way is somewhat obscure. For we shall come into His rest when we have begun to have no further need

---

4 Augustine, *De Genesi ad litteram*, Book IV, chs. 9—16, pars. 16—27, *Patrologia, Series Latina*, XXXIV, 302—306.

of any blessing. But this will be when, according to what the apostle says in 1 Cor. 15:28, "God will be all in all."

In order that we may grasp in some measure the nature of that rest, it is necessary to note that man, like Noah's ark, "has three chambers" and is divided into three men, namely, the sensual, the rational, and the spiritual man.[5] Man is called a microcosm, that is, a smaller world. Every one of those men rests and is disturbed or troubled in a twofold way, namely, either inwardly or outwardly. In the first place, the sensual man rests outwardly when he takes pleasure in something that is perceptible. This is what it means to rest positively. On the other hand, he is disturbed and troubled when that which is perceptible is disturbed or removed. But he rests inwardly when he rests negatively, that is, when, because of the work of the rational man, he has no work or nothing perceptible to be occupied with, as is clear in the case of men who think and speculate. On the other hand, he is disturbed inwardly when, alongside the disturbance of the rational man, he is confused, as is clear in the case of those who are sad and melancholy. In the second place, the rational man rests outwardly and positively in his rational and speculable objects if they are pleasant. But he is disturbed outwardly if they are sad. He rests inwardly and negatively, however, when he ceases from his work, and the spiritual man occupies himself with faith and the Word. But he is disturbed inwardly when, alongside the disturbance of the spiritual man—namely, when he is in danger of losing faith and the Word—he himself is also disturbed. For this disturbance is the most horrible of all, since it is most profound and is very close to hell. In the third place, the spiritual man rests outwardly in the Word and in faith, namely, positively, as long as the object of his faith, that is, the Word, remains fixed in him. But he is disturbed outwardly when his faith is in danger— as has been said—and when the Word is withdrawn, as happens when faith, hope, and love are tried. For this is the man who "lives by the Word of God" (Matt. 4:4; Luke 4:4). He rests inwardly, however, when he rests negatively, namely, when he is lifted up by faith and the Word into the essential work of God, which is the very birth of the uncreated Word, as He says: "This is eternal life, that they know Thee, the true God, and Jesus

[5] Cf. Augustine, *De Trinitate*, Book XII, ch. 7, par. 9, *Patrologia, Series Latina*, XLII, 1003.

Christ, whom Thou hast sent" (John 17:3), that is, the procession of the Son from the Father. And here there is no inward disturbance, for this seventh day has no evening by which it could pass over into another day. And from what has been stated one gets, in a way, a brief exposition of both kinds of theology, namely, the affirmative and the negative.[6]

11. *Let us therefore hasten to enter into that rest.*

That hastening is spiritual, and it is the hastening of spiritual feet. But here there are fervent desires like those the apostle had when he said: "My desire is to depart and be with Christ" (Phil. 1:23). And there are those words in Ps. 120:5: "Woe is me, that my sojourn has been prolonged!" These are the people for whom this life is weariness and sickness. This is how St. Augustine describes his mother in the ninth book of his *Confessions.*[7] And about himself he says in a letter: "I long for the coming of my last day." [8] Thus it is also recorded about Abraham, David, and many other fathers that they died "in good old age," "full of days," "sated with days," and "weary of this life." On the contrary, concerning those who are unbelievers, who still have a taste for this life, it is said: "Men of blood and treachery shall not live out half their days" (Ps. 55:23), because they do not get enough of this life. Therefore it should be the one desire of Christians to die to this life more and more every day and, because they are weary of it, to hasten to the life to come. Otherwise they will be numbered with those about whom Ps. 106:24 [9] says: "And they despised the pleasant land."

12. *For the Word of God is living and powerful.*

These words are explained in two ways. First as an exhortation, as Lyra, Faber, and some others do.[10] But their explanation is so

<hr>

[6] Cf. Dionysius the Areopagite, *De mystica theologia*, ch. 3, *Patrologia, Series Graeca*, III, 1032.

[7] Augustine, *Confessiones*, Book IX, ch. 10, par. 26, *Patrologia, Series Latina*, XXXII, 775.

[8] Augustine, *Epistolae ad Bonifacium*, XV, *Patrologia, Series Latina*, XXXIII, 1098.

[9] The original has "Ps. 77 [78]."

[10] Nicolaus de Lyra, *Postilla super epistolas Pauli Apostoli*, with the *Additiones* of Paulus Burgensis (Mantua, 1488), *ad* Heb. 4:12; hereafter referred to as *Postilla*.

obscure that one can scarcely believe that they themselves understand it. Nevertheless, let us help in whatever way we can. In the first place, "it is living," it gives life to those who believe. Therefore we must hasten, lest we perish in death. In the second place, it is "powerful," because it makes those who believe able to do everything. In the third place, "it is sharper than any two-edged sword," because it is nearer and more available to all than things are to themselves. In Jer. 23:23-24 we read: "Am I a God at hand . . . and not a God afar off? . . . Do I not fill heaven and earth? says the Lord." Prov. 15:11 says: "Hell and destruction are before the Lord; how much more the hearts of the children of men!" And Ps. 139, in its entirety, states this most beautifully of all: "O Lord, Thou hast searched me." Therefore since the Lord is present everywhere, one should believe in Him with all confidence; for He can help us everywhere, even if everything forsakes us everywhere. In the fourth place, "to the division of soul and spirit," that is, by separating the affections of the mind from the affection of the soul; for faith cleanses the heart everywhere, as Acts 15:9 says. And Ps. 19:8 says: "The Law of the Lord is perfect, etc." In the fifth place, "of joints and marrow," because it separates the members and the marrow from evil affections and thus purifies not only the heart but also the body. In the sixth place, "it discerns the thoughts and intentions of the heart" by rejecting evil counsels and desires, that is, one's own feeling and one's own will, which sometimes rule even in the saints.

A SECOND EXPLANATION

Secondly and better, these words are understood as a threat of cruel punishment for unbelievers. Therefore Chrysostom says: "Indeed, it is crueller than any sword: for it will fall upon (that is, will cut) the souls of those inflicting cruel wounds and fatal cuts." [11] But Chrysostom does not state what the nature of these wounds is. He says: "He need not determine what these things are; nor does he consider it necessary to mention them all, since he has such a clear account." And it is true that these horrible blows are understood only by those who in some way have experienced them, men like David, Hezekiah, and many others.

[11] Chrysostom, *Homiliae*, VII, 1, col. 62 (285).

For no punishment is on a par with the punishment which the godless endure from the mere presence of the angry countenance
of God, as Ps. 21:9 states: "Thou wilt make them as a blazing oven
at the time of Thy angry countenance." And in Wisd. 6:6 we read:
"Swiftly and horribly they will appear to you." And 2 Thess. 1:8-9
states that "those who do not obey the Gospel of our Lord Jesus
Christ shall suffer eternal punishments in their ruin, away from
the face of the Lord and from the glory of His power." Therefore
since the Word of God is above all things, outside all things, within
all things, before all things, behind all things, and therefore everywhere, it is impossible to escape to any place. But since it is
"living" and therefore eternal, it is impossible for the punishment or the cutting ever to cease. But since it is "powerful" and
potent, it is impossible to resist it. Finally, since it is "sharper
than any two-edged sword," it is impossible to hide or to be con-
cealed. And thus the unbelievers will be tortured with endless,
eternal, and incurable cutting. About this matter, St. Bernard
speaks beautifully and extensively in the fifth book of his *De
consideratione*.[12] And from this punishment there finally follows
"the division of soul and spirit, of joints and marrow," the cutting,
the disturbance, and the confusion of all internal and external
powers, according to the statement in Eccles. 9:10: "Neither work
nor reason nor wisdom nor knowledge shall be in hell." Here,
therefore, there is that trembling and confusion about which
Scripture speaks very frequently. Therefore Is. 2:10, 21 counsels:
"Enter into the rock, and hide in the dust (that is, believe in
Christ the crucified) from the face of the terror of the Lord and
from the glory of His majesty. . . . when He rises to terrify the
earth." This is the kind of counsel the apostle gives here, too, with
regard to the announced punishment when he exhorts to approach
the great High Priest.

Sharper.

"Sharper." Better: "more penetrating" or "more cutting" then
"than a two-edged sword." This means a sword that cuts twice,
or on both sides. For this is how it is in Greek: δίστομος.

[12] Bernard of Clairvaux, *De consideratione*, Book V, ch. 11, *Patrologia, Series
Latina*, CLXXXII, 802.

And piercing to the division of soul and spirit.

In conformity with philosophy it is said that substantial form, but especially the human form, is indivisible.[13] Hence those subtleties of opinions as to whether the powers of the soul differ actually, substantially, or with regard to form. A habit results from frequently repeated acts. Walking simply in faith, however, we shall follow the apostle, who, in 1 Thessalonians (5:23), divides man into three parts when he says: "May your spirit and soul and body be kept sound and blameless at the coming of the Lord." On the other hand, in 1 Cor. 14:15 he divides man into mind and spirit when he says: "I will sing with the spirit, and I will sing with the mind also." But the Blessed Virgin Mary also says: "He has scattered the proud in the mind of their hearts" (Luke 1:51). Indeed, Christ Himself divides in various ways when He says: "You shall love the Lord your God with all your heart, with all your mind, with all your soul, with all your strength, or with all your powers." Therefore Origen took more pains with regard to this matter than anyone else; [14] and after him St. Jerome says with reference to Gal. 5:17 that, as is known to all, the body, or the flesh, is our lowest part, the spirit, by which we are capable of divine things, is our highest part, but the soul is our middle part between the two.[15] If these words are understood in the way St. Augustine, too, divides man into a higher and a lower part, and also the soul,[16] they are clear and have been satisfactorily stated above.

Of joints and marrow.

Some Greek texts are said to have "of joints and members," and certainly that text would fit very well, so that "members" would be set against "joints" in the body, just as "soul" and "spirit" are set against "thoughts" in the mind and "intentions" in the heart.

---

[13] Cf. Reisch, *Margarita philosophica*, Book VIII, ch. 9: "De forma."

[14] Cf. Origen, *De principiis*, Book III, ch. 4, par. 2, *Patrologia, Series Graeca*, XI, 320—322.

[15] Jerome, *Commentaria in epistolam ad Galatas*, ch. 5, *Patrologia, Series Latina*, XXVI, 411.

[16] Cf. Augustine, *De Trinitate*, Book XII, ch. 7, par. 9, *Patrologia, Series Latina*, XLII, 1003.

13. *To whom we have to give account.*

Some want "to whom we have to give account" to mean "about whom we have to give account," just as above in ch. 1, v. 7, they want "to the angels He says" to mean "about the angels He says." [17] "To whom we have to give account" can also mean that it is the purpose of the account which we give to you to bring us to Him about whom we speak. Thus Ps. 122:6 employs the same idiomatic way of speaking and says: "Pray for the peace of Jerusalem," that is, for the things that make for peace or pertain to peace.

14. *Having, therefore, a great High Priest.*

For to those who have been terrified in consequence of the fear of that eternal judgment and that horrible cutting and division, no other refuge is left than that one sanctuary which is Christ, our Priest, in whose humanity alone we are protected and saved from a judgment of this kind, as Ps. 91:4 says: "He will cover you with His pinions, and under His wings you will find refuge." And Mal. 4:2 says: "For you who fear My name the Sun of righteousness shall rise, with healing in His wings." And He Himself says in Matt. 23:37: "How often would I have gathered your children together as a hen, etc." Hence there is that frequent statement in the Psalms (Ps. 63:7): "I will exult in the cover of Thy wings." Likewise (Ps. 27:5): "Thou hast protected me in the secret place of Thy tabernacle." To this those words in Prov. 30:24-28 also pertain: "Four things on earth are small, but they are exceedingly wise: The ants are a people not strong, yet they provide their food in the summer; the badgers are a people not mighty, yet they make their homes in the rocks; the locusts have no king, yet all of them march in rank; the lizard you can take in your hands, yet, it is in kings' palaces." Thus in Song of Sol. 2:14 the bridegroom says about the bride: "O my love in the clefts of the rocks and in the caves of affliction." Therefore the apostle also introduces Christ here more as a Priest than as a Lord and Judge, in order that He may console those who are frightened.

---

[17] Faber, *Epistolae,* f. 237 A.

CHAPTER FIVE

1. *For every high priest chosen from among men* [*is appointed to act on behalf of men in relation to God, to offer gifts — sacrifices for sins*].

THIS discourse gives the emphasis to that phrase "on behalf of men." It is as if he were saying: "Let us approach the throne of grace with confidence and without fear, because we have Jesus Christ as our High Priest." If we have a High Priest, He is certainly for us and not against us, since "every high priest," even "one appointed and chosen from among men is appointed for men," as Ex. 28:38 states: "And Aaron shall take upon himself any guilt incurred in the holy offering which the people of Israel hallow." This definitely prefigured that Christ, the High Priest, would bear the sins of all who bring offerings, that is, who believe. For He not only shows sin, as Moses does; but He also bears sins and takes them away, as Aaron does. Thus Ps. 77:20 declares: "Thou didst lead the Children of Israel by the hand of Moses and Aaron," not only by the hand of Moses but rather by the hand of Aaron; for "knowledge of sin" (Rom. 3:20) through Moses, that is, through the Law, leads no one to life unless there is both remission of sin and cleansing from it through Aaron, that is, through grace. And Num. 18:1 says: "The Lord said to Aaron: 'You and your sons and your father's house with you shall bear the iniquity of the sanctuary, and you and your sons with you shall bear the sins of your priesthood.'" Here He names "the iniquity of the sanctuary" and "the sins of the priesthood," not because the sanctuary or the priesthood have committed them, but because it is the nature and the duty of the priesthood to be the bearer and the carrier of sins. Therefore they are its sins because it bears them and takes them away from others. Here again Christ was pictured as the true Aaron and "the Lamb of God, who takes away the sins of the world" (John 1:29). Therefore in this passage the apostle describes His priesthood as having reached its peak and accomplished its work when He cried out for us on the cross, as is stated later. Thus Is. 53:4 states: "Surely He has borne our weaknesses and carried our sins." He certainly would not do this if He were not a Priest for us and not against us. Thus we read below, in ch. 12:22, 24: "You have come to . . . Jesus, the Mediator of a new covenant, and to the sprinkled blood that speaks better than Abel." For the blood of Abel cries out for wrath and vengeance, but the blood of Christ cries out for forgiveness and mercy. This is what Is. 27:2-4 says: "In that day there shall be singing to the vineyard of pure wine. I am the Lord who keeps it. Suddenly I will give it drink; lest any hurt come to it, I keep it night and day. There is no indignation in Me. Who will make Me a thorn and a brier?" Behold, He Himself keeps His church, lest any hurt come to it. For if any hurt came to it, it could not be kept. But hurt would come to it if there were any indignation in Him or He Himself were in any way a thorn. This keeping, however, is nothing else than the strengthening of a terrified conscience by His appearance. Therefore all priests should imitate this Priest and know that they are not priests for themselves but for others, in order that they may bear the iniquities of others, lest perchance they preside to their own destruction and to the destruction of others, as Ezek. 34:2-5 says: "Woe to the shepherds of Israel, who fed themselves! Should not the flocks be fed by the shepherds? You ate the milk, and you clothed yourselves with the wool, and you killed that which was fat. . . . The weak you have not strengthened, and that which was sick you have not healed; that which was broken you have not bound up, and that which was driven away you have not brought again. Neither have you sought that which was lost; but you ruled over them with vigor and with a high hand. And My sheep were scattered because there was no shepherd." Add, therefore, to this these words in Zech. 11:16-17: "I will raise up a shepherd in the land who shall not visit what is forsaken nor seek what is scattered, nor heal what is broken, nor nourish that which stands; and He shall eat the flesh of the fat ones and break their hooves. O shepherd and idol that forsakes the flock!" As for the rest, read what the apostle says in 1 Tim. 3:2 and in Titus 1:7 and 2:7: "For a bishop must be above reproach." Therefore every priest should know that he is a priest not for himself but for others, and he should strive above all to be en-

[W, LVII-3, 167, 168]

dowed with the greatest mercy, in order that he may know how to bear the sins and the ignorance of others. For thus one reads throughout the Book of Judges: "And the Lord raised up a deliverer for them." Therefore they are pictured as priests, called priests, and commanded to be priests who should have the same reputation that formerly the kings of Israel had, so that even their enemies were confident of their mercy. For in 1 Kings 20:31,[1] when the servants of Benhadad, the king of Syria, had been overcome and crushed twice by Israel, they said to their lord: "Behold, we have heard that the kings of Israel are merciful. Let us put sackcloth on our loins . . . and go out to the king of Israel, and perhaps he will save our lives." And this is how it happened. With respect to this very thing priests are reminded that, beyond other Christians, they are anointed on their fingers, not so much for the purpose of being worthy to touch the sacrament of the body of Christ as to deal gently with the matter of the same sacrament, that is, with the people of Christ. But now these consecrated hands and anointed fingers are being soaked in fury more dreadful than any poison, in such a way that they wield arms and cannon,[2] and wield these only against and in opposition to the matter of the same sacrament, that is, against the most gracious Father's beloved children in Christ. They do so with the greatest violence, namely, because they are enraged and hasten with panting piety to burn a few Jews who pierce the hosts of the sacrament with small lances or cut them with small knives.[3] But they do not slay the hosts; they slay the matter itself, and not with small lances but with cannon and all the commotion and violence of their weapons. And in all this they do not realize that what the Lord is doing in the case of the Jews is a figurative warning to teach them that they, who are persecuting the matter of the sacrament so furiously and hellishly, are seven times worthier of fire and every death. Therefore these priests chosen rather from among demons are also appointed on behalf of demons against Christ

---

[1] The original has "4 Kings [2 Kings]."

[2] Luther is objecting here to the involvement of priests and monks in feudal warfare, but later in the paragraph he singles out Pope Julius as the special target of his polemic.

[3] In 1510 there had been a pogrom in Brandenburg, brought on by such accusations, and Luther would seem to be referring to it here.

and the Christians. Julius above all.[4] For God promised those who would be His people that they would be treated in no other way by their priests than as most tender children, as Is. 66:12-13 says: "You shall be carried at the breasts, and upon the knees they shall caress you. As one whom the mother caresses, so will I comfort you, and you shall be comforted in Jerusalem." Therefore we deserved to be brought to these outcroppings of madness and to these hellish monstrosities as long as we abandoned the sacred and divine writings and preferred the writings of men. For the devil could introduce this kind of madness into the church only when he has succeeded in having that sword, the Word of God —the sword that can be turned and is more terrible to him than all hell—laid aside and allowed to waste away in rust, and when he has succeeded in seeing us occupying ourselves with the straw and stubble, with the chicks and feathers, of human calculations and arrangements, that is, with the specters and the vampires of the most trivial opinions.

Is appointed to act on behalf of men.

One should note that it is not enough for a Christian to believe that Christ was appointed to act on behalf of men unless he believes that he, too, is one of those men. For both the demons and the godless know that Christ is a Priest for men, but they do not believe this way about themselves. In a sermon about the Annunciation, the text of which is "that glory may dwell in our land" (Ps. 85:9), St. Bernard speaks axiomatically in the following way: "It is necessary for you to believe that God can remit your sins, bestow grace on you and give glory to you. And this is not enough, unless you believe with complete certainty that your sins have been remitted, that grace has been bestowed on you, and that glory is to be given to you."[5] And this is the testimony of our conscience—the testimony which the Spirit of God gives to our spirit. Concerning this the apostle says in 2 Cor. 1:12: "Our boast is this, the testimony of our conscience." For, as St. Bernard says, the testimony of the conscience is not understood as being

---

[4] Julius II, who was pope from 1503 to 1513, was noted more for his military prowess than for his churchmanship and was satirized for this in *The Praise of Folly* of Erasmus.

[5] Cf. Bernard of Clairvaux, *Sermo in festo Annuntiationis Beatae Mariae Virginis*, I, 3, *Patrologia, Series Latina*, CLXXXIII, 383—384.

of the kind that is to us from us—for this is Pelagian—and glory in shame, but as the testimony which our conscience receives, just as it receives righteousness and truth, etc. Therefore it comes about that no one attains grace because he is absolved or baptized or receives Communion or is anointed, but because he believes that he attains grace by being absolved, baptized, receiving Communion, and being anointed in this way. For that very commonly known and completely established statement is true, that it is not the sacrament but faith in the sacrament that justifies.[6] Likewise the well-known statement of St. Augustine: "It justifies not because it is performed, but because it is believed." [7] From these statements it follows that it is a most pernicious error to say that the sacraments of the new law are efficacious signs of grace in such a way that they do not require any disposition in the recipient except that he should put no obstacle in the way.[8] They call the actual committing of a mortal sin an obstacle. This is altogether false. Indeed, any sacrament requires a completely pure heart. Otherwise the recipient will be guilty of the sacrament and will incur judgment upon himself (cf. 1 Cor. 11:27). But the heart is not purified except through faith, as Acts 15:9 says. For Philip did not baptize the eunuch without ascertaining that he had faith. Nor is any infant baptized now unless one replies for it: "I believe." Therefore it does not attain grace because it is baptized, but because it believes. Thus there is also a great error on the part of those who approach the Sacrament of the Eucharist in reliance on the well-known plea that they have gone to confession, that they are not conscious of a mortal sin or have said their prayers and made their preparations beforehand. All those people eat and drink judgment unto themselves, for they do not become worthy and pure because of all this. On the contrary, through this confidence in their purity they are polluted all the worse. But if they believe and are confident that they will attain grace, this faith alone makes them pure and worthy—this faith which does not rely on those words but relies on the completely pure, holy, and firm Word of Christ, who says (Matt. 11:28): "Come

[6] Cf. Peter Lombard, *Sententiae*, Book IV, Dist. 4, chs. 4—5, *Patrologia, Series Latina*, CXCII, 847—849.

[7] Cf. Augustine, *In Joannis Evangelium Tractatus*, Ch. XV, Tr. LXXX, 3, *Patrologia, Series Latina*, XXXV, 1840.

[8] See p. 192, n. 9.

to Me, all who labor and are heavy-laden, and I will give you rest."
Therefore one must approach with confidence in these words,
and those who approach in this way will not be confounded.

4. *And one does not take the honor upon himself, but he is called
by God, [just as Aaron was].*

God calls to the priesthood in two ways. In the first place, in
such a way that he who has been called does not seek or desire
this, just as Aaron was called; for he did not know why (God) called
him. This will take place either through a miracle from God alone,
as in the case of the apostle Paul, or it will take place through
a mandate of the church. In the second place, by inspiration, so
that he who has been called desires and seeks this. This is shown
by the apostle in 1 Tim. 3:1: "He who desires the office of bishop
desires a good work." In this statement one must be careful to
observe that it gives expression to the "office" of the episcopate
rather than to the dignity. This is clear from the force of the word,
for the Greek verb ἐπισκοπεῖν means "to superintend" or "to over-
see," just as the watchmen and guards of cities are called investi-
gators or superintendents. Hence Zion, the citadel of David and
the highest point of Jerusalem, is called "a watchtower" in Latin [9]
and for this reason typifies the priesthood, whose task it is to watch
over and superintend Jerusalem, that is, the church. The same
thing is clear from the statement that follows. For it says "desires
a good work," not a good thing. This designates clearly that the
episcopate is only a work, and a "good work," but not leisure.
The others who climb, namely, out of love or desire for leisure,
pleasure, and honor, these are the ones who "take the honor
upon themselves."

6. *[Thou art a Priest forever] after the order of Melchizedek.*

That phrase "after the order" means the arrangement, that is,
according to the procedure followed by Melchizedek and according to what he did. What he did is established and recorded in
Gen. 14:18 ff. Therefore this should mean not only that Christ
offers bread and wine, as Melchizedek did, but according to everything that is recorded in the same place, as the apostle explains

[9] Jerome, *Liber interpretationis Hebraicorum nominum*, 3 Kings [1 Kings],
"S," *Corpus Christianorum, Series Latina*, LXXII, 112.

in an excellent way below, in ch. 7, namely, that he, as the greater,
blessed Abraham, even though Abraham was the father of the
priests of the Levites and had the promises. Likewise that he
received tithes from Abraham. Likewise that he was without
genealogy, without beginning and without end. Nevertheless,
in Hebrew the word דָּבָר properly means deed or the account of
a deed, or a matter, as in the well-known psalm: "They bent the
bow, a bitter thing" (Ps. 64:3). Here, however, דִּבְרָתִי is used, that
is, after the order. This certainly comes from the word דָּבָר. Paul
will set forth the rest.

7. *In the days of His flesh.*

Why the apostle says "in the days," in the plural, can seem
strange, even though he seems to be speaking about that one day,
namely, the day on which Christ offered Himself on the cross.
For He was offered only once and on one day. It can be said that
he takes the part for the whole, according to the Hebrew custom,
that is, that "days" are taken collectively for the whole time of
His life, during a part of which He offered Himself. For this is
a very common way of speaking in the Scriptures, as is clear in
the Book of Kings (2 Kings 24:1): "In his days the King of Syria [10]
came up," and the like. For we say that what happens during
a part of a month, a year, and a day happens in a year, in a month,
and on a day. In fact, it is our custom to say: "This thing took place
in my days, that is, during the time in which I lived, but not during
the whole time or on all the days." But why does he speak with
such care that he says "in the days of His flesh" when "in His
days" would seem to be sufficient? The answer is that he did this
as one learned in the Scriptures, since just as Christ is a Person
of a twofold nature, a temporal and an eternal nature, so Scripture
attributes to Him two kinds of days, times, and ages. For in Micah
5:2 it is stated: "His going forth is from the beginning, from the
days of eternity." Here again he speaks of "days" collectively,
namely, the eternal brightness itself. He calls this "the days of
eternity" to distinguish it from the days of temporality, when He
began "to go forth in Bethlehem as Ruler in Israel." Thus Is. 26:4
distinguishes the ages clearly and says: "You have hoped in the

---

[10] Although the original has *rex Syriae* and we have translated accordingly,
2 Kings 24:1 speaks of "Nebuchadnezzar king of Babylon."

Lord in eternal ages," that is, you have hoped in eternal ages in Him who is the Lord. Hence the Psalms use the expressions "for an age" and "for ages of ages." And Titus 1:4 says: "which He promised before the times of the ages and of the world." Here, therefore, Paul calls "the days of Christ's flesh" the time of this present life to distinguish it from the days of His divinity.

[Jesus offered up] prayers and supplications, [with loud cries and tears, to Him who was able to save Him from death].

How the apostle wants these two to differ is uncertain, unless perhaps they differ in the way Phil. 4:6 distinguishes them. There we read: "But in every prayer and supplication with thanksgiving let your petitions be made known to God." Consequently, by "prayers" he means the petitions by which we show what we want; but by "supplications" he means the entreaties and prayers with which we strive to influence a judge and to get what we ask for by adducing our need, due, the violence of our opponent, etc., as in rhetoric. And His words "Father, forgive them; for they know not what they do" (Luke 23:34) seem to support this meaning. But with the word "Father" He wins for Himself very briefly and most efficaciously the affection of Him to whom He is praying, for no affection is more efficacious than the affection between a son and a father. With the words "Forgive them" He designates the petitions or prayers; for they point out what is being asked for, namely, the remission of sins. But with the words "for they know not what they do" he points out the supplication in a beautiful manner, for He humbly acknowledges and admits their guilt but extenuates it and makes it excusable. This is the best way to make supplication. One should also note that this text elucidates beautifully the mystery of the old sacrifices. For against the gifts and sacrifices which "the priests chosen from among men" offered, Paul here sets the "prayers and supplications" which Christ, who was mystically prefigured through them, offered. Therefore calves, goats, and the other sacrifices—in addition to the fact that they signify tropologically the mortification of the flesh and the members on earth, as is taught in Rom. 12:1 and Col. 3:5—also prefigured offerings of prayers and praises. For Christ made the justification of the new law so easy that we can accomplish with the mouth what they could scarcely obtain with everything they

[W, LVII-3, 174, 175]

had, even with their physical goods. Therefore Hos. 14:2 says: "Take away all iniquity, and receive the good; and we will render the calves of our lips." The apostle comes close to this explanation below in ch. 13:15 when he says: "Through Him, then, let us continually offer up a sacrifice of praise to God, that is, the fruit of lips that acknowledge His name." Ps. 50, in its entirety, also applies to this. There we read: "Hear, O My people, and I will speak. O Israel, I will testify against you. I am God, your God (that is, I am not an idol or your creature, that I need your calves). I will not reprove you for your sacrifices; your burnt offerings are continually before Me (that is, the things you offer are already before Me, because 'they are all Mine')." And for this reason He concludes below (v. 23): "He that offers praise as a sacrifice will glorify Me." And again (v. 14): "Offer to God praise as your sacrifice" (that is, "what else do you offer when you offer yourself than praise of Me?"). In the same vein Is. 1:11 says: "What to Me is the multitude of your sacrifices?" And in the last chapter of Isaiah we read: "What is this house which you will build for Me?" (They, namely, the Jews, would reply: "This house built of stone and wood.") But the Lord continues: "All these things My hand has made, and all these things were made, says the Lord" (Is. 66:2). Nevertheless, this "sacrifice of praise" does not mean that praise with which even a godless person blesses God, as the well-known words in Ps. 48:19 state: "He will praise Thee when Thou hast done well to him." On the contrary, it means praise in the midst of sufferings, as the well-known words in Is. 48:9 prove: "For My name's sake I will remove My wrath far off from you (I will not condemn you); and for My praise I will bridle you, lest you perish," namely, in sufferings and chastisements; that is, when a man in the midst of bitterness of heart and in the agony of death even sings to God, saying (Ps. 119:137): "Righteous art Thou, O Lord, and right is Thy judgment." This is what the thief did on the cross and what David did in Ps. 119:54, when he said: "Thy punishments (that is, my tribulations) have been my songs in the place of my pilgrimage." Thus Ps. 42:8 [11] says: "By day the Lord commanded His mercy and by night His song," that is, praise and joy in tribulation. Hence hell is hell not because punishment is there, but because praise of God is not there, as Ps. 6:5 states: "For in death there is no one who re-

---

[11] The original has "Ps. 43 [44]."

members Thee." For God, with His justice, displeases them. Thus heaven is heaven not because joy is there, but because praise of God is there, as Ps. 84:4 states: "Blessed are those who dwell in Thy house, ever singing Thy praise." For God gives them pleasure, and for this reason they rejoice. Therefore a Christian, as a child of God, must always rejoice, always sing, fear nothing, always be free from care, and always glory in God.

And He was heard for His godly fear.

This ambiguous term "godly fear" gives rise to various meanings. For some take Christ's godly fear to be passive, namely, because He is the Son, then because He was called to the priesthood through God Himself.[12] For this very reason His Person should also be revered by all creatures. Others go to the ambiguous term in Greek. For the Greek word εὐλάβεια means "godly fear" as well as "dutiful love." [13] Therefore they take it to mean dutiful love, namely, the love the Father naturally has for the Son. And in my judgment this meaning seems to be the best, so that the meaning is that even though we were completely deserving of wrath, yet it was proper for the Father's love to hear the Son for us, so that the love He could not deny the Son is set against our iniquity, because of which He could have denied everything to every one of us. Therefore with this word the apostle calls forth for us confidence in God because God considered His love, not our iniquities. In the third place,[14] the word can be taken in an active sense, namely, the godly fear with which Christ revered the Father, so that because there was no man who did not despise God, He alone revered Him, as Is. 11:3 [15] states: "And the spirit of the fear of the Lord shall fill Him." But about all of us the well-known words of Ps. 36:1 [16] are said: "There is no fear of God before their eyes." Again, it is stated about Christ in Ps. 16:8: "I set the Lord ever before Me"; but about men Ps. 54:3 says: "They set not the Lord before their eyes." But the fear of God is the highest worship of God, so much so that there are some who say

12 Paul of Burgos, *Additio* I on Heb. 5:7, in Lyra, *Postilla.*

13 On *pietas*, see also p. 10, n. 5.

14 Cf., among others, Lyra, *Postilla,* ad Heb. 5:7.

15 The original has "Is. 7."

16 The original has "Ps. 13 [14]," probably referring to Ps. 14:2-3; Luther quotes the words of Ps. 36:1 as they appear in Rom. 3:18.

that it surpasses love. For in Gen. 31:42 even Jacob calls God "Fear" when he says: "If the God of my father Abraham and the Fear of Isaac had not been on my side, perhaps you would have sent me away empty-handed." Therefore even the Hebrews number "Fear" among the names of God.[17] To this even Is. 8:12-14 alludes in a manner that is not obscure. There we read: "Do not fear their fear or be in dread. Sanctify the Lord of Hosts Himself, and let Him be your Dread and your Fear. And He will be a sanctification to you." Hence the saints of the old law are commended more highly because of their fear of God. Besides, in 2 Sam. 23:3 David foretold among his last words that the kingdom of Christ as praised in his greatest and final proclamation would consist in the fear of God, saying: "The Ruler of men, the just Ruler in the fear of God." Therefore the meaning will be that Christ was heard, not because we were worthy – indeed, we were completely unworthy on account of our irreverence – but because His godly fear was worthy and was so great that He was heard for the sake even of those who were altogether unworthy and irreverent.

9. [*And being made perfect,*] *He became the source of salvation to those who obey Him.*

The man Christ is the mediating cause of salvation, as one says; [18] for as the Sign He is wont to be the cause of understanding and love. Thus Is. 11:10 speaks of "the Root of Jesse who stands for an Ensign of the people." In the same chapter (v. 12) we read: "The Lord will raise an Ensign for the nations and will assemble the outcasts of Israel." Likewise in Zech. 8:23: "In those days ten men of all languages of the Gentiles shall take hold of the robe of a Jew, saying: 'We will go with you.'" And in Jer. 13:11 the people of Christ are compared to "the girdle that sticks close to the loins of a man." In Is. 22:23-24 Christ is compared to a peg on which diverse kinds of vessels are hung. All this betokens that drawing of the Father by which as many as are saved are drawn through the revelation of Christ and cling to Him through faith. For this clinging is what the apostle means here with the words "to those who obey Him."

[17] Luther is probably referring to Gen. 31:42, as his comments on that passage (W, XLIV, 51—55) suggest.

[18] Cf. Peter Lombard, *Sententiae*, Book IV, Dist. 1, ch. 2, *Patrologia, Series Latina,* CXCII, 839.

11. [*About this we have much to say which is hard to explain,*] *since you have become dull of hearing.*

This is better expressed in Greek with the words "since you have become sluggish," so that it is properly in accord with what follows. For because of the time they ought to have been teachers if they had been watchful and eager in the understanding of the Scriptures. Now, however, they have been sluggish and have not worked that land of promise flowing with milk and honey, that is, Holy Scripture. For this reason what is stated in Prov. 24:30-31 has happened to them. There we read: "I passed by the field of the slothful man, and by the vineyard of the slothful man; and behold, it was all filled with nettles, and thorns had covered the face thereof, and the stone wall was broken down." By this it is pointed out that neglect of Scripture leads to nothing but thorny opinions, involved questions, and burning controversies, and causes Scripture in its entirety to have the look of being horribly uncultivated.

12. [*For though by this time you ought to be teachers, you need someone to teach you again*] *the first principles of God's words.*

Here the apostle makes a clear distinction, namely, that there are words of God for those who are perfect, for beginners, and necessarily therefore also for those who are making progress. This difference is not understood more easily than in accordance with that threefold theology also mentioned above, namely, symbolic, proper, and mystical theology [19]; or in the following way: sensual, rational, and spiritual theology. Dionysius calls the last type ἄλογος,[20] that is, illogical, namely, because it can be communicated or grasped neither by word nor by reason but only by experience. Symbolic theology is that which teaches how to learn to know God by means of figures and perceptible images, as formerly among the Jews in the temple, the tabernacle, the ark, in sacrifices, and the like. Today, too, these things are tolerated among Christians in the images that adorn the churches, in songs, in organs, and the like.

[19] Apparently a reference to p. 163, n. 6.

[20] Dionysius the Areopagite, *De coelesti hierarchia,* ch. 2, *Patrologia, Series Graeca,* III, 14—15.

CHAPTER SIX

1. *Therefore let us leave the elementary doctrines of Christ [and go on to maturity, not laying again a foundation of repentance from dead works and of faith toward God,*

2. *with instruction about ablutions, the laying on of hands, the resurrection of the dead, and eternal judgment].*

SOME think that the apostle is saying this to those who took for granted that Baptism should be repeated rather frequently and that catechetical instruction in the faith should take place again and again.[1] For these matters which the apostle adduces, namely, to believe in God, to believe in Christ, to believe in the Holy Spirit, to believe in one Baptism, to believe in the remission of sins, to believe in eternal life, are the things communicated to those who are to be catechized and baptized. Therefore they are also called the rudiments of faith in which those who are still uninformed are instructed, as is clear in the Apostles' Creed. And formerly, when adults were baptized, the rudiments were treated of in a solemn way; but now, because those who are baptized are baptized as little children, they are only read over those who are to be baptized. These are "the first principles of God's words" and "the elementary doctrine of Christ." But once this has been done, it is impossible to repeat it anew. Therefore all theologians say that the Sacrament of Baptism and Confirmation cannot be repeated.[2] And Chrysostom, too, seems to concur in this opinion when he says: "Since those who believe could perhaps be induced to lead an evil life or to live carelessly, he says: 'Be vigilant.' One should not say: 'Because we are living carelessly, we will be baptized again, be catechized again, and receive the Holy Spirit again. For if we fall from faith to the slightest degree, we shall be able to

[1] Faber, *Epistolae,* f. 238 B.

[2] See, for example, Peter Lombard, *Sententiae,* Book IV, Dist. 23, ch. 3, *Patrologia, Series Latina,* CXCII, 899—900, contrasting Extreme Unction with Baptism, Confirmation, and Ordination.

be baptized again, to wash our sins away, and to receive the same blessings we had received at first!' 'You are mistaken,' he says, 'if this is what you think.' 'It is impossible,' he says. Therefore you should not hope for what is impossible. He did not say: 'It is not proper, it does not profit, it is not permitted.' No, he said: 'It is impossible.' Therefore he led them into despair." [3] But the apostle mentions "baptisms," in the plural. He does this either because he has used the plural for the singular or, as some suppose, for the sake of those who thought that they could be baptized with many and repeated baptisms.

Let us go on to maturity.

He calls "maturity," as Chrysostom says, "the completely good life." [4] But what that life is St. James explains when he says in ch. 1:4: "Patience has a perfect work." Therefore Christ also said that this good ground will bear fruit in patience (cf. Luke 8:15). And here the apostle immediately says below (v. 11): "We desire each one of you to show the same earnestness in realizing the full assurance of hope." For through tribulations patience divests the soul of the figure and all visible things and transfers it into the hope of the things that are invisible, as Rom. 5:4-5 states: "Experience works hope, but hope does not put to shame."

6. *To restore again to repentance those who have fallen away.*

Some think that these words are spoken by the apostle about those who in any way have fallen into sin.[5] And in order to counteract the error of the Novatians they are compelled to distort the word "impossible" and to declare that it was used instead of the word "difficult." But because it is dangerous to twist clear words of Scripture into a different meaning, one should not readily permit this, lest in the end the authority of all Scripture vacillate, except where the context demands it. St. Augustine, writing to St. Jerome, did not permit the apostle's well-known words "I do not lie" in Gal. 1:20 to be understood as referring only to a pernicious lie but said that they should also be understood as referring to a lie that is obliging and deceptive or, as St. Jerome

[3] Chrysostom, *Homiliae,* IX, 2, col. 78 (300).

[4] Chrysostom, *Homiliae,* IX, 2, col. 77 (299).

[5] Cf. Lyra, *Postilla, ad* Heb. 6:6.

says, prudent.[6] Furthermore, in this way they still neither escape
nor refute [7] the Novatian error, since it is no less difficult for
God to justify any godless person again, and it is impossible for
man to rise from any sin. Therefore the truth must be asserted,
and heresy must be refuted, and not till then should one, so far
as possible, harmonize this text. But that repentance remains for
those who have fallen is clear, in the first place, from what the
apostle Paul says in 2 Cor. 12:21-22: [8] "Lest perhaps . . . God
should humiliate me . . . and I should mourn over many of you
who have not repented of the . . . fornication." And in 1 Cor. 5:5
he delivered the fornicator along with his stepmother to Satan
for the destruction of the flesh, in order that his spirit might be
saved. And in like manner he instructs Timothy and Titus to use
the Word of God with gentleness (cf. 1 Tim. 3:5; 2 Tim. 2:25;
Titus 1:7 f.; Titus 3:10), in the hope that in some way the godless
and the heretics may be converted. Indeed, if there were no repentance, the entire Epistle to the Galatians would amount to
nothing, since it is not the so-called actual sins that are censured
in this epistle but the greatest sin, namely, the sin of unbelief,
because of which they had fallen away from Christ to the Law.
Thus we read in the Old Testament that the very saintly David
fell three times and rose again just as often. In like manner the
brothers of Joseph, although they were fratricides, were restored
through repentance. And lest the heretics reason captiously that
their opinions are in accord with the New Testament, behold,
Peter, along with all the apostles, fell from faith; and they all
fled. Yet they were restored. Therefore one must understand that
in this passage the apostle is speaking about the falling of faith
into unbelief, namely, because of their opinion that they can be
saved without Christ by their own righteousnesses, which is altogether impossible. For this reason he says at the beginning (6:1)
that he will omit the words about faith and the elementary doctrines of Christ. This means that it is "impossible" for him to be
restored who at one time began with Christ and, after backsliding,
seeks someone else. And that this is his meaning he seems to point
out clearly enough below, in ch. 10:26, where he says: "If we

---

[6] Cf. *Luther's Works*, 26, p. 84, n. 3.

[7] Although the text has *contundunt*, "crush," we have followed the emendation suggested by the Weimar editor, *confutant*.

[8] The original has "1 Cor. 4."

sin deliberately . . . there no longer remains a sacrifice for sins."
Accordingly, it was the need of the primitive church that compelled the apostle to speak so severely against those who had
fallen. Here there was danger not only with regard to the changing of morals after faith had taken root but more so with regard
to the newly planted faith itself. The apostle also shows this concern abundantly enough in the rest of his epistles.

8. *For land which has drunk the rain that often falls upon it* [*and*
brings forth vegetation useful to those for whose sake it is cul-
tivated receives a blessing from God].

That "rain" in Scripture means doctrine Chrysostom and Augustine prove from the well-known words in Is. 5:6, where we
read: "And I will command My clouds to rain no rain upon it." [9]
It is clear, however, that here He is speaking about the synagog
when He says: "The vineyard of the Lord of Hosts is the house
of Israel. . . . I looked that he should do judgment, and behold,
iniquity; and do justice, and behold, a cry" (v. 7). This is what
he calls "briers and thorns" here. Thus Is. 45:8 says: "Shower,
O heavens, from above, and let the clouds rain righteousness";
that is, let them teach faith in Christ, which is righteousness.
Ps. 68:10: "Willing rain wilt Thou, O God, set apart for Thine
inheritance." And in Micah 2:11 we read: "I will cause wine to
drop for you and will be for this people the one who causes it to
drop." This is said in order that we may be instructed to understand the mysteries of Scripture, namely, what this statement in
Ps. 78:23 means: "He opened the doors of heaven and rained upon
them." For this figure of speech means that the doctrine of faith
is given from heaven. Thus these words in Deut. 11:10-11: "The
land which you are going to enter is not like the land of Egypt
from which you have come and water it as in a garden. No . . .
it is a land of hills and valleys that look for rain from heaven."
This means that the church does not teach itself with its own
doctrines but is taught by God, as Is. 54:13 states: "All your children shall be taught by the Lord."

---

[9] Chrysostom, *Homiliae*, X, 1, col. 83 (305), including the words quoted in
the next paragraph; Augustine, *Enarrationes in Psalmos*, LXXVI, 18, *Corpus Chri-*
stianorum, Series Latina, XXXIX, 1064, quoting Is. 5:6.

9. [*Though we speak thus*] *yet in your case, beloved, we feel sure of better things* [*that belong to salvation*].

He says this because, as Chrysostom states: "He who strikes a slow man makes him slower." Therefore "after he has frightened and stricken, he cares for them again, lest he cast them down all the more and throw them to the ground." For sinners should not be upbraided in such a way that they are only wounded and driven to despair; but they should be cherished again, so that they are encouraged to be obedient. But this will happen if they are never reproved without mixing in some praise of them. On the other hand, they should never be praised without being reproved to some extent. Thus here the apostle does not strike them in all cases. Nor does he flatter them in all cases. Thus in Rev. 2 and 3 John praises and censures the seven angels of the churches, and in the Epistle to the Galatians the apostle first reproves, then praises. Indeed, in nearly all his epistles he observes these two things. But the prophets also have the same custom. Now they say the best things about the people. Soon they say all the worst things, and vice versa. Therefore sores should not be cut and left, but they should much rather be soothed with plasters.

10. *For God is not so unjust as to overlook your work* [*and the love which you showed for His sake in ministering to the saints, as you still do*].

Although, according to what the apostle says in Rom. 15:25, this ministry to the saints is understood to be the very contribution or offering that was administered to the apostles and other saints, yet we must accustom ourselves to the way of speaking usually employed in Scripture.[10] According to this way of speaking, all those who bear the name of Christ are called "saints," as Chrysostom also mentions with reference to this passage.[11] For both Christ and our neighbor are wronged if we do not regard as a saint him of whom we confess that he has been baptized in His holy name. Therefore this ministry is also understood to be every service shown to a neighbor in his needs.

---

10 Cf. *Luther the Expositor*, pp. 75—77.

11 Chrysostom, *Homiliae*, X, 4, col. 87 (308).

11. *And we desire each of you [to show the same earnestness in realizing the full assurance of hope until the end].*

Again the apostle, whose purpose it is to teach, teaches on the basis of his own example. For he does not say: "We want" (as Chrysostom says). For "I want" expresses authority, but "we desire" expresses "fatherly" or rather brotherly "love." It is the exact opposite when one, out of fondness for correcting, rules violently and impatiently without the service of love. And it usually happens that those who do not want a single syllable of what they say to be disregarded have not heeded a single syllable themselves.

12. *[So that you may not be sluggish, but imitators of those] who through faith and patience will inherit the promises.*

How beautifully he combines the two, faith and patience! For faith causes the heart to cling fast to celestial things and to be carried away and to dwell in things that are invisible. For patience is necessary in order that by it the heart may be sustained not only in its contempt for the visible things that attract but also in its endurance of those that rage. For this is how it happens that the believer hangs between heaven and earth, and, as Ps. 68:13 says, "sleeps among the sheepfolds," that is, that in Christ he is suspended in the air and crucified.

13. *For when God made a promise to Abraham.*

Chrysostom says: "Just as by means of what he said above the apostle terrified with punishment, so by means of these words he comforts with rewards by showing God's customary way of doing things. But it is not His custom to fulfill His promises swiftly but to do so after a long time." [12] Therefore he who wants to serve God must learn to know His will and His custom. For who can in any way serve a master whom he does not know? Furthermore, to learn to know God as a dog learns to know its master or in the way the philosophers learned to know His power and His essence, as is recorded in Rom. 1:20, is not enough. For this is a sensual, crude knowledge which is harmful to those who have it. But one must learn to know what His will or what His plan is. This, however, He shows in His commandments, as Ps. 103:7 [13] states: "He made

[12] Chrysostom, *Homiliae*, XI, 1, col. 89 (310).
[13] The original has "Ps. 130 [131]."

known His ways to Moses and His will to the Children of Israel."
But no one understands His commandments, either, unless he is
illumined anew from above, as Wisd. 9:13 says: "For who among
men will be able to know the counsel of God, or who will be able
to think what God's will is?" Likewise 1 Cor. 2:16: "Who has
known the mind of the Lord?" Likewise (1 Cor. 2:11, 10): "The
things of God no one knows but the Spirit of God. But God has
revealed them to us through His Spirit." And this is what Christ
meant when He said in John 14:26: "That Spirit will teach you
all things and bring to your mind whatever I have said to you."
This means that you cannot yet bear and understand My words,
even though they are the commands and the will of the Father.
But you will understand them when the Holy Spirit teaches. And
this was beautifully pointed out beforehand in Ex. 20:19 [14] and
in Deut. 18:15, where, when the Jews could not endure God
when He spoke, they desired an interpreter, and God promised
one, who was to be Christ. And for this reason Ps. 143:8 teaches
that one should pray: "Teach me the way I should go." And
throughout Ps. 119 we read the words "Teach me," "Instruct
me," "Give me understanding," etc., and there are many similar
words. But with all these words not only God's essence but especially His will is commended. Therefore those who presume to
grasp Holy Scripture and the Law of God with their own intellect
and to understand them by their own effort are exceedingly in
error. For this is the source of heresies and godless dogmas, since
they approach, not as receptive pupils but as bustling teachers,
although in Ps. 92:14-15 it is written: "They shall be vigorous
and sturdy to declare, etc.," that is, they shall be teachable in
order that they may teach.

But although it is impossible for those without experience to
tell why man of himself cannot understand the will or the Law
of God, yet one must try in one way or another. In the first place,
His will is expressed in every command that He Himself alone
should be loved and preferred above all things. When He has
begun to bring this about and to fulfill this will, He strips and
divests man inside and outside of every work of his. And by doing
this He "brings to nought the plans of nations and foils the de-
signs of peoples" (Ps. 33:10). Here in the depths a man says:

---

[14] The original has "Ex. 19."

"Thy judgments are like the great deep" (Ps. 36:6). Here he "comprehends with all the saints what is the breadth and length and depth" (Eph. 3:18). In brief, he is confounded and disturbed to such an extent that it is impossible for him to persist and persevere in the will of God unless "the Holy Spirit helps him in his weakness" (Rom. 8:26) and, as Isaiah says, "bridles his mouth with praise" (cf. Is. 48:9). Here, however, as is stated in Job 3:23,[15] he becomes "a man whose way is hidden, and God will surround him with darkness." Therefore how can he understand God, to say nothing of loving Him, then, when all His counsels and thoughts have been rejected? Therefore to understand this invisible will of God in such darkness, this is nothing else than the function of the Spirit. And surely this will of God is still bearable in one way or another. At all events, it leaves words of consolation, namely, "For a brief moment I forsook you, but with great compassion I will gather you," as in Is. 54:7 and similar passages. But that final will, which removes the very word of consolation and promise, is the will concerning which Christ's well-known statement can be understood, namely, that "if those days had not been shortened, no flesh would be saved" (Matt. 24:22).

15 The original has "Job 4."

CHAPTER SEVEN

1. *For this Melchizedek, king of Salem.*

THE Hebrew word מֶלֶךְ means "king," just as שָׁלֵם means "at peace" and צֶדֶק means "righteousness." But one must note that in Holy Scripture these words "righteousness" and "peace" are understood only of divine righteousness and peace, and in such a way that "righteousness" is the very grace by which a man is justified, that is, faith, hope, and love, as in Ps. 31:1: "In Thy righteousness deliver me." And in Ps. 71:1: "Give the king Thy judgment, O God, and Thy righteousness to the king's son." Again, in Ps. 24:5: "He will receive blessing from the Lord and mercy (righteousness in the Hebrew) from the God of his salvation." According to the rule, therefore, one must observe that in Scripture the grace which the scholastic doctors call "justifying" or "formed faith" [1] is called "the righteousness of God," "the mercy of God," "the salvation of God," "the power of God," and the like. But this righteousness is the righteousness about which it is written in Rom. 1:17 that it is from faith, as is stated that in the Gospel "the righteousness of God is revealed from faith to faith." This is erroneously explained as referring to the righteousness of God by which He Himself ·is righteous,[2] unless it were understood in such a way that faith so exalts man's heart and transfers it from itself to God that the heart and God become one spirit and thus in a way are the divine righteousness, the "formative" righteousness, as they call it,[3] just as in Christ the humanity, through the union with the divine nature, became one and the same Person. Therefore it follows that this Melchizedek could not be a "king of righteousness" except by representing Christ in name and in type—Christ, who alone is "the Sun of righteous-

---

[1] Cf. *Luther's Works,* 26, p. 88, n. 7.

[2] Cf. also *Luther's Works,* 34, pp. 336—337.

[3] Cf. Peter Lombard, *Sententiae,* Book III, Dist. 23, ch. 3, *Patrologia, Series Latina,* CXCII, 805.

ness" (Mal. 4:2) and "the King of righteousness" (Heb. 7:2), who justifies all who are righteous. Thus even the shoes must be loosened from our feet (cf. Ex. 3:5), that is, the notion concerning human righteousness acquired through elicited acts.[4] Similarly, "peace" does not mean the peace that can be spoken of, written about, and thought of by man, nor that which can be given by some creature; but it is the peace "that passes all understanding" (Phil. 4:7), that is, that passes the mind and is hidden under the cross and death just as the sun is hidden under a cloud. Therefore concerning the godless it is stated in Ps. 14:3: "The way of peace they do not know" (cf. Rom. 3:17). But it is impossible for one to have this peace without faith, that is, the righteousness of God. Ps. 85:10 says: "Righteousness and peace have kissed each other." For since God takes away all our goods and our life through many tribulations, it is impossible for the heart to be calm and to bear this unless it clings to better goods, that is, is united with God through faith. Thus the apostle is wont to begin his epistles with "Grace and peace" (Rom. 1:7; Gal. 1:3). And Christ says (John 14:27): "My peace I give to you; not as the world gives, etc."

He deduces the superiority of Christ and His priesthood from four things:

namely
{
the eternal existence (Heb. 7:3)
the blessing (Heb. 7:3)
the perpetuity
the tithing
}

The eternal existence consists in the fact that Christ was prefigured through Melchizedek, whose beginning is not described. The blessing, however, consists in the fact that Abraham was blessed by Melchizedek and that in this way all the children of Abraham except Christ were blessed. The tithing consists in the fact that Abraham and Levi, but not Christ, paid tithes to Melchizedek as the worthier one. The perpetuity consists in the fact that Abraham and Levi died, but that Christ lives forever. And in this way he excludes the vain confidence of the Jews, who had arrogant thoughts about the Law and about their priesthood, although both they themselves and their patriarch were on a lower plane than the other person, who gave the blessing. Thus the Master of the Sentences also says in Book III, Distinction 3, 3, that Christ did not pay tithes along with Levi, although He was

[4] Cf. p. 125, n. 6.

with Levi in the loins of Abraham; for He was not in the loins of Abraham according to the same law.[5] For Levi was there according to the law of carnal concupiscence, but Christ was there according to the law of love. Therefore, as St. Augustine says on Genesis: "Just as when Adam sinned, all who were in his loins sinned, so when Abraham paid tithes, all who were in his loins paid tithes";[6] that is, they showed that they were on a lower plane and were devoid of the blessing. For it was necessary for Christ to be the natural Son of Abraham and David—the Son who had the true flesh of both; for it was necessary for Scripture to be fulfilled. According to Scripture, God promised the blessing and the kingdom to Abraham. On the other hand, it was impossible for Him to be the Son of both through the Law and the work of the flesh, that is, through concupiscence and sin; for in this way He would have been born with sin and would not have been blessed but would rather have had to be blessed. And thus what was necessary and what was impossible were engaged in a struggle in which the one contradicted the other, just as happens to every work of God. Only the wisdom of God found the solution, namely, that He should be born from the woman alone, without a man, and both things should be accomplished: that, on the one hand, He was the natural Son of Abraham and, on the other hand, was worthier and greater than Abraham and all because He was without sin, "full of grace and truth" (John 1:14). Hence it is clear that the Blessed Virgin had to be a mother whose virginity was unimpaired. Otherwise "the fruit of her womb" (Luke 1:42) would not have been "blessed." In the course of time, therefore, when the truth has been revealed to a greater extent, this very thing is stated more clearly, as in Ps. 132:11:[7] "Of the fruit of your womb I will set upon your throne." And in Ps. 127:3: "Lo, sons are a heritage from the Lord, the fruit of the womb a reward." According to the Hebrew, Ps. 110:3 says: "Thy people will offer themselves freely on the day of Thy power in holy brightness; from the womb of the morning the dew of Thy childhood will

[5] Peter Lombard, *Sententiae,* Book III, Dist. 3, ch. 3, *Patrologia, Series Latina,* CXCII, 761—762.

[6] Cf. Augustine, *De Genesi ad litteram,* Book X, ch. 19, par. 34, *Patrologia, Series Latina,* XXXIV, 423, quoted in the form given by Peter Lombard (see note 5 above).

[7] The original has "Ps. 121 [122]."

come to Thee." The prophetic vision pictures the same thing, where "a stone was cut out of a mountain without hands" (Dan. 2:34), that is, Christ from the Virgin without the work of a man. And Ps. 22:9: [8] "Thou art He who took me from the womb," not like Job, who said (10:10): "Hast Thou not milked me as milk?" And just as a bee gathers honey from a flower, so the Spirit drew the body of Christ from the completely pure streams of blood of the Virgin Mary. And this is "the water of strife" near which the Jews "contend with the Lord" (Num. 20:13) up to the present day. And it was prefigured in Ex. 17 that they refused to believe that Christ was born as the natural Son of Abraham without a law or a work of the law, that is, of the flesh. But this birth of flesh that took place in a wonderful way through the Holy Spirit without flesh also betokens the spiritual birth concerning which John 1:13 says: "Who were born, not of blood nor of the will of the flesh, but of God."

12. *When the priesthood is changed, a change of law must also take place.*

With five distinguishing characteristics he elevates the priesthood of Christ above the Levitical priesthood: first, because He is another (Heb. 7:12-14); secondly, because He is eternal (Heb. 7:15-19); thirdly, because He is bound by an oath (Heb. 7:20-22); fourthly, because He is the one and only (Heb. 7:23-25); fifthly, because He is perfect (Heb. 7:26-28). Therefore one must note here that the word "law" used in this context can be taken in two ways.

In the first place, according to the lower understanding, by which he means only the ceremonials, namely, the vestments and external adornments of the priests, likewise the offerings and sacrifices of the flesh of beasts, likewise the judgments and teachings pertaining to leprosy and the uncleanness resulting from touching the dead, and the like. Thus the meaning is that the law has been changed; that is, ceremonies of this kind prescribed by the law have been abrogated, and the things that were signified by these have themselves been instituted, that is, the spiritual and inner garment and adornment of the priests. Concerning this Ps. 132:9 says: "Let Thy priests be clothed with righteousness," that is to say, not with purple and blue, like the

[8] The original has "Ps. 121 [122]."

priests of the Law. For in the new law a priest does not differ from the people in the matter of vestments or attire but rather because of his outstanding sanctity and righteousness. For the ceremonies and the vestments we see have been established by the church, and in the course of time their number has been increased. Thus the offerings and sacrifices of the new law are not rams or calves but rather the hearts or souls of believers and sinners, as is written in Acts 10:13, where unclean animals were shown to St. Peter, to whom it was also said: "Rise, Peter, kill and eat." It is clearly apparent from what follows that this was said about the centurion and the Gentiles who were to be slain with the Word of the Gospel and thus offered to the Lord, as Is. 66:20 states: "And they shall bring your brethren from all nations for a gift to the Lord . . . just as the Children of Israel bring their offering in a clean vessel." Likewise the statement in Ps. 45:15: "The virgins shall be led to the king." Thus the law that consisted in judgments and in teachings concerning the justification of the flesh has certainly been changed; for the cleanness or the uncleanness which the Priest of grace judges and teaches do not pertain to leprosy, the flesh, hair, attire, house, etc., but to sins of uncleanness of the spirit and the conscience. For in the new law there is no difference between a leprous Christian and one who is not leprous, or a menstruous woman and a young woman in childbed, or a filthy garment and a garment that is clean. In short, the only thing that makes a difference among Christians is sin, which pollutes the conscience. Although everything else, so far as it is outside in the flesh, formerly made a distinction between Jew and Jew, yet now it makes no distinction whatever between Christian and Christian.

COROLLARY

From this there follows the corollary which states how one should understand the well-known statement of the Master of the Sentences and the teachers who comment on him. "The sacraments of the Law," he says, "did not justify; but the sacraments of the new law confer grace on all who put no obstacle in the way." [9] For this is either not properly understood or is very falsely

---

[9] Cf. Peter Lombard, *Sententiae*, Book IV, Dist. 1, ch. 5, *Patrologia, Series Latina*, CXCII, 840.

stated, since the sacraments of grace benefit no one but rather harm all unless "they draw near in full assurance of faith" (Heb. 10:22). But faith is already the grace that justifies. Therefore it is more correctly understood in this way, that the sacraments of the law justified only the flesh, namely, by distinguishing between leprous and clean flesh, between skin and skin, between garment and garment, between hair and hair. Although all these things are clean, yet, because they are external and in the flesh, they contribute nothing whatever to the cleanness of the heart. But the sacraments of grace justify the heart by distinguishing between heart and heart, between conscience and conscience, between faith and faith, between hope and hope, between love and love. If these are clean, they make a person acceptable before God, even though the others are completely unclean. Thus the apostle has the courage to state confidently in Titus 1:15: "For the clean all things are clean, but for the unclean nothing is clean; but both their mind and their conscience is defiled." The reason for all this is that in the sacraments of grace we have the promise of Christ, which states: "Whatever you bind on earth, this shall also be bound in heaven, etc." (Matt. 18:18). The old Law did not have this promise; for man was not clean in heaven because through the priesthood he was pronounced clean on earth, but was clean only on earth. Therefore the apostle calls Christ "the Surety of a better covenant" (Heb. 7:22) as the One who promises the remission of sins and cleanness of heart through the word of His priest. He who believes him is altogether righteous and clean before God.

Secondly, "law" can be understood according to the higher understanding with which the apostle proceeds in the Epistle to the Romans and in the Epistle to the Galatians, where by "law" he understands simply whatever is commanded by God and by man, whether it is ceremonial or judicial and moral.[10] Thus the sense is that "the Law has been changed," that is, has been fulfilled through Christ. For He "is the end of the Law" (Rom. 10:4), as Matt. 5:17 says: "I have not come to abolish the Law, but to fulfill it." With reference to this 1 Tim. 1:9 says: "The Law is not laid down for the righteous"; that is, insofar as a righteous man has all that the Law requires, he is now outside the Law. For he

10 Cf. *Luther's Works,* 27, pp. 187—188.

owes the Law nothing; but he keeps the Law, and his life is the Law itself, living and fulfilled. Properly speaking, therefore, it is not the office of the new priest to teach the Law but to point out the grace of Jesus Christ, which is the fulfillment of the Law, as Ps. 92:2 states: "To proclaim Thy mercy at dawn and Thy truth throughout the night." Thus we read in Is. 9:4: "The staff for his shoulder, the yoke of his burden, and the rod of his oppressor (that is, of the Law) Thou hast broken as on the day of Midian." Therefore John the Baptist, "the voice of one crying in the wilderness" (Matt. 3:3), that is, the word of a preacher among sinners, points with his finger and says: "Behold, the Lamb of God, who takes away the sins of the world" (John 1:29). But this change has not yet been carried out, as the previous one was; but it is being carried out from day to day. Therefore the new priest partly teaches, partly points along with John the Baptist, since in this time that righteous man for whom the Law has not been laid down makes no more than a beginning.

13. *For the one of whom these things are spoken [belonged to another tribe, from which no one has ever served at the altar].*

"Of whom" could be translated with "to whom," considering that it is a way of speaking commonly used by the apostle. Thus above, in the first chapter (v. 7), he has "but of the angels," that is, to the angels. And above, in the fourth chapter (v. 13), he has "All things are laid bare to the eyes of Him of whom we have to give account," that is, to whom. For in this way he points out that a word comes into use after the manner of a movement toward its subject matter. Thus also in Gal. 3:24: [11] "The Law has been a custodian to Christ" and often in other places.

22. *This makes [Jesus] the surety of a better covenant.*

One should note that where it is recorded in the Holy Scriptures that God makes a will, there it is pointed out somewhat obscurely that at one time or other God will die and arrange the inheritance, as below in chapter 9:6: "Where there is a testament, the death of the testator must intervene." This has been fulfilled in Christ. Hence the words "testament," "inheritance," "part,"

[11] The original has "Gal. 4."

[W, LVII-3, 193, 194]

"portion," "cup," etc., occur so frequently in Scripture. All this points to the death of Christ and to faith in His resurrection.

26. [*For it was fitting that we should have such a High Priest,*] *holy, blameless, unstained.*

According to the usage of Scripture that which is clean and sacred to God is called "holy." On the other hand, that which is open to uses other than divine is called "profane." Therefore it is frequently recorded in the Law that the people and the priests are sanctified, likewise the temple, the tabernacle, the vestments, and the vessels. And in this way it connotes in a mystical manner the sanctification of the Spirit, by which they become a new creature. A person who is irreprehensible is called "blameless"; for a saint can use his sanctity in an improper manner, just as a Christian can use his Baptism and the newness of the spirit in an improper manner. Therefore "blamelessness" is the irreprehensible use and the work of the saint himself, so that "holy" points out the substance, and "blameless" points out the performance, as in Ps. 24:4: "He who has blameless hands (that is, irreprehensible in what he does) and a clean heart," that is, one who is holy. And Ps. 18:26 says: "With the blameless Thou shalt be blameless." Therefore Christ is "the blameless Lamb," that is, irreprehensible and unaccusable. This, as Isaiah and Peter say, means that "He committed no sin; no guile was found on His lips" (1 Peter 2:22; Is. 53:9). He who cannot be polluted by others either is called "untainted." For even if a priest of the Law were clean and irreprehensible so far as he himself was concerned, he could be polluted by something else if, for example, he were to touch a corpse or a leper. But just as Christ was free from uncleanness because no inner filth of His own made Him unclean, so He cannot be polluted by the filth of others either.

Separated from sinners.

He says this because Christ is sitting in heaven, where there are no sinners. But just as the priests on earth are themselves sinners, so they are mingled among sinners and dwell among them. Is. 6:5 says: "Woe is me, because I have held my peace," that is, I have not mentioned the good things. This is expressed in the Hebrew text with "because I am a man of unclean lips, and I dwell in the midst of a people of unclean lips." Why, then, does the apostle say: "It was fitting that we should have such a High Priest"? Or what was the nature of that fittingness? In the first place, for the sake of God, in order that He might be a worthy Priest who would be heard and accepted in our stead; for "God does not listen to sinners," as John 9:31 says. Ps. 5:4 says: "For Thou art not a God who delights in wickedness, for no evil will sojourn with Thee." In the second place, for our sakes, in order that He might be able to sanctify us, to make us blameless, untainted, separated, and like Him in all respects. This happens when we cling to Him with faithful hearts and set our minds "not on things that are on earth but on the things that are above, where Christ is seated at the right hand of God" (Col. 3:1-2). This is what it means to be sanctified.

CHAPTER EIGHT

1. *Now the main point in what we are saying is this.*

HERE "the main point," which is called κεφάλαιον in Greek, means "the sum" and what it was commonly customary to call "the sum total." Thus the apostle uses the same way of speaking in Rom. 13:9 when he says that "every commandment is summed up in this one word." In Greek the word is "recapitulated," that is, summed up or brought together. "You shall love your neighbor as yourself." This means that love for one's neighbor is the sum and concise statement of the whole Law, as is stated in the same place: "Love is the fulfilling of the Law" (Rom. 13:10). In Gal. 5:14 he points this out in another statement—but it has the same meaning—when he says: "For the whole Law is fulfilled in one word: 'You shall love your neighbor as yourself.'" And in conformity with this way of speaking St. Jerome, writing on Matt. 17:4, says: "The Law and the prophets must be recapitulated in the one tabernacle of the Gospel," [1] must be summarized and reduced to a concise statement or epitome. Christ, too, makes such a recapitulation (ἀνακεφαλαίωσις) or summary (κεφάλαιον) when He says in Matt. 7:12: [2] "Whatever you wish that men would do to you, do so to them; for this is the Law and the prophets."

10. *I will put My laws into their minds and write them on their hearts.*

The grace of the New Testament consists in this, that what is spoken and written there teaches the things that are of the Spirit, and the words of grace are spoken according to the well-known statement in Ps. 45:2: "Grace is poured upon your lips." Not so Moses, who stammers and is not eloquent, and, as he says

---

[1] Jerome, *Commentaria in Evangelium S. Matthaei*, Book III (on Matt. 17:3), *Patrologia, Series Latina*, XXVI, 122.

[2] The original has "Matt. 5."

in Ex. 4:10: "I am slow of speech and of tongue." Hence the apostle has the courage to say that "the Law works wrath" (Rom. 4:15) and is a "law of sin" (Rom. 7:25; 8:2), and that Moses is a servant of sin, so that one could say: "Wrath is poured upon your lips." Therefore it happens in the New Testament that while the Word of life, grace, and salvation is proclaimed outside, the Holy Spirit teaches inside at the same time. Therefore Isaiah says (Is. 54:13): "All your sons shall be taught by the Lord." And in Jeremiah we read: "I will give My laws. . . . And they shall all know Me" (cf. 31:33-34). Hence Christ refers to these two prophets when He says in John 6:45: "It is written in the prophets: 'They shall all be taught by God.'" Likewise in 2 Cor. 3:3: [3] "You are a letter from Christ delivered by us, written, not with ink but with the Spirit of the living God, not on tablets of stone but on tablets of human hearts." Thus we read in 1 John 2:27 that "His anointing will teach you all," and in John 14:26: "But the Counselor, the Holy Spirit . . . will teach you all things." Accordingly, this is how Scripture must be understood when it says that the laws are written in the minds and in the hearts. For by "mind" and "heart" (for this is how we are speaking now) it means intellect and feeling. For to be in the mind means to be understood; to be in the heart means to be loved. Thus to say that the Law is in the mouth means that it is taught; to say that it is in the ear means that it is heard; to say that it is in the eyes means that it is seen. Therefore it is not enough for the Law to be in the soul and to state objectively that it is there. No, it must be in the soul formally,[4] that is, the Law must be written in the heart out of love for the Law.

[3] The original has "2 Cor. 4."

[4] That is, it must present in actuality; for an analogous use of *formaliter*, see, for example, Thomas Aquinas, *Summa Theologica*, I-I, Q. 89, art. 5.

CHAPTER NINE

2. *For a tent was prepared, the outer one, [in which were the lampstand and the Table and the bread of the Presence; it is called the Holy Place].*

THE tent of Moses has been explained in various ways by various commentators.[1] For some think that it refers to the universe. Then the "Holy of Holies" would represent the celestial and invisible things themselves, and the cherubim would represent the angelic choirs themselves. Therefore Scripture frequently addresses God with the words "Thou who art enthroned upon the cherubim" (Ps. 80:1; Is. 37:16). But the "Holy Place" would represent the visible world, and the "second curtain" itself would be the starry heaven.[2] The "seven lamps" would be the seven planets, and the "table of the showbreads" would be the four elements, etc. Yet this explanation, whether true or not, is somewhat forced and does violence to the text. Others prefer to understand the "tent" tropologically and take it to mean the smaller world, that is, man himself, who, according to the higher part of reason, dwells among the things that are invisible and belong to God. For thus God alone, as Augustine declares in many places,[3] dwells in and fills man's higher mind; and in this way such a man is truly the ark of the Lord, which has the mercy seat, the cherubim, the manna, and the rod of Aaron. But the "Holy Place" refers to the lower reason, which, as they say, is illumined by the light of natural reason. This light is represented by the lampstand. Finally, however, the court is taken to be the perception of the flesh, and to typify this the court was five cubits in height, because there are only five senses. In short,

[1] Cf. Lyra, *Postilla, ad* Heb. 9:2.

[2] Faber, *Epistolae,* f. 247 A-B.

[3] Cf. Augustine, *De Trinitate,* Book XII, ch. 3, par. 3, *Patrologia, Series Latina,* XLII, 999—1000; see also *Luther's Works,* 21, pp. 303—304.

in this way the court is the faculty of perception, the Holy Place is reason, the Holy of Holies is the intellect. These are those three men frequently mentioned by Paul, namely, animate, carnal, and spiritual man.[4] And each has his own rite, his own theology, and his own worship of God. To these the well-known threefold division of theology corresponds: symbolic theology to the faculty of perception, proper theology to reason, mystical theology to the intellect.[5] In the third place, here others, together with the apostle, take the tent to mean a kind of spiritual world, which is the holy church of God. And thus the Holy of Holies is the church triumphant, the Holy Place is the church militant, and the court is the synagog. With this, in turn, the fact that the court is five cubits high is in agreement; for the synagog was based on what is written in the five books of Moses.

The lampstand with its shafts and seven lamps signifies either the Word of God (namely, the spoken Word) by which the church is illuminated, as 2 Peter 1:19 states: "We have the prophetic Word made more sure. You will do well to pay attention to this as to a lamp shining in a dark place." But the number seven, which is characteristic of the sevenfold spirit, signifies universality (that is, that all the spoken proclamations throughout all the churches have one meaning in common and shine with the same light). Or, if they are connected with Rev. 1:20, the seven golden lampstands are, as is stated in the same place, the "seven churches," that is, the churches taken collectively. Or, thirdly, as is stated in Zech. 4:10, "the golden lampstand and its seven lamps" are "the seven eyes of the Lord, which range through the whole earth." But the eyes of the Lord are called the priests of the churches. For just as the eye directs the body, so the priest directs the church, as is stated in Job 29:15: "I was an eye to the blind and a foot to the lame." Jer. 15:19 says: "If you separate the precious from the vile, you shall be as My mouth." Fourthly, one can take the lamps to be the consciences of individual persons, as Luke 11:34 states: "Your eye is the lamp of your body."

The table and the bread of the Presence is either the same Holy Scripture that the believers receive from the mouth as from a table, according to the well-known words in Mal. 2:7: "The lips

4 See p. 162, n. 5.

5 See p. 179.

of the priest shall guard knowledge, and they shall seek the Law from his mouth"; or it is Christ Himself, who is our Altar, Sacrifice, and Bread, as John 6:35 states: "I am the Bread of life." For we receive Him in the sacrament and feast ourselves on Him in this life. Therefore Ps. 23:5 states: "Thou hast prepared a table before me against those who oppress me." Perhaps this verse gives expression to the mystery which consisted in the fact that the table was placed on the north side and the lampstand on the south side; for in the Scriptures "the north" represents enemies and oppressors, as Jer. 1:14 states: "From the north every evil shall break forth." For truly there is neither consolation nor victory in any trial unless we approach the sacrament and "the table prepared against those who oppress us."

This, too, should be noted, that the Hebrew text is said to have "bread of the countenances" where we have "bread of the Presence." Yet in reality this amounts to the same thing. For that bread was designated in this way because Christ should always be kept in sight and before our faces, and should be remembered by us. This is what the verse already mentioned speaks of when it says: "Thou hast prepared before me," that is, before my face. And Christ says: "Do this in remembrance of Me" (1 Cor. 11:25). This is why it is also called by another name a memorial of the Lord's Passion, as in Ps. 111:4: "The Lord has caused His wonderful works to be remembered." Others, however, think that it was called "bread of the countenances" because the Sacrament was made completely visible and ready, and was directed toward and instituted for us and our needs. For He does not turn His back to us or forsake us. No, He turns His countenance toward us when He comes to us every day in the Sacrament. And the plural "of the countenances" is used because He comes this way in many places.

The ark of the covenant (v. 4) made of incorruptible acacia wood overlaid on all sides with gold is the very same Christ who was born from the completely pure and uncorrupted flesh of the Virgin. This means that on all sides He was adorned with the heavenly gold of wisdom and grace "within and without" (Ex. 25:11), that is, in His heart and in His work, especially when He hangs on the cross. For then most of all He is the ark of the covenant, that is, of reconciliation. He Himself is also the *mercy seat* (v. 5) on which He is .enthroned, and, as the apostle says,

"in Him the whole fullness of the Godhead dwells bodily" (Col.
2:9). Thus Rom. 3:25 states: "Whom God put forth as a propitiation through faith in His blood." It also means that in Him are
the tables of the covenant (v. 4), since, as the apostle says in Col.
2:3, it is understood that "within are hidden all the treasures of
wisdom and knowledge." For the Law and the wisdom of God
cannot be understood either except in Christ, whom, as the apostle
says in 1 Cor. 1:30, "God made our wisdom and righteousness."
Finally this also means that the Law cannot be fulfilled except
in Christ. Just as the external Word and the Sacrament, which
are meant by the lampstand and the table, are shared by the worthy
and the unworthy, so they are not enough if we do not taste Christ
in the things that are hidden and, as we read in Col. 3:1, "seek
the things that are above, where Christ is." Though *the manna*
and *the golden urn* (v. 4) were in the ark, they also mean Christ
Himself, in whom alone there is consolation and refreshment for
the soul, since they call "manna" that gift of the experiential
tasting of eternal life "which no one knows except him who receives it," as Rev. 2:17 [6] states: "To him who conquers I will give
the hidden manna . . . and a new name, which no one knows except
him who receives it." *The rod of Aaron* (v. 4) is also Christ Himself, who blossomed forth from a barren and untouched virgin,
as we read in Is. 11:1: "There shall come forth a rod from the
root of Jesse." And Num. 24:17 says: "A star shall come forth out
of Jacob, and a staff shall rise out of Israel and shall smite the
princes of Moab." But many apply all this at the same time to
the Blessed Virgin.[7] Nor is this strange, since it can be applied
to every Christian because of his faith in Christ, in which he has
all that is Christ's.

Many take *the cherubim* (v. 5) to be the angels in heaven,
and today it is not certain what form they had, except that it is
recorded in the Scriptures that they had wings. For this reason
some assumed that they had the form of birds; others, that they
had the form of winged angels. Therefore one can take the position of later interpreters and understand the cherubim to be
the contemplative wisdom of Christ. For, as St. Gregory says,

---

[6] The original has "Rev. 3."

[7] See, for example, Bernard of Clairvaux, *De consideratione*, Book V, ch. 10,
par. 23, *Patrologia, Series Latina*, CLXXXII, 801—802.

flying means contemplation.[8] Thus Ps. 18:10 says that "He arose and flew on the wings of the winds," that is, on the contemplations of the spirits. The name points out enough. For "the cherubim" are understood to be "the fullness of knowledge." Therefore here he also calls them "the cherubim of glory," and in this way he indicates that the wisdom of Christ in glory is one thing, and that the wisdom of Christ crucified is something else. For through the latter the flesh is depressed, through the former the spirit is lifted up. Furthermore, prudence of the spirit is necessary above all when one contemplates Christ, lest we follow the "face" of the one, lose that of the other, and be drawn into a different error. This usually happens to those who neglect to harmonize the contradictions of Scripture in Christ and rush in only one direction. For example, it is stated about Christ that He is the most glorious King of all. The Jews follow this face of the cherubim in such a way that they depart very far from the crucified Christ, since they pay no attention to the other face of the cherubim, where, as is stated in Is. 53:2, "He has no form or comeliness." This is also true with reference to other contradictions and opposites that agree in Christ because of His humanity and His divinity. Therefore it is written that the faces of the cherubim were turned toward the mercy seat. And again: "At the mouth of two or three shall every word be established" (cf. Deut. 19:15). The first *curtain*, which was in front of the Holy Place, pointed out the concealment and the faith of the future church, of the future Gospel, and of the future sacraments. For the synagog did not see these as being present. Therefore during the Passion of Christ this very curtain was "torn in two, from top to bottom" (Matt. 27:51); for then the church appeared, and the synagog came to an end. But the second curtain, which was in front of the Holy of Holies, points out this concealment of our faith in which Christ reigns as man. It will be removed in like manner when He appears in glory. Thus we learn to know Christ according to His flesh and according to His divinity, but only through faith, as 2 Cor. 3:18 [9] states: "But we, with unveiled faith, reflecting" — namely, through faith — "the glory of the Lord, are being changed into the same likeness from glory to glory."

---

[8] Gregory, *Moralia*, XXXV, 2, *Patrologia, Series Latina*, LXXVI, 751.

[9] The original has "2 Cor. 4."

Having the golden censer.

One should note that the apostle says here that the golden censer was in the Holy of Holies. This has caused many to think that Paul is not the author of this epistle, since Moses seems to have said nothing about such a censer.[10] But the text itself speaks in an obscure manner, so that it is uncertain whether the tabernacle had only two altars or had three. For the altar for the burnt offerings, which was of bronze and stood in the court, is described with sufficient clarity in Ex. 27. But the second altar, namely, the one on which incense was burned and which was overlaid with gold, is placed by all in the Holy Place, namely, between the lampstand and the table. Thus Ex. 30:6-7 says: "And you shall place the altar in front of the curtain that hangs before the ark before the mercy seat, and Aaron shall burn fragrant incense on it." It is also written in the same place that perpetual incense should be burned on it in the morning and in the evening. This cannot be taken to mean the Holy of Holies, into which the priest entered only once a year. But that there was also a third altar in the Holy of Holies can be surmised in the first place from Lev. 16:12-13, where that solemn rite at the Feast of the Atonement is described, and where, among other things, it is stated: "And he shall take a censer full of glowing embers from the altar" — for the burnt offerings and for the incense — "and, taking in his hand the incense mixed for burning, shall go beyond the curtain into the Holies" — that is, the Holy of Holies — "so that when the spices have been placed on the fire, the smoke and vapor arising from them covers the mercy seat that is above the covenant." There is no doubt that the apostle took what he said here, namely, "having the golden censer," from this text. In the second place, at the end of Ex. 30, where instruction is given regarding the mixing of this incense, it is stated: "You shall put some of it before the tabernacle of the covenant at the place where I shall appear to you," that is, before the mercy seat. "The incense shall be for you a holy of holies." Therefore it seems that there was an altar in that place. In the third place, here the Greek word θυμιαστήριον means not only a censer but also an altar or a place where incense is burned, because the apostle speaks of it as

---

[10] Cf. Jerome, *Commentaria in Isaiam prophetam,* Book III (on Is. 6:9), *Patrologia, Series Latina,* XXIV, 98—99.

"having the golden altar." In the fourth place, because Zechariah, the father of John (Luke 1:5), is thought to have been the high priest; for it is written that the angel Gabriel, "standing on the right side of the altar of incense," appeared to him. And the context seems to do much to compel one to reach this conclusion. But I am well aware of the fact that all these points can be invalidated with ease, for those texts that have been adduced do not say that there was an altar or a censer in that place, but rather that it was outside and that the incense with the glowing embers had to be received by the priest who was to go in and that it had to be burned inside. Nor is this sufficient reason for thinking that the incense was placed on the fire in the Holy of Holies, "so that the smoke and vapor covered the mercy seat," as stated above; for it means the fire received outside in the censer and brought in by the priest. Nor is it thought to have been a hanging censer such as the church now has; but it is thought to have been stationary, like the vessel or the cup into which the incense was put. What, then, shall we say with regard to the apostle, who states that there was a golden censer in the Holy of Holies? Therefore one can say that the censer was in the Holy of Holies, since it belonged there and was brought there by the priest on the Feast of the Atonement. And this is what I think until I am better informed.

Furthermore, it is customary to draw attention to the fact that in 1 Kings 8:9 it is written that in the ark there was nothing but the two tables of the covenant.[11] But the apostle says that a golden urn holding the manna and Aaron's rod were also in it. Here Faber distorts the preposition and understands "with which" instead of "in which," so that in this way he could maintain that it was not in the ark but was with the ark. And certainly Ex. 16:33 simply says: "Take a jar, and put an omer of manna in it, and place it before the Lord, to be kept throughout your generations. . . . And Aaron placed it in the tabernacle." Although one cannot gather from this text or, in my recollection, in any other Scripture passage that a golden urn is meant, yet it is clearly stated that there is a jar for the manna. Therefore it follows that although it is recorded that there was nothing but manna in the ark, yet one should not understand that the manna was kept without its jar (which he calls a golden urn here); and thus there is agreement with

11 Paul of Burgos, *Additio* on Heb. 9:4, in Lyra, *Postilla.*

1 Kings 8:9. But concerning Aaron's rod Num. 17:10 says: "Put back the rod of Aaron into the tabernacle of the covenant, to be kept there as a sign for the rebels of the Children of Israel." One cannot hold on the basis of this text that the rod was in the ark unless one takes the ark to be "the tabernacle of the covenant," just as one must understand Ex. 16:34, when it said about the manna: "And Aaron placed it in the tabernacle," as quoted above. Yet others say [12] both that they were outside at the side of the ark and that they can be said to have been in the ark because they were at the side of the ark, as is stated in Deut. 31:26: "Take this book, and put it by the side of the ark of the covenant." Or one can say according to 1 Kings 8:9 that after Solomon had built the temple, he transferred Aaron's rod from the ark, not because this can be proved with any.text, but because it can be shown that a similar thing happened in the case of this Book of Deuteronomy, which, as is recorded (cf. 2 Kings 22:8), was found, at the time of King Josiah, not at the side of the ark but behind the altar.

7. [*But into the second only the high priest goes, and he but once a year, and not without taking blood*] *which he offered for his own and the people's ignorance.*

This "ignorance" means physical sins against the Law, that is, impurities in dress, drink, food, flesh. For, as the apostle says below in ch. 10:4, "It is impossible that the blood of bulls and goats should take away sins," namely, of the conscience. Therefore the Law was a very heavy burden, and yet it justified and sanctified only carnal and temporal things.

9. [*According to this arrangement, gifts and sacrifices are offered*] *which cannot perfect the conscience.*

From this text, as has also been stated above, one has a clear statement of the proper distinction between the old and the new law; for then the sins, righteousness, sacrifices, sacred rites, promises, doctrines, and priests were all carnal and did not sanctify "according to the conscience" but according to the body. Now, however, our sins, righteousnesses, sacrifices, sacred rites, promises, and doctrines, and our Priest are all spiritual and sanctify according to the conscience. Yet both were commanded by

[12] Cf. Lyra, *Postillae, ad* 1 Kings 8:9.

God, but the former were "imposed" — as he states here — "until the time of reformation." And hence what the Master of the Sentences says in his fourth book is true in some measure — although he is censured by all — namely, that the sacraments of the old Law, "even though they were performed in faith and love," did not make righteous.[13] For it is completely true that they did not make righteous because of their sacraments and sacrifices, even when these were performed in love, but that love itself and faith accomplished this. Nor is this strange, since in the New Testament it is not the sacrament but faith in the sacrament that makes righteous.[14]

13. *For if the . . . sprinkled ashes of a heifer sanctify those who are defiled.*

In Num. 19:2 ff. we read: "Tell the people of Israel to bring you a red heifer without defect, in which there is no blemish, and upon which a yoke has never come" — for this reason the apostle prefers to call it a heifer here, evidently because it is a young animal — "and you shall give it to Eleazar the priest. He shall lead it outside the camp and sacrifice it in the sight of all, and dipping his finger in the blood he shall sprinkle the blood seven times toward the tabernacle and shall burn the heifer in the sight of all, after consigning her skin and her flesh as well as her blood and her offal to the fire. And the priest shall also throw cedar wood and hyssop and scarlet stuff dyed twice into the fire which consumes the heifer." And below (cf. v. 9) we read: "But a man who is clean shall gather up the ashes of the heifer and deposit them outside the camp in a place that is completely clean, to be kept for the multitude of the Children of Israel and for a water of sprinkling, because the heifer has been burned for sin." And later (cf. vv. 17-19) it is stated: "And they shall take some ashes of the burnt sin offering and add running water in a vessel, and a man who is clean shall dip hyssop in this water and sprinkle with it every tent, all the furnishings, and every man polluted by contact of this kind; and in this way the clean man shall sprinkle the unclean on the third and on the seventh day." Likewise (cf. vv. 11-12): "He who has touched the dead

13 See p. 172, n. 6.
14 Cf. p. 172, n. 6.

body of a human being and for this reason has been unclean for seven days shall be sprinkled with this water on the third and on the seventh day and in this way shall be made clean. If he has not been sprinkled on the third day, it will not be possible for him to be made clean on the seventh day." From this one understands from what source David took this statement in Ps. 51:7: "Purge me with hyssop, and I shall be clean." For all teachers agree that by this heifer the humanity of Christ was meant.[15] For on the seventh day the humanity of Christ was offered for us. On the seventh day, says Burgensis, because during the whole time of the Law up to the time of Christ only six heifers were offered in this way.[16] The first was offered by Moses in the wilderness. Its ashes lasted up to the time of the Babylonian captivity. The second was offered by Ezra for the second temple, and the remaining four were offered by others up to the time of Christ.

14. *How much more shall the blood of Christ cleanse our conscience!*

He gives a beautiful description of the difference between the purity of the New Testament and that of the Old Testament, and he deduces it by pointing out the contrasts. For the purity of the Old Testament lay in the flesh, in clothing or vessels; the new purity lies in the conscience, in the heart or mind. The impurity of the Old Testament is contracted by touching a dead or an unclean person, that of the New Testament by dead works or sins. The purity of the Old Testament tended to serve creatures or desires, that of the New Testament to serve the living God.

Let us, too, run through these points one by one. First the purity of the conscience. This means that a man is not bitten by the recollection of his sins and is not disquieted by the fear of future punishment, as Ps. 112:7 states: "The righteous shall not be afraid of evil tidings." For, as the prophet says,[17] an evil conscience is caught and troubled between a sin committed in the past and future punishment as between difficulties, just as the apostle says in Rom. 2:9: "There will be tribulation and distress."

---

[15] See, for example, Peter Lombard, *Collectanea in epistolam ad Hebraeos, Patrologia, Series Latina,* CXCII, 472.

[16] Paul of Burgos, *Additio* II on Num. 19, in Lyra, *Postillae.*

[17] A reference to Lam. 1:3.

For since it cannot change a sin committed in the past and in any way avoid the future wrath, it cannot escape being distressed and troubled, no matter where it turns. Nor is it freed from these difficulties except through the blood of Christ; and if it looks at Him through faith, it believes and realizes that its sins have been washed away and taken away [18] in Him. Thus through faith it is at the same time purified and made calm, so that out of joy over the remission of sins it no longer dreads punishments. Accordingly, to this purity no law, no works, and nothing at all except this blood of Christ alone can contribute; nor indeed can the blood itself do this unless the heart of man believes that this blood has been shed for the remission of sins. For one must believe Him who makes the covenant when He says (Matt. 26:28; Luke 22:20): "This is the blood which is shed for you and for many for the forgiveness of sins." Secondly, by "dead works" he undoubtedly means sins; for he surely calls those works dead which pollute the conscience and from which it is cleansed through the blood of Christ. But nothing except sin pollutes the conscience. From this exceedingly weighty statement it evidently follows that even good works done outside grace are sins, so much so that they can also be called dead. For if the conscience is mortally unclean without the blood of Christ, it can do only what it itself is, that is, what is unclean, as the apostle also teaches in Titus 1:15: "To the unclean nothing is clean." It is certain, however, that he is not speaking about venial impurity but about impurity that is mortal. Otherwise even to the clean and the saintly nothing is clean, that is, without venial sin, since even their righteousnesses are unclean, as Is. 64:9 [19] says. And thus the opinion of those who call good works outside grace dead but not mortal [20] comes completely to nothing, for here the apostle manifestly makes "dead" and "mortal" identical when he uses the phrase "from dead works." Otherwise if "dead" is identical here with what is "not meritorious," as they say, it follows that the blood of Christ will cleanse, not sinners but those who have done "good works in general" (as they call them). Consequently, they would also be

[18] We have been unable to reproduce in English the play on *abluta* and *ablata*.

[19] The original has "Is. 44."

[20] Cf., among others, Peter Lombard, *Sententiae,* Book IV, Dist. 15, ch. 4, *Patrologia, Series Latina,* CXCII, 875, as well as various commentators on him.

compelled to say that "unclean," "sin," "transgression," etc., are identical with "not meritorious," which amounts to nothing else than completely overturning all Scripture by means of a new meaning of words. From this it follows that a good, clean, quiet, and joyful conscience is nothing except faith in the remission of sins. This faith can be put only in the Word of God, which proclaims to us that the blood of Christ was shed for the remission of sins. For no matter to what extent we were to see or hear that the blood of Christ was shed, the conscience would by no means be made clean as a result of this unless the words "for the remission of sins" are added. For the Jews saw, all the Gentiles heard, and they were not made clean. Indeed, it is not enough either to believe that it was shed for the remission of sins unless they believe that it was shed for.the remission of their own sins. Behold, only the blood of Christ that was shed makes the conscience clean through faith in the Word of Christ. Therefore here, too, the apostle has previously mentioned "the blood of Christ, *who through the Holy Spirit offered Himself.*" And Rom. 3:25 speaks of Him "whom God put forward as an expiation through faith in His blood." One should note by all means that he does not simply say "through His blood" (which amounts to the same thing, although it is stated somewhat obscurely) but "through faith in His blood, etc.," that is, through the faith that is in His blood, namely, in the blood that was shed for us, just as He Himself also says in John 6:55-56: "My flesh is food indeed, and My blood is drink indeed. He who eats My flesh, etc." For he means this "eating" and "drinking" in a spiritual sense, that is, believing, just as St. Augustine expressly explains when commenting on this passage. He says: "To what end do you prepare your belly and your tooth? Believe, and you have eaten." [21] Therefore one should also pay special attention to the pronouns "His," "His own," "My," etc. For not all flesh or all blood, but only Christ's, that is, that which was shed for the remission of sins, makes clean and nourishes. From this it follows that those who meditate on Christ's Passion only in order that they may suffer with Him or gain from it something else than faith meditate in a way that is nothing short of fruitless and heathenish. For even what heathen could not suffer this way with Christ in His suffering? But one should think of His Passion

[21] Augustine, *In Joannis Evangelium Tractatus,* Ch. VI, Tr. XXV, 12, *Patrologia, Series Latina,* XXXV, 1602.

with the desire that faith be increased, namely, that the more frequently one meditates, the more fully one believes that the blood of Christ was shed for one's own sins. For this is what it means to drink and eat spiritually, namely, to be enriched and incorporated into Christ by means of this faith, as stated above. This is certainly true to the extent that purification under the Law also resulted from a kind of faith. For nothing was taken away from the body, the clothing, or the vessel polluted by contact with an unclean corpse except an opinion and a certain consciousness of wrong remaining as a result of contact of this kind. For actually they were unclean only because the Law had decided that they were. Here, where there has been true uncleanness, the conscience is cleansed far more.

Thirdly, *to serve the living God.* From this it manifestly follows that without Christ one does not "serve the living God" but either creatures or idols, that is, the things "that are nothing in the world" (cf. 1 Cor. 8:4), even though they seem to be doing what is good. Therefore the notion which says that one can serve God without grace and not sin is destroyed again. For if not to sin means not to serve the living God, nay, rather to serve someone other than God, the well-known commandment that "you shall worship your God, and serve Him alone" (Matt. 4:10; cf. Deut. 6:13) will be false. Finally, although the apostle wrote to the Philippians [22] (3:6) that he had lived blameless in the righteousness of the Law, yet, on the other hand, he confesses in Titus 3:3 ff. that formerly he had served passions, etc. Therefore he also says: "We, too, were once foolish, disobedient, led astray, slaves to various passions and pleasures, passing our days in malice and envy, hated, and hating one another. But when the goodness and loving-kindness of God our Savior appeared, He saved us, not because of the deeds of righteousness we did but according to His own mercy."

15. [*Therefore He is the Mediator of a new covenant, so that those who are called may receive the promised eternal inheritance, since a death has occurred*] *for redemption from the transgressions* [*committed under the former covenant*].

[22] The original has "Colossians."

The apostle should not be understood to be speaking here of the transgressions that are committed by touching a corpse and, in general, as he stated above (v. 10), "in food, drink, various baptisms" — that is, ablutions — "and righteousnesses of the flesh." For transgressions of this kind were figures of those transgressions by which the heart and the conscience are polluted, that is, which are contrary to the commandments of the Decalog, which Christ took away with His new covenant, although He also abrogated those ceremonials and terminated them completely with the same new covenant. But although He began to put an end to transgressions of the conscience and the Decalog, yet He does not terminate them as yet; for He Himself is the end of sins and the beginning of righteousness, as Gabriel said in Dan. 9:24, "to put an end to sin and to bring in everlasting righteousness."

Therefore he touches, though somewhat obscurely in passing, on the nature and power of the Law when he mentions the transgressions *committed under the former covenant.* But by this he means what he states more clearly in Rom. 5:20: "The Law came in that the offense might abound." And in Gal. 3:19 we read: "The Law was enacted on account of transgressions." And again in Rom. 4:15: "The Law works wrath." And this was beautifully prefigured through the ceremonial laws of the old covenant. For if there had been no law which prohibited contact with a corpse, a menstruous woman, a woman in childbed, a man who has an emission of semen, an unclean vessel, garment, and house, it would be no sin to have touched these. The same thing would be true if the Law made no distinction between clean and unclean animals, just as in those days the Gentiles did not sin, and today the Christians do not sin because they touched, ate, touch, and eat such things. Just as it is altogether true concerning those laws that "the power of sin is the Law" (1 Cor. 15:56) and that "where there is no law, there is no transgression" (Rom. 4:15), so the true and spiritual Law of the Decalog is "the power of sin," yet in a different way; for the Law of the Decalog is the power of sin through the knowledge of oneself. Not so the Ceremonial Law; for whether the Decalog is known or not known, still there is sin in the human race, and it is through the Law that one learns for the first time that it is there. But the Ceremonial Law made only that a sin which was not a sin without it.

17. *For a testament takes effect only at death.*

This passage gives a clear illustration of the allegorical understanding of the Law of Moses, by which we learn that everything contained in that Law was promised and prefigured with reference to Christ and in Christ, and that for this reason (as has been seen above) under the name "testament" and "promise" the death of Him who would be true God and true man was determined long ago. For since He cannot die, yet promises (namely, by making a testament) that He will die, it was necessary for Him to become man and thus to fulfill what He had promised. Therefore let us follow Chrysostom, who, investigating the distinguishing features of both testaments, says: "For a testament is made when the day of death is near. Moreover, such a testament regards some as heirs but disinherits others. Again, a testament contains certain provisions on the part of the one who makes it and certain requirements to be met by the heirs, so that they receive certain things and do certain things. Again, a testament must have witnesses." [23] Let us look at these three points in order. For Chrysostom says no more about the well-known fact that Christ made His testament when the day of His death was near. The evangelists, you see, relate unanimously that when Christ passed along the cup which had been blessed by Him, He said: "This cup is the new testament in My blood" (Luke 22:20), and this at the Last Supper. But Chrysostom also touches too briefly on why He made a testament, on what was to be received. This should have been discussed most of all. Therefore one should know that He made a will and left immeasurable blessings, namely, the remission of sins and eternal life, when He made His completely trustworthy testament. For in Luke 22:20 He said: "This is the blood which will be shed for you." Mark says "for many" (14:24). But Matt. 26:28-29 contains the clearest statement of all. There He said: "For this is My blood of the new testament, which will be shed for many for the remission of sins. But I tell you I shall not drink again of this fruit of the vine until that day when I drink it new with you in My Father's kingdom." With these most delightful words He bequeathes to us, not the riches or the glory of the world but once and for all absolutely all blessings, that is, as I have said, the remission of sins and possession of the future kingdom. Thus

---

[23] Chrysostom, *Homiliae*, XVI, 1, col. 123 (341).

[W, LVII-3, 212, 213]

He also says in Luke 22:29: "And I appoint for you (He says: "I appoint," not "I shall appoint"; for it is proper to use the verb in the present tense when making a testament) as My Father appointed a kingdom for Me." These are the precious and inestimable things about which 2 Peter 1:3-4 says: "Even as His divine power has granted to us all things that pertain to life and godliness through the knowledge of Him who calls us by His own glory and power, through whom He has granted us the very great and precious promises, that through these you may become partakers of the divine nature by escaping from the corruption of that lust which is in the world."

Let us return to Chrysostom. In the first place, He did not make a testament for all, because "He disinherits some," as He says in John 17:9: "I am praying for them, not for the world." Likewise in John 17:20: "I do not pray for these only, but also for those who are to believe in Me through their word." Likewise because He did not say "for all" but "which will be shed for many" (Mark 14:24; Matt. 26:28). And here (Heb. 9:15) we read: "So that those who are called may receive the promised eternal salvation." But this touches on the subject of predestination, which is either too difficult or too harsh for our feeble intellect to be able to grasp. Therefore, to speak rather humbly, He left the legacy only to those who fear His name and believe in Him, as John 1:12 states: "He gave power to become children of God to those, etc." And Ps. 25:14 says: "The Lord is a support for those who fear Him, and He makes His covenant known to them," where the Hebrew is said to have: "The secret of the Lord is for those who fear Him." In the second place, the witnesses of this testament are the Holy Spirit Himself and the apostles, as John 15:26 states: "The Spirit of truth, who proceeds from the Father, He will bear witness concerning Me, and you will bear witness, because you have been with Me from the beginning." Therefore they said in Acts 3:15: "To this we are witnesses." And in Acts 1:8 we read: "And you shall be My witnesses in Jerusalem, etc." In the third place, what those for whom He made the testament do He also expressed when He said: "Do this in remembrance of Me" (Luke 22:19; 1 Cor. 11:24); that is, they are to proclaim His death (1 Cor. 11:26), preach penitence, the remission of sins, and eternal life. Then they are not to receive in vain the grace bequeathed by the testament but to make use of it against lusts.

For this is what He said: "This is My commandment, that you love one another" (John 15:12), likewise the other things He teaches them about bearing persecutions, about love, and about peace in a very beautiful discourse in John 12 — 18. Behold, this is what the Old Testament prefigures, where by means of the blood of calves they were cleansed for the remission of sins of the flesh and in this way became clean and remained worthy possessors of the Promised Land and its blessings.

23. *Thus it is necessary for the copies of the heavenly things [to be purified with these rites, but the heavenly things themselves with better sacrifices than these].*

Chrysostom: "But what things does he now call heavenly? They are not heaven, are they? They are not the angels, are they? No, they are the things that take place among us. Therefore the things that are ours are in heaven, and these things of ours are heavenly, even though they are celebrated on earth." But how this can take place follows in the same place: "To be on earth and not to be takes place in a certain way and voluntarily." "If we draw near to God, we are in heaven. For what do I care about heaven when I see the God of heaven? Thus Christ said: 'We will come to Him and make Our home with Him' (John 14:23)." [24] This is what Chrysostom says. Therefore to be heavenly is to love heavenly things and to set one's mind on things that are divine, as Col. 3:2-3 states: "Set your minds on things that are above, not on things that are on earth. For you have died, and your life is hid with Christ in God." Likewise Phil. 3:20: "But our commonwealth is in heaven." Likewise 1 Cor. 15:47-49: "The first man was from the earth, earthly. . . . the second man is from heaven. As was the earthly man, such also are the earthly; and as is the heavenly, such also are the heavenly. Therefore just as we have borne the likeness of the earthly, let us also bear the likeness of the heavenly." We read about this again in 2 Cor. 3:18: "But we, with unveiled face reflecting the glory of the Lord, are transformed into the same image from glory to glory, as by the Spirit of the Lord." Therefore "the heavens" are mentioned in many places in the Old Testament. Ps. 19:1: "The heavens are telling the glory of

24 Chrysostom, *Homiliae,* XVI, 2-3, col. 125 (343—344).

God." Is. 45:8: [25] "Drop down dew, O heavens, from above, and let the clouds rain righteousness." In short, therefore, to be heavenly is to despise the visible things, yes, even their images, and to cling to God alone, the divine Good, that is, the divine will, in prosperity as well as in adversity, in life and in death. To be earthly is to despise the invisible things, that is, the divine will, and to cling to the visible things, to set one's mind on the good fortune of the world. Therefore Christ bears witness everywhere that He does the will of His Father, and He teaches others to do the same thing, as He says in John 4:34: "My food is to do the will of My Father." To cling to God is to be freed from the world and all creatures; to bear the image of Christ is to live according to the love and the example of Christ. "He who says that he loves God, and does not keep His commandments is a liar," says 1 John 2:4. But since these divine blessings are invisible, incomprehensible, and deeply hidden, nature cannot attain or love them unless it is lifted up through the grace of God. For the same reason it happens that the spiritual man can be judged, known, and seen by no one, not even by himself; for he remains in the deepest darkness of God. David learned this and bears witness to it when he says in Ps. 31:20: "Thou shalt hide them in the covert of Thy presence" (that is, in the covert which is before Thee). To be sure, this begins in this life; but it will be completed in the life to come. Therefore it is a great thing to be a Christian and to have one's life hidden, not in some place, as in the case of the hermits, or in one's own heart, which is exceedingly deep, but in the invisible God Himself, namely, to live amid the things of the world and to be nourished by what appears nowhere except by means of ordinary verbal indication and hearing alone, as Christ says in Matt. 4:4: "Man does not live by bread alone but by every word." Thus the bride says in the Song of Solomon (5:2): "I am sleeping (because she is not aware of the things that are visible) and my heart is awake." On the other hand, those who are earthly are sleeping, and their heart is sleeping. Therefore it is evident that Christ's believers are most properly called heavenly because if "the soul is present more where it loves than where it lives," [26]

[25] The original has "Is. 43."

[26] Although Luther and others attributed this play on words to Augustine, its immediate source seems to be Bernard of Clairvaux, *Liber de praecepto et dispensatione*, ch. XX, par. 60, *Patrologia, Series Latina*, CLXXXII, 892.

and if it is the nature of love to change one who loves into what is loved,[27] it is true that those who love heaven and God are and are called heavenly and divine, though not because they are heavenly by nature or in a metaphysical sense. For in this sense, nothing except heavenly bodies would be heavenly; indeed, even the demons and absolutely all the souls of men would be heavenly, since they are of a certain heavenly, that is, incorporeal, nature.

24. [*For Christ has entered, not into a sanctuary made with hands, a copy of the true one, but into heaven itself, now*] *to appear in the presence of God in our behalf.*

As has been stated, some learn to know Christ through speculation, others through practice.[28] The former believe that Christ appears in the presence of God in behalf of others, but the latter believe that Christ has appeared in the presence of God in our behalf. Therefore a Christian must be sure, yes, completely sure, that Christ appears and is a Priest before God in his behalf. For as he will believe, so it will happen to him. Therefore Mark 11: 23-24 says: "Whoever does not doubt in his heart, but believes that what he says will come to pass, it will be done for him. Therefore I tell you, whatever you ask in prayer, believe that you receive it, and you will." In Matt. 8:13 Christ says to the centurion: "Go; be it done for you as you have believed." And in James 1:6-7 we read: "But let him ask in faith, with no doubting; for he who doubts is like a wave of the sea that is driven and tossed by the wind. For that person must not suppose that . . . he will receive anything from Him." For this reason one must observe most prudently and circumspectly the opinion of those who apply the well-known statement in Eccles. 9:1, namely, "Man does not know whether he is worthy of love or of hatred," to the circumstances of the present hour in order that in this way they may make a man uncertain with regard to the mercy of God and the assurance of salvation.[29] For this amounts to a complete overturning of Christ and of faith in Him. For Ecclesiastes is not speaking about present circumstances. No, it is speaking about perseverance and future

[27] Cf. Dionysius the Areopagite, *De divinis nominibus,* ch. 4, par. 15, *Patrologia, Series Graeca,* III, 713.

[28] See pp. 215—217.

[29] See Luther's comments on Eccl. 9:1-2 (*W,* 20, 158).

circumstances, which are certain for no one, as the apostle says: "Let anyone who thinks that he stands take heed lest he fall" (1 Cor. 10:12). And Rom. 11:20 says: "You stand through faith. Do not be high-minded" — that is, boast — "but fear." This is sufficiently clear from the very text of Ecclesiastes (9:1-2), for it says: "There are righteous men, and their works are in the hands of God; yet man does not know whether he is worthy of love or of hatred. But all things are kept uncertain for the time to come." Therefore those who despise their prayers and efforts, and reject them as uncertain, act very wickedly. For this is contrary to what the apostle says in 1 Cor. 9:26: [30] "I do not run aimlessly; I do not fight" — that is, strike in fights — "as one beating the air." Hence St. Bernard, in his sermons on the Song of Solomon, admonishes his brothers not to despise their prayers in any way but to believe that they are written and have been written in heaven before they are completed, and that they should expect with the greatest certainty that their wish, namely, that their prayers, have either been heard and are to be fulfilled in their own good time or that it is better if they are not fulfilled.[31]

There are two questions. In the first place, one asks how the saints of the old law were justified.[32] Here the apostle denies that the saints were righteous and perfect through the Law, although it is certain that their works, that is, the works of the Law and of obedience, were meritorious. Indeed, many, like Zechariah and Elizabeth in Luke 1:6 and others, were made blameless through those works. On the basis of what has been said, the answer is easy. For those who lived by faith truly good works were meritorious, that is, as long as they kept the Law spiritually on the inside as well as physically on the outside. Thus Rom. 2:25 says: "Circumcision is of value if you keep the Law." Yet it is of no value if you do not keep the Law. For what does it mean when one says that keeping the Law is of no value if you do not keep the Law, and that keeping the Law is of value if you keep the Law? Nothing else than that external ceremonies have been prescribed, not because there is salvation in them but to the extent that there

---

[30] The original has "1 Cor. 12."

[31] Bernard of Clairvaux, *Sermones in Quadragesima,* V, 5, *Patrologia, Series Latina,* CLXXXIII, 180.

[32] Cf. Peter Lombard, *Sententiae,* Book III, Dist. 25, *Patrologia, Series Latina,* CXCII, 809—811.

is occasion to practice faith and love, and to curb sins more effectively. But where one has begun to observe them with another end in view and to practice them for another purpose, as is done by the hypocrites, then they should be completely abrogated and removed. Thus today, too, one can say about ecclesiastical ceremonies with all possible justification that tonsure, adornment, and other ceremonial displays are indeed of value "if you keep the Law"; that is, keeping the laws of the church is of value if in this way you practice the Law of God, fulfill it more, and sin less. But if you cling to these things alone, then "your circumcision has become uncircumcision" (Rom. 2:25); that is, the keeping of the Law has become a transgression of the Law. Therefore we read in the same place (Rom. 2:23): "You who boast in the Law, do you dishonor God by breaking the Law?" In this way one can pass judgment on the words for which the Master of the Sentences is censured by all when he teaches in the fourth book that works of the old Law were of no value, even if they were done in faith and love.[33] For if he understood this to mean that because of their nature they contributed nothing at all to grace and merit, his understanding was altogether right; for absolutely nothing external is of value to the soul. But if he meant that they could not become meritorious and pleasing to God through those who were in faith, he was completely wrong; for "all things work together for good for the saints" (cf. Rom. 8:28), and "all the paths of the righteous are mercy and truth" (cf. Ps. 25:10). For it is impossible for him who is in the grace of God to do anything else than a good work, as that passage in John (1 John 5:18) states: "He who is born of God does not sin."

The second question. How is it that even now our sacrifice does not cease, when we are perfect and righteous through the grace of Baptism and repentance? For Christ is offered for us every day. To this question Chrysostom replies: "We sacrifice indeed, but for the remembrance of His death; and this is the one sacrifice that was offered once." [34] This is how I understand his statement: Christ was offered only once, as stated in a preceding chapter (Heb. 7:27). But what is offered by us every day is not so much a sacrifice as the remembrance of that sacrifice, as He

---

[33] See p. 207, n. 13.

[34] Chrysostom, *Homiliae*, XVII, 3, col. 131 (349).

said: "Do this in remembrance of Me" (Luke 22:19; 1 Cor. 11:24). For He does not suffer as often as He is remembered to have suffered. But it is far more necessary for this remembrance to be repeated than it formerly was, when the repetition of the remembrance of the Passover of the Lord and of the exodus from Egypt was prescribed. Furthermore, the sacrifice of the New Testament is perfect and has ceased completely so far as the Head of the church, who is Christ, is concerned; but the spiritual sacrifice of His body, which is the church, is offered from day to day, when the church dies constantly with Christ and celebrates the mystical Passover, namely, when it slays lusts and passes over from this world to the future glory. The apostle also touches beautifully on the difference between the two sacrifices when he says that in the sacrifices of the Law a remembrance of sins took place (cf. Heb. 10:3), but that in our sacrifice a remembrance of the remission of sins took place and takes place through the word which He spoke: "Father, forgive them" (Luke 23:34). Likewise "It is finished" (John 19:30). Likewise "which will be shed for you for the remission of sins" (Matt. 26:28). There, accordingly, the consciousness of sins remains and grows; here it passes away and is diminished.

CHAPTER TEN

5. [*Consequently, when Christ came into the world, He said:*] *Sacrifice and offering Thou hast not desired but a body Thou hast prepared for Me*].

B EFORE we discuss [these words] separately, we shall arrange them in the proper order, as they occur in the Hebrew text. "A sacrifice" — the Septuagint has "sacrifice"; Jerome has "victim" — "and offering Thou hast not desired." "But Thou hast perfected my ears" (Ps. 40:6). The Septuagint has "But a body Thou hast prepared for me." Jerome has "But Thou hast dug out my ears." "Burnt offering and sin offering Thou hast not required. Then I said: 'Lo, I come, in the roll of the book it is written of Me. I have desired to do Thy will, O God, and Thy Law is within My heart' " (Ps. 40:6-8). Emphasis and a raising of the voice must be observed at the words "it is written of me" and at the words "I have desired." Indeed, the last two verses must be read with emphasis, so that they mean: "Away with the beasts! I, I am He who is described and required there! On the contrary, it is about Me that it is written in the roll of the book!" Therefore also "Lo, I come, and although others are rebellious and obstinate either when they hear or when they speak, I, on the other hand, have Thy Law within My heart, namely, in the inmost affection of My heart; that is, I love Thy Law most perfectly — Thy Law which is odious to all others." To understand this, it is helpful to know that for the Hebrews some verbs are neutral and have the nature of nominals, and that the best way to understand them is to change them into their nominals. Thus "I have desired" means "I have had the desire or have been willing." Thus in Ps. 118:25 we have "Make me saved, O Lord!" In the Hebrew this is "Hosannah!" that is, "Save!" that is, "Be the Savior!" or "Make salvation! Bring it about that there is salvation!" One learns this beautifully from Matt. 21:9, where we read: "Hosannah to the Son of David!" That is, "Make salvation for this Christ, the Son of David!" Likewise in Ps. 22:31,

[W, LVII-3, 219, 220]

where we read: "To the people which shall be born, which the Lord has made," they say in Hebrew "because" or "for the Lord has made," that is, because the Lord is the Maker who makes all things in all, and we make nothing. Thus the Blessed Virgin also says in Luke 1:49: "He who is mighty has done great things for me," that is, "He, the mighty One," which means "He, the Doer of all things."

But that phrase "at the head of the book," which has tormented many, is clearly understood from the Hebrew, namely, "in the roll of the book." [1] This word gives expression to the fact that even those things that were written on the sheets of parchment were written about Christ and are to be fulfilled, unless someone wants to understand "roll" in a mystical sense as meaning the coverings of the Law. In this way the translations could be brought into agreement, namely, that the Septuagint has taken "the head of the book" to mean the mystical sense itself, and the Hebrew text has taken "the roll" to mean the external sense of the Law — the sense which would be the tail and the hind feet of the Law, so to speak. For they are usually brought into agreement in the same way everywhere. And one can see that this was prefigured in Ex. 4:4, where Moses is commanded to take hold of the tail of the staff that was turned into a serpent. On the other hand, however, in Gen. 47:31 [2] Jacob "did obeisance to the top of the staff." Likewise in Esther 5:2.[3] But the Law is undoubtedly meant by the staff. Accordingly, if "the head of the Law," "the end of the Law," as the apostle says, the top of the Law, is Christ, surely the tail of the Law, the feet of the Law, are the letter itself, that is, Moses. Thus the wise man says: "If you are asked twice, let your answer have a head" (Ecclus. 32:7-8).

It is still necessary to explain how "Thou hast perfected my ears" agrees with "a body Thou hast prepared for me." In the Hebrew the word is identical in meaning with "to adapt," "to prepare," "to adjust," likewise with "to dig out" and "to open," likewise with "to buy." For this reason the Septuagint followed the first meaning and said "body" instead of "ears." For the Hebrew has the word "ears" but does not have the word "body."

---

[1] Cf. Paul of Burgos, *Additio* on Heb. 10, in Lyra, *Postilla.*

[2] The original has "Gen. 49."

[3] The original has "Esther 1."

Here, therefore, the apostle follows the understanding of the Septuagint by taking the adapted body of Christ to be what was offered on account of sins instead of the bodies of beasts, as follows in the text. But the Hebrew word has a different meaning. For "to dig out" and "to open the ears" is nothing else than to cause one to hear, just as the earth is opened and dug out, as in Mark 7:34: "Ephphatha," that is, "Be opened." And the statement "And his ears were opened" follows. But this opening means to cause one to be obedient and to believe. For faith is obedience, as Rom. 1:5 states: "To bring about obedience to the faith." And thus the meaning will be that in the New Testament the offerings of beasts are not pleasing to God. Indeed, they are never pleasing to Him. But He takes pleasure in the offering and obedience of faith. Thus we read in Jer. 5:3: "O Lord, Thy eyes have regard for faith." Therefore throughout Scripture the Spirit has only one aim: that we hear the voice of God, that is, that we believe. "For he who believes will be saved" (cf. Mark 16:16). But the words "Thou hast opened My ears" can be understood actively or passively. Actively in this way: "Thou hast opened my ears," that is, "Thou hast made Me obedient to Thee." This sense is a bit forced. Passively in this way: "Thou hast opened My ears," that is, "Thou hast brought it about that people were made to believe Me and in Me, and that in this way through Me, not through beasts, remission of sins and salvation were accomplished for those who believe in Me." And this is the sacrifice that is pleasing to God, namely, faith in Christ. Thus Matt. 17:5 states: "This is My beloved Son, with whom I am well pleased; listen to Him." In Gen. 49:10, where our text has "And He will be the Expectation of the peoples," other texts have "And to Him shall be the hearing and the gathering of the peoples." It is as if he were saying: "The ears of the peoples will be opened, and they will believe in Him." For no one listens to Christ except when the Father digs out and opens his ears, that is, "draws him" (John 6:44). Therefore what the Septuagint has said about Christ's own body, this the Hebrew text says about the mystical body of Christ when it speaks of a digging out of the ears. But both are one mystical body, which is constantly offered with Christ. Therefore both senses can be called one sense, and thus it is evident that in Hebrew all three meanings can have one sense: "Thou hast adapted," "Thou hast dug out," "Thou hast bought my ears." Alternatively: "Thou hast adapted," "Thou hast dug out," "Thou hast bought My body" — the mystical body — adapted, dug out, bought with My own body, which was offered and adapted for it.

But the word "ears" is emphatic and forceful to an extraordinary degree; for in the new law all those countless burdens of the ceremonies, that is, dangers of sins, have been taken away. God no longer requires the feet or the hands or any other member; He requires only the ears. To such an extent has everything been reduced to an easy way of life. For if you ask a Christian what the work is by which he becomes worthy of the name "Christian," he will be able to give absolutely no other answer than that it is the hearing of the Word of God, that is, faith. Therefore the ears alone are the organs of a Christian man, for he is justified and declared to be a Christian, not because of the works of any member but because of faith.

19. *Therefore, brethren, since we have confidence to enter the sanctuary by the blood of Christ.*

With these somewhat obscure, nay, I should rather say exceedingly beautiful and rich words, the apostle evidently wants us to imitate Christ, who suffered and by dying crossed over to the glory of the Father. The meaning, of course, is brief and clear, namely, what is written in Col. 3:3: "You have died with Christ, and your life is hidden with Christ in God." But one must observe with what grace and power of expression the apostle discusses this. In the first place, that figurative veil of the temple was a sign of the flesh of Christ, as the apostle plainly shows here. But the removal of the veil by him who enters, namely, the priest, signifies the death of the flesh of Christ — the death by which He Himself was removed from us and entered the invisible sanctuary. And that way or entrance of the priest in former days was old and dead; it signifies that this way and entrance of Christ is new and alive. And in this manner He fulfilled the figure and took away the shadow. But at the same time this whole fulfillment and figure of the truth (for he beautifully connects them both at the same time and discusses them with the same words) has a meaning that goes beyond this and is the sacrament of the imitation of Christ. His flesh, of course, which He assumed, signifies the weaknesses of our flesh — the weaknesses which we assumed through sin and because of which it comes about that we walk on the old and dead way, that is, by following the lusts of the flesh. Therefore "a new and living way" had to be prepared; and in order that this might come about, lust had to be slain. Therefore the suffering of Christ's flesh, His death and removal, is the sacrament of the slaying of the conscience, of the same death. But Christ's entry into heaven through death is also the sacrament of our new life and way, by which we are to seek only heavenly things and love them with absolutely all our affection after entering into the heavenly things, so that, "our commonwealth," as the apostle says, "is in heaven" (Phil. 3:20). Of this mystical and exemplary suffering of Christ Paul is full throughout nearly all his epistles, as in Rom. 6:4; 8:10; Eph. 4:22 ff.; Col. 3:3; and Phil. (3:10 f.); and everywhere he teaches about the slaying of the old man and the renewing of the inner man. Therefore what Christ did according to the flesh alone (for He did not cross over at some time or other from sins, as we do, but He was always in heaven, as John 3:13 says: "No one has ascended into heaven but the Son of Man, who is in heaven"), through this He, with His single act, is in agreement with our double act, as Augustine says in the fourth chapter of the third book of his *On the Trinity*.[4] For we cross over according to the flesh and according to the spirit, but Christ crossed over only according to the flesh. Therefore the crossing over of our flesh is an example—for we shall be like Him (1 John 3:2)—yet by the crossing over of Christ's flesh the crossing over of the spirit is signified as by a sacrament. Hence arise those various concepts of lives and deaths (so to speak). For life and death at the present time is the workshop in which two other lives and two other deaths fight with each other, so that if love lives, lust dies, and this means to live to God and to die to the world. But if lust lives, love dies, and this means to live to the world and to die to God. For one of the two must either die or live. And these two are called spirit and flesh. Thus in addition to physical life and death there are two lives and deaths, the death of the flesh and the death of the spirit, the life of the flesh and the life of the spirit. The apostle speaks of this very often.

But the apostle challenges us with a twofold exhortation to

---

[4] Augustine, *De Trinitate*, Book IV, ch. 3, pars. 5—6, *Patrologia, Series Latina*, XLII, 889—891; apparently Luther reversed the numbers of the book and the chapter.

enter this new life. For it is an arduous and exceedingly hard thing, especially for those who are inexperienced, to put everything, even life, on Christ. Therefore he first sets forth the example of Christ, our Leader, who fights in the forefront. Although under no compulsion, yet for the purpose of buoying up our confidence He crossed over first of all, and He smooths the exceedingly rough road. Then the apostle points out that Christ not only gave an example by crossing over, but that He also holds out His hand to those who follow. Therefore he says that we "have confidence to enter," for He Himself opened this way for us (Heb. 10:20) and at the same time is for us the Priest who sympathizes with our weaknesses (Heb. 4:15) and is able to help those who are tempted (Heb. 2:18). For this reason we have no excuse for delaying, since He certainly cannot do more for us than He is doing. For while others can teach and exhort to cross over, this Christ alone is not only the Companion but also the One who leads the way, not only the Leader but also the Helper, yes, the Ferryman, as we read in Deut. 32:11: "As an eagle incites its nestlings forth by hovering over its brood, so He spread His wings to receive them and bore them up on His pinions." For he who relies on Christ through faith is carried on the shoulders of Christ, and He will cross over successfully with the bride, of whom it is written that "she comes up through the desert leaning on her beloved" (cf. Song of Sol. 8:5).

24. *Let us consider how to stir up one another to love.*

The church of this time has been gathered from the diverse believers of the world, and very many who are weak, impotent, imperfect, and sinful have been intermingled, as Christ says in John 12:8: "The poor you will always have with you, but Me you will not always have." But because human nature is constituted in such a way that it prefers to deal with those who are good and perfect to dealing with those who are imperfect and difficult — because of this sin it comes about that those who are weaker cause those who are more perfect to be haughty, to despise, to judge, etc., while, on the other hand, those who are more perfect cause those who are weaker to envy and disparage — for this reason the apostles strove with all their might to counter this evil, lest schisms and heresies arise in the church. These, of course, are prevented only by mutual love. Furthermore, the love that is shown to equals or betters is (as one sees everywhere) either no love at all, or it is not Christian, as Matt. 5:43-47 states: "You have heard that it was said to those of old: 'You shall love your friend and hate your enemy.' But I say to you: 'Love your enemies, do good to those who hate you, pray for those who persecute and slander you. For if you love only those who love you, what reward will you have? Do not even the tax collectors do this?'" This, therefore, is the Christian love that is shown to those who are contemptible and unworthy of love; this, in fact, is the kindness that is bestowed on those who are evil and ungrateful. For this is what Christ and God did for us; and we, too, are commanded to love as He did. In the same place we read: "You, therefore, must be perfect, as your Father is perfect" (Matt. 5:48).

26. *For [if we sin] deliberately [after receiving the knowledge of the truth, there no longer remains a sacrifice for sins].*

Commenting on this passage, Chrysostom says in opposition to the Novatians: "Here those who take away repentance rise up again. . . . To them we shall say that here he excludes neither repentance nor the propitiation which comes about through repentance. . . . But he does exclude a second Baptism. For he did not say: 'There is no further remission,' but he says that 'there is no further sacrifice,' that is, there is no second cross." [5] And this refutation of his can be strengthened from the preceding text, where the apostle spoke of "not forsaking our assembly, etc." Here he seems to be speaking about those who forsake the church, outside which there certainly is no repentance or remission. Likewise from the text which follows, where he said: "Recall the former days, etc." Here he clearly calls them—as though they had fallen away—to the repentance which they seemed to deny. But here enough has been said for those who are willing and peaceable. Against those, however, who are contentious one must deal on the basis of other Scripture passages, as we have adequately done in the sixth chapter.[6] For it is certain that every mortal sin is contempt for the Son of God and treads Him underfoot (cf. Heb. 10:29), which the apostle mentions here, just as is clearly proved in 2 Sam. 12:9, where it is said to David:

[5] Chrysostom, *Homiliae*, XX, 1, col. 143 (361).

[6] See p. 182.

"Why, then, have you despised the Word of the Lord?" For he did not sin against faith. No, he sinned against the Fifth Commandment and the Sixth.

One can simply say that the words are to be understood as meaning what is stated in the last chapter of James (5:14 ff.), namely, in the way the apostle says that love "never ends, bears all things, etc." (1 Cor. 13:8, 7). In like manner, the evangelist John says that "He who is born of God does not sin" (1 John 3:9), and the like. From the opposite point of view one can also say that he who is outside Christ cannot repent. In both cases one must understand that there is perseverance; that is, just as he who is in grace cannot sin, no matter what he does, but remains in grace, so he who is in sin, cannot do good, no matter what he does, but remains in sins. Thus in both cases he is describing the existing state of affairs, not declaring a change to be impossible.

CHAPTER ELEVEN

1. *But faith is the substance of things hoped for, [the argument of things not seen].*

MORE recent commentators interpret these words in various ways. Some take "substance" to be "the cause" or "the foundation." [1] And it is true, of course, that faith is that foundation of the apostles and the prophets on which, as the apostle writes in Eph. 2:20, we are built and the "foundation that has been laid," of which he speaks in 1 Cor. 3:11. Thus Christ Himself says in Matt. 16:18: "On this rock I will build My church," that is, on the firmness of faith. But whether this is the meaning of "substance" in this passage we shall leave to others. Here, however, they want "argument" to be the "proof," the "demonstration," and, in general, what in dialectics is called the argument, so that there is some sure knowledge that certain things, that is, "things invisible," exist, namely, because this is how the patriarchs and other saints believed.[2] This view does not please me, not only because from this opinion it would follow that Adam and Abel did not have faith—for, since they were the first believers, their faith was not certain for the reason that others had believed this way, but especially because it seems to be self-contradictory. For this way faith would be nothing else than one person's credulity that has been established and proved by means of the credulity of another person; and thus the apostle would be speaking, not about the faith of all but only about a persuasion, and the proof would be passive, not active. Those who take "argument" to mean reproof hold to the same view. Thus we read in John 8:46: "Who of you will argue Me of sin?" namely, so that faith reproves either its own credulity or that of others. For

1 Peter Lombard, *Collectanea in epistolam ad Hebraeos, Patrologia, Series Latina,* CXCII, 487—488.

2 See, for example, Peter Lombard, *Sententiae,* Book III, Dist. 23, ch. 8, *Patrologia, Series Latina,* CXCII, 806—807.

one must rather say that all these things are properly spoken about the power and the work of faith. For when faith is present, it works mortification and convicts those who do not believe.

Chrysostom, however, takes "substance" in the sense of "reality" and as being identical in meaning with "essence." [3] The Master of the Sentences follows him in his third book, except that he takes "argument" to mean "conviction." [4] Chrysostom takes it to mean "connection," [5] unless perchance the manuscript of the one or the other has been corrupted. For ἔλεγχος, which the apostle has placed here, means "argument," "comprehension," and "indication."

"If these things to be hoped for are thought to be without substance, faith gives them substance. Over and above this, however, it does not give them substance but is their very essence. For example, the resurrection has not yet taken place and does not yet exist in substance; but hope makes it a reality in our soul. This is what he meant by substance." And again: "O what a wonderful word he used when he said: ['Faith is] the conviction of things not seen'! For there is conviction in things that are manifest. Therefore faith is the seeing, he says, of things which do not appear." [6]

In the third place, let us follow the very common use of this noun "substance," which in the Scriptures nearly always means possession, namely, property, as in the preceding chapter (10:34): "Since you knew that you had a better substance and an abiding one." And in Luke 8:43 we read about a woman "who had spent all her substance on physicians." 1 John 3:17 says: "He who has this world's substance." With this word he — in agreement, as it were, with this passage — certainly distinguishes "the substance of this world" from the substance that is not of this world but of the other world. Therefore since faith is nothing else than a clinging to the Word of God, as is stated in Rom. 1:17, it follows that the possession of the Word of God, that is, of the everlasting

[3] Chrysostom, *Homiliae*, XXI, 2, col. 151 (369).

[4] Peter Lombard, *Sententiae*, Book III, Dist. 23, ch. 8, *Patrologia, Series Latina*, CXCII, 806—807.

[5] Cf. *Patrologia, Series Graeca*, LXIII, 369, note (a).

[6] This is a continuation of the quotation from Chrysostom begun at note 3 above.

goods, is at the same time also the taking away (at least so far as affection and clinging are concerned) of all present goods, as Ps. 73:28 states: "For me it is good to cling to God." Therefore the apostle, as a wise and faithful agent of his Lord, properly calls the Hebrews, who founded their substance on this world, back to "a better substance, which is the gaining of the soul" (cf. Heb. 10:34, 39), yes, of all goods, in order that in this way he may divest them of their affection for temporal things and transfer them to heavenly things. Jerome follows this interpretation in his commentary on the Epistle to the Galatians.[7]

3. *By faith we understand that the world was fashioned by the Word of God, [so that visible things were made out of things which do not appear].*

In this passage "the things which do not appear" does not mean "chaos" and that "primordial matter"[8] of nature from which they say the world was created. No, it means the same thing that is stated in Rom. 1:20, namely, that "the invisible things of God are clearly understood through the things that are made." Thus in 1 Cor. 2:9 the apostle also quotes from Isaiah (64:4): "Eye has not seen nor ear heard, nor has it entered into the heart of man what things Thou hast prepared for those that love Thee." And in the same place (1 Cor. 2:10) he says: "The Spirit searches everything, even the depths of God." But how it is that the very simple unity of God is properly spoken of in the plural number— it is safer to be ignorant of this with a pure faith than it is to investigate it with inquisitive speculation. Nor should the apostle's words "out of things which do not appear" disturb us, as if the preposition "out of" denoted the material; for we must put off the shoe of this false notion when we, together with Moses, approach the burning bush of divine Scripture (cf. Ex. 3:5). But what the words "Thy hand created the world out of invisible matter" in Wisd. 11:18 mean I leave to others. The author of the Book of Wisdom Platonized very much. Some say on the basis of little authority that Philo was the author of this book.[9]

[7] Jerome, *Commentaria in epistolam ad Galatas*, Book III (on Gal. 5:20), *Patrologia, Series Latina*, XXVI, 420.

[8] Cf. Reisch, *Margarita philosophica*, Book VIII, ch. 4: "De concordia dictarum opinionum."

[9] This opinion is cited but rejected by Jerome, "Praefatio in libros Salomonis," *Patrologia, Series Latina*, XXVIII, 1307—1308.

4. By faith Abel offered to God a more acceptable sacrifice than Cain.

Here the apostle determines clearly that the importance of the sacrifices and the entire value of the merit did not lie in the worthiness or the greatness of the work, but that faith is the cause; for God weighs the spirits and looks at the hearts. Ps. 7:15 states that He "loves the righteous and searches the hearts." And in 1 Sam. 16:7 He says to Samuel: "Man looks at the outward appearance, but God looks at the heart." Therefore He requires nothing of man except the heart. In Prov. 23:26 we read: "My son, give Me your heart," not your tongue or your hand. Therefore when David had said in Ps. 18:20: "He will reward me according to the works of my hands," he immediately, by way of spiritual precaution, added the word "in the sight of His eyes" (v. 24), lest he seem to be teaching purity of works without purity of the heart, since "in the sight of God" the hands are not pure unless the heart is pure. Therefore in Is. 1:15 He finds fault with so many sacrifices and with nearly all the works of the Law (which surely were good); for, He says, "your hands are full of blood." Therefore the believer is described as being "upright in heart" in Ps. 7:10: "Who saves the upright in heart" and in Ps. 11:2: "To shoot in the dark at the upright in heart." For the uprightness of the heart does not deceive. But every outward person, every appearance, and any title at all—like priest, layman, master, servant—deceives.

Therefore it is clear that these words of the apostle have the same meaning that is recorded in Gen. 4:4: "God had regard for Abel"—namely, first because of his faith, not because of his work, for this follows—"and for his offerings." Accordingly, this is the crossroad where the truly righteous and the hypocrites separate. For those who are truly righteous press forward to works through faith and grace; the hypocrites, with perverse zeal, press forward to grace through works, that is, to what is impossible. But that endless tradition of decretals, decrees, statutes, etc., has multiplied us work-righteous [10] hypocrites like "locusts out of the smoke," as Rev. 9:3 writes, and thus has darkened for us the sun of the completely pure faith, so that the spirit also sobs anew for the church, as in Ps. 12:1: "Save me, O God; for there is

---

[10] The Latin word is *operarii*.

no longer any that is godly, for the faithful have vanished from among the sons of men."

Through which he obtained a testimony.

St. Jerome asks how God gave a testimony to the gifts of Abel, or how one should understand that He had regard for his gifts.[11] And he replies that the translation of Symmachus [12] makes this clear. It says: "And the Lord was inflamed about Abel, etc." For the apostle seems to have followed him when he says that the testimony was given by God. Thus Chrysostom also says with reference to this passage: "It is said that fire descended and consumed his sacrifices. . . . For the language of the Syrians has 'set fire to,' namely, where one would have 'had regard for.' " [13]

That he was righteous . . . and through that faith, though he is dead, he still speaks.

By means of a remarkable example God proves that He cares for those who are oppressed, since after the death of Abel He Himself speaks for him. Even though in this way He points out somewhat obscurely that the soul is immortal and that there is eternal life, yet He does so with power. Thus a righteous man lives, acts, and speaks more truly and better when he no longer lives, acts, and speaks in himself, but when he lives, acts, and speaks in God. For that Abel lives in God he shows by reason of the fact that he also speaks in God. Thus "though he is dead, he still speaks," so that he who, when he was alive, could not teach his one brother through his faith and example, now that he is dead, that is, lives far more vigorously, teaches the whole world. So great a thing is faith, that is, life in God. For this reason it is altogether fitting to sing (Ps. 112:6): "The righteous shall be in everlasting memory" (that is, in the memory of eternity). Thus Chrysostom says: "How does he who is dead still live? For the fact that he is in the mouths of all shows that he is alive. For if

[11] Jerome, *Liber hebraicarum quaestionum in Genesin* (on Gen. 4:4), *Corpus Christianorum, Series Latina,* LXXII, 6—7.

[12] In the passage cited in note 11, Jerome attributes this to Theodotion rather than to Symmachus.

[13] Chrysostom, *Homiliae,* XXII, 1, col. 155 (373).

he had a thousand tongues when alive, he would never be held in such great admiration as he is now held when he is dead." [14] But by this we are all exhorted, not only that death should not be feared, but that it should even be desired as what for Abel and every righteous man is a door and a crossing over from humanity to divinity, from the world to the Father, from wretchedness to glory. For in this way God has shown from the very beginning of the world and of Scripture what great blessings He can make out of a few evils. For Abel had to be slain in order that the glory of life might be shown in his death and that this consolation of life might be greater in Abel than the perturbation of the death that was brought in had been in Adam.

5. *By faith Enoch was taken up* [*so that he should not see death*].

Chrysostom says: "Many ask to what place Enoch was taken up, why he was taken up, and why neither he himself nor Elijah died. And if they are still alive, how are they alive and in what kind of state? But it is needless to ask such questions. The Scriptures have said (Gen. 5:24; 2 Kings 2:11) that Enoch was surely taken up and that Elijah, too, was assumed but they have not added where and in what condition they are. Nothing more, however, is stated than what is necessary." [15] Therefore whatever is stated about them outside the Scriptures must be the opinions or notions of people who do not know, and it is better to have no knowledge of these opinions and notions than to be troubled in vain by idle curiosity. But God wanted his taking up to be recorded in the Holy Scriptures for our sakes, namely, "in order that the human soul," says Chrysostom, "might get the hope that death would be destroyed and the tyranny of the devil would be condemned." For all this took place in order that in the beginning faith concerning the Savior's future redemption might be nourished and sustained, and that the human race might not see itself completely deserted and despair of redemption. For the elect never lacked consolation. Nor did they lack tribulation. Thus although in Abel the human race saw death, yet in him it saw

[14] Chrysostom, *Homiliae*, XXII, 2, col. 156 (374).

[15] Chrysostom, *Homiliae*, XXII, 3, col. 157 (375).

a better life. Although in Enoch it saw no death, yet in him it saw life.

6. *For he who comes to God must believe [that He exists and that He rewards those who seek Him].*

"To believe that God exists" seems to many to be so easy that they have ascribed this belief both to poets and to philosophers, as the apostle also asserts in Rom. 1:20. In fact, there are those who think that this is self-evident. But such human faith [16] is just like any other thought, art, wisdom, dream, etc., of man. For as soon as a trial assails, all those things immediately topple down. Then neither reason nor counsel nor faith has the upper hand. Ps. 107:27 says: "They reeled like a drunken man, and all their wisdom was swallowed up." For this reason the apostle James calls this faith "dead" (2:17), and others call it "acquired" faith.[17] But in man there is nothing that is not vanity and a lie. In the second place, such faith believes nothing about itself but believes only about others. For even if it believes that God exists and rewards those who seek Him, yet it does not believe that God exists and rewards it itself. Therefore, as the saying goes, it is faith about God, not in God.[18] For this reason another faith is needed, namely, the faith by which we believe that we are numbered among those for whom God exists and is a Rewarder. But this faith does not come from nature; it comes from grace. For nature is terrified and flees from the face of God, since it believes that He is not God but is a tyrant, a torturer, and a judge, as the well-known words in Deut. 28:65 state: "The Lord will give you a trembling heart . . . and your life shall hang in doubt before you." And let us give a simile applicable to the two kinds of faith. Just as a candle exposed to the wind loses not only its rays but all light, while the sun shining from above can be disturbed by no power of the winds either in its rays or in itself, so the first kind of faith is extinguished, the second kind never.

[16] *Fides humana* was a faith based on reasoning, persuasion, or some other human ground, rather than on the converting work of the Holy Spirit, which was *fides divina.*

[17] Luther is referring to the notion in Franciscan theology of a *fides [naturaliter] acquisita,* such as that of the demons (cf. James 2:19).

[18] For a related distinction, cf. Peter Lombard, *Sententiae,* Book III, Dist. 23, ch. 4, *Patrologia, Series Latina,* CXCII, 805.

7. *By faith Noah, being warned by God* [*concerning events as yet unseen, took heed and*] *constructed an ark* [*for the saving of his household; by this he condemned the world and became an heir of the righteousness which comes by faith*].

The words of Holy Scripture should not be treated carelessly. For since they are the words of the Spirit, they are necessarily full of weight and majesty. Therefore since He commends to us the faith of the fathers, we must understand that this faith is completely perfect in every way, that is, has been exercised in all trials, so that it became worthy of being described with such great glory as an example for the whole church. In the first place, therefore, the glory of the faith of Noah was such that he believed and stood firm for 100 years, whereas one finds some do not believe for even a moment, like those about whom we read in Ps. 106:13 [19] that "they did not wait for His counsel." For this reason those words "Wait for the Lord" (Ps. 27:14), "Wait for Him if He tarries" (Hab. 2:3), "Be strong" (Ps. 27:14), "Bear up with the Lord" (Ps. 27:14), and the like, are repeated so often in the Holy Scriptures. The second reason is that Noah preached this faith so forcefully and was not listened to. For that he preached is certain from 2 Peter 2:5. Peter calls him "a preacher of righteousness"; and for this reason Noah felt that the more he was tried and tormented, the less he was heard. Moreover, the outcome, namely, that all perished in the Flood, proves that he was not listened to. For if they had believed, they would not have perished. Therefore their greatest sin was unbelief, just as Noah's righteousness was supreme faith. Consequently, the apostle also praises him very highly not so much because he constructed an ark but because he "constructed an ark in faith" by expressly adding faith as the sum and substance of the work. Furthermore, the apostle praises him because he condemned the world through faith, not through any good work, as if he were saying with the greatest clarity that no sin they had committed was as great as their refusal to believe Noah when he preached. Thus Christ says in John 15:22: "If I had not come and spoken to them, they would not have sin." For where there is faith, even sin is not sin. On the other hand, where there is no faith, not even righteousness is righteousness, as Rom. 14:23 says: "Whatever does not proceed from faith is sin." In the third

[19] ·The original has "Ps. 77 [78]."

place, now those things are prone to follow that usually follow
when there are unbelieving listeners and believing teachers,
namely, outcroppings of mocking and slander, of blasphemy, contempt, and disgrace, especially since the delaying of the threat-
ened evil increased the courage of those people but assailed the
faith of this man with completely manifest evidence. As often as
he was condemned as a fool, as a liar, as a babbler, not only by
one person but by all—especially because he, relying only on his
own understanding contrary to the understanding of all, constantly busied himself with the construction of the ark—so often
he saw, heard, and experienced above all the Word of God alone
and constantly and persistently preferred it. For St. Peter also
commends God's patience highly when he says (1 Peter 3:20)
that in the days of Noah this patience with believers and unbelievers was waited for. But that the people were like this can
be understood from those words in Luke 17:26-27, where Christ
says: "As it was in the days of Noah, so will it be in the days of
the Son of Man. They ate, they drank, they married, they were
given in marriage, until the day when Noah entered the ark, and
the Flood came and destroyed them all." With these words He
shows that the faith of this one man was vehemently assailed by
means of the morals of the whole world. And scarcely any battle
is greater than this one, since it is regarded as the height of folly
to think that only one man among all, yes, in opposition to all,
is wise. Therefore the faith of Noah was not that "quiet quality
of the soul" [20] (as we are wont to dream about faith) but the life
of the heart, "as a lily among thorns" (Song of Sol. 2:2), like Jerusalem in the midst of the heathen.

By faith Noah took heed.

That is to say, he took heed by faith which had been constantly tried and tested through many tribulations as through fire.
For this reason the apostle commends the purity of his heart highly
and says that he "took heed" with regard to the things which did
not appear. For to have faith in things that are invisible certainly
means having a heart cleansed and separated from all things that
are visible. This purity of heart is perfect righteousness, as Acts
15:9 says: "He cleansed their hearts by faith."

[20] Cf. Peter Lombard, *Sententiae*, Book III, Dist. 23, ch. 5, *Patrologia, Series
Latina*, CXCII, 805.

8. *By faith Abraham obeyed when he was called to go out to*
a place [which he was to receive as an inheritance; and he went
out, not knowing where he was to go].

In the first place, it was hard to leave his native land, which
it is natural for us to love. Indeed, love for the fatherland is numbered among the greatest virtues of the heathen.[21] Furthermore,
it is hard to leave friends and their companionship, but most of all
to leave relatives and one's father's house. With this example Abraham complied with what is taught in Ps. 45:10: "Hear, O daughter,
consider, and incline your ear, and forget, etc." In the second
place, he went out with no knowledge of where he was going,
with nothing for him to follow except the Word of God concerning
things which were nowhere to be seen. For just as for us the
place where Enoch and Elijah are is situated in darkness, in gloom,
in ignorance, and in the invisible things of God, so to Abraham
this place to which he was called was completely hidden. And
this is the glory of faith, namely, not to know where you are going,
what you are doing, what you are suffering, and, after taking
everything captive — perception and understanding, strength and
will — to follow the bare voice of God and to be led and driven
rather than to drive. And thus it is clear that with this obedience
of faith Abraham gave a supreme example of an evangelical life,
because he left everything and followed the Lord. Preferring the
Word of God to everything and loving it above everything, he was
a stranger of his own accord and was subjected every hour to
dangers of life and death.

Now, however, because every righteous man has his devil and
adversary, it is certain that Abraham had many who found fault
with and condemned this faith and purpose, who either accused
him of folly or out of some pernicious piety advised him not to
believe that what was happening was from God. For the greatest
of all trials is the trial of faith, against which the devil employs
both his own strength and that of all men and all things. Therefore Abraham's faith was tried "as gold in the furnace" (Wisd. of
Sol. 3:6), especially also because, while all the others lived and
acted differently, he alone opposed such numerous examples of
all. For the fact that an example greatly opposed to his life as
a stranger is observed is also the most powerful attack on him

---

[21] Cf. Cicero, *De officiis,* Book I, ch. 17.

whose purpose it was to serve God. The attack is so powerful that Ps. 73 in its entirety cries out against the force of this stumbling block. "As for me," says the psalmist, "my feet had almost stumbled, my steps had well-nigh slipped; for I was envious of the wicked when I saw the peace of sinners" (vv. 2-3). And Ps. 37 — "Be not vexed over evildoers, etc." — is full of exhortations and arguments against the same tempest of stumbling blocks that Jer. 12:1 censures: "Why does the way of the wicked prosper? Why do all who are treacherous thrive?" Moreover, after they had entered the Promised Land, the varying trial of faith not only did not come to an end but was also increased. For "He gave him not even a foot's length," as is stated in Acts 7:5,[22] but as a stranger he endured many evils and dangers in the same land. Besides, he was compelled to journey to Egypt and to return (Gen. 12:10; 13:1). Furthermore, his wife was twice taken away by kings (Gen. 12:15; 20:2). But neither in his son Isaac nor in his grandson Jacob did he see the promises fulfilled. Finally there was the greatest trial of all: he was commanded himself to sacrifice his own son, whom he undoubtedly loved most dearly, none other than the very son in whom he had received the promise of the blessing. Therefore he is most rightfully called and was appointed to be "the father of many nations" (Gen. 17:4; Rom. 4:17-18), "the father of our faith" (cf. Rom. 4:16), and "Abraham's bosom" (Luke 16:22) (which is undoubtedly the same faith that is commended in the Gospel).

On the basis of these arguments one must refute those carnal questions and complaints of ignorant people, especially of the Jews, who, with their eyes fixed on the external works of Abraham, not also on his faith, consider only this, that, as one reads, Abraham took his maid to wife (Gen. 16:2) and again took another woman to wife after the death of Sarah.[23] Likewise that Jacob married two sisters, together with their maids. For they are wont to engage in completely useless discussions without paying any attention to the fact that it would have been very easy for those men, who because of their great faith despised everything, also to despise the flesh of a woman if they had not acted either out of obedience to God or because of the mystery of things to come. For in this way God laughs and scoffs at Behemoth, as is written

22 The original has "Acts 8."
23 Cf. *Luther's Works*, 3, pp. 46—54.

in Job 41, that is, at the hypocrites; and He who is "wonderful in His saints" (cf. Ps. 68:35) shows in the outward life of the saints the things because of which those people are generally made to stumble. But the things He does inside, He hides, as Ps. 31:20 says: "In the covert of Thy presence Thou wilt hide them from the plots of men." Thus it happens that "the spiritual man judges all things and is judged by no one" (1 Cor. 2:15). Therefore it is the height of rashness to judge one's neighbor, since even the elect are hidden and are sometimes saved through the most manifest sins.

24. [*By faith Moses, when he was grown up, refused to be called the son of Pharaoh's daughter,*

25. *choosing rather to share ill-treatment with the people of God than to enjoy the fleeting pleasures of sin.*

26. *He considered abuse suffered for the Christ greater wealth than the treasures of Egypt, for he looked to the reward*].

In the first place, Chrysostom commends the faith of Moses because in the ardor of his faith he despised the royal court where he was son and master, namely, able to live in pleasure and honor; in fact, he had the right to spend his whole life at court.[24] For thus Stephen the martyr says, among other things in Acts 7:22-23, that Moses was instructed in all the wisdom of the Egyptians and was mighty in his words and deeds up to the fortieth year of his life. From this it is clear that he was an important man at the court of the king, was brought up with great care, and was honored with the high regard of all. Nevertheless, because of his faith he held all this and all the splendor of the court in contempt. In the second place, Chrysostom commends him because he despised all this, not for the sake of certain other visible things, whether greater or equal, but for the sake of the cross and the things that are nothing but misfortunes. Even then he was fulfilling the well-known words of the apostle in 1 Cor. 1:27-28: "He chose what is weak to shame the strong. . . . He chose things that are not, to bring to nothing things that are." And he chose the wisdom, or rather the foolishness, of the cross to reject the wisdom with which he

---

[24] Chrysostom, *Homiliae*, XXVI, 2-3, cols. 179—181 (397—398).

was endowed. In the third place — and this was the greatest thing —
he was rejected even by his brethren, for whose sake he had
even despised all those things and had subjected himself to dangers. They said, as we read in Acts 7:27: "Who made you a ruler
over us?" For it was on this account that he was also compelled
to flee to Midian (Ex. 2:15).

Index

By HILTON C. OSWALD

INDEX TO SCRIPTURE PASSAGES